W9-BRA-135

For Bea,
great meeting you.

Arthur Schwartz

Linda Eckhardt's 1995 Guide to America's Best Foods

LINDA ECKHARDT'S 1995 GUIDE TO AMERICA'S BEST FOODS

Includes recipes, serving suggestions, mail-ordering information

HOW TO SHOP COAST TO COAST

Linda West Eckhardt

Wings Books

New York • Avenel, New Jersey

For Shirley Barr, the best in the business

It is expected that the recipes in this book are to be followed as specified. Neither the publisher nor the author make any representation for results or accuracy if the recipes are not followed as specified.

Copyright © 1994 by Linda West Eckhardt

All rights reserved. No part of this work may be reproduced or transmitted in any form or by any means, including photocopying and recording, or by any information or retrieval system, except as may be expressly permitted by the 1976 Copyright Act or in writing by the publisher.

This 1994 edition is published by Wings Books, distributed by Random House Value Publishing, Inc., 40 Engelhard Avenue, Avenel, New Jersey 07001, by arrangement with the author.

Random House
New York • Toronto • London • Sydney • Auckland

Printed and bound in the United States of America

Library of Congress Cataloging-in-Publication Data

Eckhardt, Linda West, 1939–
[1995 guide to America's best foods]
Linda Eckhardt's 1995 guide to America's best foods.
p.   cm.
Includes index.
ISBN 0-517-09334-0
1. Food—Catalogs.   2. Food industry and trade—United States—
Directories.   3. Mail-order business—United States—Directories.
4. Cookery.   I. Title.   II. Title: 1995 guide to America's best foods.
III. Title: Guide to America's best foods.
TX353.E28   1994
641′.029′473—dc20   93-44031
CIP

8   7   6   5   4   3   2   1

ACKNOWLEDGMENTS

Thanks to the food purveyors of America, without whose cooperation, guidance, and help this book would not have been possible. Thanks also to Kate Hartson, editorial director and vice president of Random House Value Publishing, Inc., whose vision for the book matched my own. Thanks also to LaVonne Carlson and Bill Akunevicz Jr. of Random House Value Publishing, Inc. for shepherding the book through the publication process. As always, thanks to my agent, Mildred Marmur, friend first, business partner as well. And thanks to the Focus Group in Ashland who taste tested every single food item that came in the door. Without their energy and discriminating palates, the choices would not be so clear. Thanks to my husband Joe and my son Jay who also ate their share of the food tests. And thanks to our dogs Asher and Afton who ate what the humans couldn't and who helped in the process of selection—such as the day they buried our offering instead of eating it. Way to go dogs.

Books can not always please, however good; minds are ever craving
for their food.
—GEORGE CRABBE (1754–1832)

TABLE OF CONTENTS

4. THE PROTEIN PURVEYORS

Patés and sausages, hams and bacon. Corn-fed Midwestern beefsteaks. Poultry, including Thanksgiving turkeys, game, and chickens. Fish and shellfish, fresh, canned, and smoked. Using old family recipes and newfangled shipping techniques, these people will send to you fresh patés, free-range poultry, buffalo, whole lamb, milk-fed veal, live lobsters, fresh littleneck clams, and live crawfish. All guaranteed. All fresh.

5. HOT STUFF

Salsa, chili, and steak sauces. Dry spices. Ethnic herbs and spices. Chili peppers every which way. Chutneys and fruit sauces. Pickled fruits and vegetables. Relishes. Fruit and berry vinegars, mustards, mayos, olives, oils, and salad dressings. Some of the most innovative concoctions occur within this category, including many salt-free, fat-free, and sugar-free salad dressings and jams. Raspberry walnut. Lemon chardonnay. Champagne mustard. Yum.

6. THE CONFECTIONERY

All the sweet goodies: ice cream, custom-made chocolate gifts, truffles, nuts, hand-dipped chocolates, dessert sauces and ice cream toppings, old-fashioned hard candies, toffees, taffies, caramels. Newfangled candy bars. Even chocolate in a jar. Other great snacks: real Pennsylvania pretzels, popcorn balls. Other good stuff.

7. ESPRESSO BAR

Besides mail-order sources for fine coffee beans, there are flavored cocoas and teas from the world over. Crackers and biscuits, shortbreads, cookies and fruitcakes, mousse cakes, bundt cakes, loaf cakes, jam cakes, and other sweet delights.

8. GREAT GROCERIES

Forget Fauchon. Forget Harrod's. Every single thing you ever imagined available by mail order and to the local shopper in America's grand grocery stores. Best local and regional sources for American and imported goods. All ethnic supplies, exotic hardware from Europe, Africa, and Asia. Strange things you never thought you needed. Available here with one phone call or one mind-boggling visit.   285

9. INDEXES

INTRODUCTION

I tell you what. It's just like Christmas, your birthday, and Valentine's Day all rolled into one. You order something on the telephone and before you know it, the doorbell rings, the Federal Express man stands there with a smile on his face, package in hand, and there's your present. A package that came overnight, perhaps cloaked in a portable Styrofoam refrigerator, fresh, just made. It might be six dozen Texas tamales. Or fresh Patés from New York. Or a live lobster from Maine. Or a box of fresh chanterelles from Oregon. or an entire crate of organic, fresh produce from California—lettuces, purple potatoes, carrots, artichokes, asparagus. Or fresh fruit—a perfect pear, dripping sweet Texas grapefruit. Some handmade cheeses.

Open it up. The package is cold. The aroma is sweet. You say you got a paté and cornichons? What more do you need? A fresh baguette . . . a bottle of wine . . . a piece of fruit . . . your best friend. It's a picnic you won't soon forget.

And the next time you think about taking a vacation, take along this book. Let it be your guide to the real regional specialties of America. You can take the kids on a tour of a sucker factory in Arizona. Let them pet lambs in Virginia. See the pears put into gift packs in Oregon. Pick fruit on an organic California farm. Visit a bakery in Chicago. Stop in for a pastrami sandwich in Ann Arbor. Don't fail to visit Park Kerr's El Paso Chile in El Paso. He'll regale you with stories. He'll tell you everything about his part of the world.

Use the maps you'll see in the sidebars to guide you to the real America. Eat your way from place to place. What better way to understand your country and all its regional specialties.

And when you get to know the food purveyors in America's cities and towns, ask them to sign their copy of this book at their listing. It's really their book. I only report what I've tasted and seen.

Thanks to the improvements in fast shipping and shipping techniques, the availability of products in America is changing fast, and an entire food business has developed as a result. In the last five or six years, UPS, Federal Express, and all their cousins have blossomed and made it possible to have delivered to you fine, fresh, regional specialties grown and made in far-flung locations.

Live crawfish and Cajun specialties to go with them. Blue Corn from

Mexico, with peppers fresh and dried galore. Small batch jams made from wild and local fruits and berries. Buffalo berries from South Dakota, muscadine grapes from the South. Some of these jams are sweetened without sugar, using only fruit juices instead. You'll find handmade cheeses of a quality you may have thought you'd have to go to the countryside of France to get. Family-made ethnic sauces and spice blends, so that you don't have to go to Africa to find a genuine *Berbere*, or to an Indian restaurant to have an authentic Indian meal. All the indigenous ethnic foods and ingredients are yours with a phone call.

Alice Waters is largely responsible for beginning the trend towards market gardening in this country. For *Chez Panisse*, she began asking local farmers to grow organic produce for her. Other chefs followed. Then food co-ops began to develop between growers and restaurant operators so that new and greater varieties of fresh foods were grown and presented to enthusiastic restaurant goers. It was a short hop to the kitchen after restaurant diners began badgering the waiter: Where can I get this? I want to cook this at home. . . .

The new generation of farmers and cooks have rejected mass production. They've taken a great leap backward to pure, fresh, unadulterated local foods, grown carefully, prepared without artificial additives, and presented to a population of diners who care enough to insist on the very best. Purity, goodness, and small-batch cooking are the principles that guide these food purveyors. They guarantee that what you receive from the Fed Ex man, sight unseen—a pig in a poke as they say—will in fact be a better food product than you can buy in your local supermarket. Hands down.

Look in this book and you'll find the same sources for fresh and fine foods that many restaurants use every day. You can get everything at the same superior quality demanded by the finest chefs.

Because, right this very minute, real people in real kitchens are stirring together real food to package and ship out today to really discriminating diners who are sophisticated about food, interested in regional specialties, health conscious, and probably like to eat out. If that describes you, then you'll probably get as excited as I did, trying for the first time the best foods that America has to offer. Think of it this way: it's home cooking, only you don't have to do it. All you have to do is eat.

How to Use This Book

Within each chapter of this book, you'll find subdivisions that contain listings for particular food items—cheeses, for example—with full descriptions of the food products and complete addresses from where to get them. Some companies sell more than one kind of product. In this case, I've listed the company under its primary product type and told you about their other products. You can look in the index if you're interested in one particular product and it will tell you the companies that sell that product.

You won't find exact prices in this book. They change too fast. Call or write the companies for a current quotation of prices. Note that I've listed whether or not companies take credit cards and if they accept phone orders. Most do. But the ones who don't are worth the trouble or they wouldn't be listed in this book.

The focus group that taste-tested every single item that was accepted for this book worked on this premise: Does the product taste good? Did it arrive in a safe condition? Last but not least, does the package look good? We did not concern ourselves with cost. We're after value here, that's the real bargain. In some notable cases, the costs are equal to or lower than local supermarket prices for products that so far surpass supermarket quality it's ridiculous. We've tried to note that where possible.

You'll find directions and maps to the stores, farms, and factories that welcome guests. Flip through the book and check out the area maps. Don't fail to check out the extra special grocery stores listed in the last chapter of the book. You may even discover one of these stores close to your home. These grocers are specialists who offer excellent quality products—usually organized around an ethnic or quality theme.

Use this book to plan your next weekend outing away from home, or to consider your next vacation trip to a new area of the United States. Stick this book in your car or motor home when you start across America and you can munch your way across the land. What is a vacation for if not to find something great to eat? Happy grazing.

BREAD AND BREAKFAST

Great breads, pancake and waffle mixes. Terrific flours, meals, seasonings, and bakers' supplies. Granolas and cereals. Fresh fruit and berry jams, marmalades, conserves, and crystal jellies. Honeys, maple syrups, and sugars. Fine butters and handmade cheeses.

What are you going to do—shoot something for breakfast.

—MARIE WINDSOR to Charles McGraw in *The Narrow Margin,* 1952

GREAT BREADS, PANCAKE AND WAFFLE MIXES.

This chick is toast.

—BILL MURRAY right before zapping an Amazonian deity with his laser gun in *Ghostbusters*, 1984

Dan Leader didn't worry about moving 100 miles away from New York City to bake for city customers. He demonstrates that breads made with starters—not yeast and not chemical additives—have a keeping quality second to none. Do as Dan says. Slice into the bread. Stand the cut side down on the counter. The bread will stay good up to a week. Every time you cut another slice, you'll find a deepening crisp crust, a soft, redolent wheaty middle, and a complex taste that makes me feel like praying. Thank you God. Thank you Dan. This is bread.

BREAD ALONE

BREAD ALONE, INC.
Rt. 28
Boiceville, NY 12412

Can Dan Leader bake bread? Does a wild bear live in the woods? Yes to both. Dan sells his bread in another wild woods—Manhattan—at green markets and in fine grocery stores. He's an indefatigable worker, sometimes baking breads, then driving the two-plus hours from the forests of the Catskills to city markets. And he loves it. The bread begins from homemade starters and is that classic rustic type bread made from organic grains. Located near Woodstock, his bread is a part of a revolution going on in this country as profound as Woodstock was to music.

Order Pain Levain, Peasant Bread, Raisin Pumpernickel, Sour Rye with Caraway, Whole Wheat Walnut, Currant Buns, Farm Bread, Mixed Grain, Miche, or Onion Levain. You won't be disappointed.

The Miche is particularly recommended. A whole wheat loaf that is simplicity itself, it has a depth of flavor rarely found. Perhaps it's because Dan is such a stickler for quality that he sometimes oversees the harvest of the organic grains he uses in the breads. Perhaps it's his time-consuming method for making his own slow starters. Perhaps it's because Dan bakes the breads in brick ovens he built with his own two hands. Or perhaps it's because Dan Leader has found a way to package passion. In a loaf of bread.

CREDIT CARDS: **Yes**

CALL FOR CATALOG

RETAIL STORE: **Call for directions**

PHONE: **914-657-3328**

FAX: **914-657-6228**

MINIMUM ORDER: **6 loaves**

Bread and Breakfast

H&H BAGELS

2239 Broadway at
80th St.
New York, NY 10024

~~~~~~~~~~~~~~~

CREDIT CARDS: **Yes**

CALL FOR CATALOG

RETAIL STORES: **Other
store located at 639
West 46th St. Corner
of 12 Ave., NY**

PHONE: 800-692-2435
212-595-8000

FAX: 212-765-7391

MINIMUM ORDER: **2 dozen**

BEST NEW YORK BAGELS

Does Dustin Hoffman know his bagels? Anne Meara? Bernadette Peters? Would Michael J. Fox lie to you? All these people plus 8 million New Yorkers who voted H&H Bagels the best in New York all say—if you're out of New York and you want a bagel—just dial 1-800-NY-BAGEL and your worries are over.

No kidding. When you're in New York, these bagels are everywhere. The Rainbow Room. The Omni Park Central. N.Y.U.'s med school and law school. Dean & Deluca. They're nothing fancy. They're just plain and simple bagels made the way bagels should be made and coming at you in the mail almost as fresh as you'd get them in the store.

The shop looks as plain as your old bathrobe, but the aroma is devastatingly good, and as comfortable as Mama. The shop's located on the Upper West Side of Manhattan in an area of fine foods that are ultimate New York. For me, a visit to the Big Apple is not complete without swinging through H&H for a fast bagel fix. The ten varieties are all water-boiled before they're baked. Choose from plain, garlic, poppy seed, raisin, pumpernickel, whole wheat and oat bran. The bagels are big, they're chewy, and they're certified kosher.

Get two dozen minimum then store them in the freezer. Pop one in the toaster and before you know it, you'll be whistling "New York, New York, it's a wonderful town."

**EMPIRE BAKING
COMPANY**

4264 Oaklawn Ave.
Dallas, TX 75219

~~~~~~~~~~~~~~~

CREDIT CARDS: **Yes**

CALL FOR CATALOG

RETAIL STORE: **Call for
directions**

PHONE: 214-526-3223

FAX: 214-526-3394

MINIMUM ORDER: **No**

REAL BREAD

Real bread has come to Texas. And about time too. Michael London's bakery on Oaklawn has 'em lined up to buy this wondrous creation. A bread with heft and crunch, the result of a love affair with bread that began for London when he was yet a literature professor. Now, after seven years practice in a Greenwich, New York bakery, London has done the American thing—he's franchised real bread! Move over McDonald's. As London says, "The ideal to which I aspire is changing the face of baking in America. I feel I'm here to rescue breadmaking traditions."

Made with natural starters and sour doughs, London's bread is sold in several varieties. First of all the sourdough round, then a pecan raisin, a calamata olive, a Jewish rye, a Pan Aux Raisin and others. Call and ask what's in the oven today.

If you're in a city with Whole Foods stores, they sell Empire Breads. They bake in franchise stores in Atlanta, Washington D.C., Ann Arbor, Nashville, and Dallas. Wanna start your own biz? Why not a bakery? You too can learn to bake real bread.

AUTHENTIC CHICAGO-EUROPEAN BREADS

NEW BAKERY
2022 W. 51st St.
Chicago, IL 60609

CHECKS OR MONEY ORDERS
  ONLY

CALL FOR CATALOG

PHONE: 312-925-0064

MINIMUM ORDER: 5 loaves

A few bakeries in this country classify as better than the best. The New Bakery is one of them. Reflecting perfectly the mixed heritage of Chicago, they offer more versions of rye bread than you ever imagined. And every one of them authentic. Russian rye, Latvian rye, a rectangular rye, and a two-pound rye that keeps for up to a week. Each of these breads is different and distinct.

Eugene Kniuksta and his bakers know that bread sustains and they put their heart and soul into it. Bagels, Polish rye, an exceptional Raisin Twist, and the best pumpernickel in America. It's rich, it's crusty, it's full of good brown grains. All you need is a little sweet butter.

SWISS BAKERY

NEW GLARUS BAKERY & TEA ROOM
534 First St.
New Glarus, WI 53574

CREDIT CARDS: Yes

CALL FOR CATALOG

RETAIL STORE: Visit the
  tea room year round in
  New Glarus, WI.
  Located half way
  between Madison and
  the Illinois border

PHONE: 608-527-2916

MINIMUM ORDER: No

Howard Weber is a classically trained baker who just happened onto this bakery established in 1915 and located in a restored Swiss town of 1900 people right outside of Madison. Like other independent craftsmen, he opted for life in the slow lane and the chance to perfect his craft. He employs local talent and has trained them in the procedure for making fine Swiss pastries, including the stollen which he'll mail to you from November 1 through December 31.

Not only is the bread laced with marzipan, light and dark raisins, and almonds with a buttery yellow crumb, but the instant these loaves come from the oven, the New Glarus bakers form a mini-assembly line. First they dip each hot, pungent loaf into pure melted butter, then pass it on to be rolled in powdered sugar. It is set aside to cool, then shrink-wrapped, tied with a bow, boxed and put into the mail. They'll even put in a gift card for you. Each loaf serves eight.

Visit New Glarus and you'll feel like you're in a foreign country, Switzerland to be exact. Walk in and out of the neat tourist stops, then pop into Howard's bakery and tea room. It's small, it's warm, it's dripping with the aroma of yeast, butter, and nuts. You may eat more than you expected to when you first started looking into the glass cases, but that's all right. It's a small indulgence. Enjoy.

VALLEY BAKERY

502 "M" St.
Fresno, CA 93721

CREDIT CARDS: **Yes**

CALL FOR CATALOG

RETAIL STORE: **Call for directions**

PHONE: **800-354-4787**

FAX: **209-485-0173**

MINIMUM ORDER: **No**

ARMENIAN CRACKER BREAD

Janet Saghatelian, second-generation Armenian baker, has made her reputation with flat cracker bread known as *lahvosh*. This is the most amazing stuff. She sent me a case of it when I was writing my last book, and even a year later the last pack tasted as good as the first. Made from Montana spring wheat flour, water, cane sugar, vegetable shortening, salt, yeast, malt, sesame seeds, and dry milk, this ancient type of flat bread is rolled thin, sprayed with a milk wash and sprinkled with sesame seeds before baking. Once it enters the special 30-foot oven that Janet's father devised, the batter develops surface bubbles that give the bread its special crisp light texture. It comes in 15-inch rounds and in Janet's own cracker-sized hearts sprinkled either with seeds or with cinnamon. You can use it for cheese, as a palate cleanser at a wine tasting, or you can moisten the big rounds, as Janet's mother did, and use them in a variety of sandwich rollups Janet calls Valley wraps. The paper wrapper offers dozens of recipes for Valley Wrap sandwiches. Or you can invent your own.

Linda
Eckhardt's
1995
Guide to
America's
Best Foods

TERRIFIC FLOURS, MEALS, SEASONINGS, AND BAKERS' SUPPLIES.

If you want to find an outlaw, you call an outlaw. If you want to find a Dunkin' Donuts, call a cop.

—RANDALL "TEX" COBB in *Raising Arizona*, 1987

THE BAKERS FIND

139 Woodworth Ave.
Yonkers, NY 10701

CREDIT CARDS: Yes

CALL FOR CATALOG

RETAIL STORE: Yes

PHONE: 800-966-2253

FAX: 914-423-3227

MINIMUM ORDER: No

BAKERS GOLD MINE

So you've always wanted to start your own home bakery business. The only thing holding you back was a steady supply of rainbow sprinkles and Arrow-thermo decorating bags and Davis double-acting baking powder and meringue powder and sturdy cardboard boxes and doilies in every size and shape. Hold the phone. You're only a call away from every conceivable baker's supply you ever dreamed of and a good many you didn't know to dream for.

Until you read Rose Berenbaum's cookbooks. Here's everything. For three generations, the Socolows, owners of The Bakers Find, have supplied bakeries and restaurants with high-quality baker's necessities. Now, they'll supply you. And not only that, they pride themselves on creating care packages. Got a kid in college? A cousin whose nuts for nuts? Let The Bakers Find have at it. They'll create a care package to your specs or theirs, and UPS it with a gift card from you to that special person.

Only a half hour north of midtown Manhattan in Yonkers, they're a great place to visit for baking fiends.

KING ARTHUR FLOUR

P.O. Box 876
Norwich, VT 05055

CREDIT CARDS: Yes

CALL FOR CATALOG

PHONE: 800-827-6836

FAX: 802-649-5359

MINIMUM ORDER: No

*Linda
Eckhardt's
1995
Guide to
America's
Best Foods*

FINE FLOURS AND BAKING SUPPLIES

King Arthur flour is found in grocery stores in the Northeast as frequently as the giant miller's products. But anybody who ever baked one whit knows that King Arthur is the only flour to buy. Whether you can get their products from the grocery store, or if you have to mail order it, you'll get superior breads, pastries, and other baked goods if you start with the King.

I am particularly smitten with their white whole wheat. This is a new strain of whole wheat that isn't exactly snow white, but it's a darn sight lighter in texture and color than most whole wheat flours. The flavor is nutty and nice. I like it.

King Arthur puts out a catalog that could bankrupt me it's got such good baking supplies. Whenever I work on bread machine recipes or other baking recipes, I reach for the King Arthur.

Beginning with their famous Excalibur flour, to pancake mixes, King Arthur's products are pure gold. Here's your source for diastatic malt powder, Parrish pans, a good baker's bench knife, and a decent bread knife. Get your La Cloche here, and your pizza stone and peel.

They have a good library of baker's cookbooks for sale—including my own *Bread in Half The Time,* winner of the 1991 Julia Child Award for the Best Cookbook of the Year by the IACP.

If it has to do with baking, King Arthur's the place.

Perfect Biscuits Every Time

Preheat the oven to 450°F. Spritz an 8-inch glass pie plate with cooking spray and set aside. Combine in the food processor bowl fitted with the steel blade the flour, salt, sugar, soda, and baking powder. Pulse to mix and aerate the mixture.

Arrange tablespoons of shortening around the top of the flour mixture, then process 10 seconds exactly. Now, with the motor running, add buttermilk through the feed tube and continue to process until the mixture forms a loose ball that rides the blade around. Stop immediately and turn the dough out onto a lightly floured surface. Pat into a 9-inch disk about ⅔-inch thick. Cut the biscuits using a biscuit cutter or a small glass and arrange them, sides touching, in the prepared pan. Bake in the preheated oven 12–15 minutes until golden brown.

2 cups White Lily all-purpose flour

½ teaspoon salt

1 teaspoon sugar

¼ teaspoon soda

1 tablespoon baking powder

5 tablespoons shortening

1 cup buttermilk

Bread and Breakfast

THE WHITE LILY
FOODS CO.

P.O. Box 871
Knoxville, TN 37901

~~~~~~~~~~~~~~~~

CREDIT CARDS: No

CALL FOR CATALOG

PHONE: 615-546-5511

FAX: 615-521-7725

MINIMUM ORDER: No

PURE WHITE FLOUR

Ever since I discovered this lily white flour for baking biscuits I've been taking along an extra suitcase when I go to the south, so I can smuggle a case full up to the Pacific Northwest where it's not available. Yes, there is that much difference in southern soft wheat made into pure all-purpose flour and other flours. Biscuits just pop right up. Open up a steamy hot biscuit and it will be flaky and lily white inside. It will, indeed, melt in your mouth.

And to top it all off, White Lily makes a self-rising flour that's basically their all-purpose flour with baking powder added. They buy this stuff by the gross in the South for biscuits and pancakes. Try it a time or two and you'll want a case of it too.

White Lily's newest product that I've been baking with everyday for a new bread machine cookbook is called Bread Flour and it's a blend of spring and winter wheat with a higher protein content than their all-purpose. This will develop gluten better and make yeast breads leap out of the pan. They do not use bromation.

In addition to the Four Star flours, White Lily sells a cornmeal mix guaranteed to produce Southern style cornbread—the only kind as far as I'm concerned that's fit to eat.

BICKFORD
FLAVORS

19007 St. Clair Ave.
Cleveland, OH 44117

~~~~~~~~~~~~~~~~

CHECKS OR MONEY
ORDERS ONLY

CALL FOR CATALOG

RETAIL STORE: Call for
directions

PHONE: 216-531-6006

FAX: 216-531-2006

MINIMUM ORDER: No

FINE FLAVORINGS

You want old-fashioned pure flavors to cook and bake with, Bickford's the place. It's an Ohio company that nearly closed when its founder became too old to operate his one-man band any more. But a fellow named Steve Sofer, who owned a health food store, stepped in and bought the place. It's a godsend for bakers.

Bickford's vanilla is second to none. I wouldn't think of making a yellow cake or a batch of ice cream without it. The vanilla's strong. You can probably cut back on the amount your recipe calls for.

And, if you're looking for more exotic flavors, Bickford's probably got them. Ask for black walnut, clove, mango, and a bunch of other flavors, available in bottles from 16 oz. to 5 gallons. Just how much baking did you plan to do?

GREAT BAKING MIXES

NORTHWEST SPECIALTY BAKERS

15425 SW Koll
Parkway, A1
Beaverton, OR 97006

CREDIT CARDS: **Yes**

CALL FOR CATALOG

PHONE: **800-666-1727**

FAX: **800-955-9945**

MINIMUM ORDER: **No**

I f you're a kitchen clod, or perhaps just a baking wanna-be, here's your secret weapon. Northwest packages everything from brownies to bread machine mixes. Mix with a wooden spoon and your own two hands and people will swear you just came back from a pastry course with George Geary, the famous Walt Disney pastry chef.

Why? Because Mark Bonebrake and the bakers at Northwest Specialty have premixed natural, good ingredients so that most of the hard work is done. They made their reputation with great beer breads, in a line they call *Dassant*—dump the mix in and stir together with a bottle of beer. The flavors include Classic, Whole Wheat, and Garlic Provencal. These breads are wonderful with soups and salads.

Our hands down favorite, however, is the *Dassant* Belgian Truffle Brownie. It's rich, it's dark, it's complex in flavor. When the *San Francisco Chronicle* taste-tested this box mix against five grocery store mixes, the *Dassant* was so much better it wasn't even in the same league. Yes, you do have to add butter and eggs to this mix. Trust me on this. It's worth it.

Among their satisfactory bread machine mixes are Old Fashion Cinnamon Raisin, Danish Almond Poppyseed, Italian Garlic Basil, Northwest Multigrain Honey, Farmhouse Oatmeal Wheat, and Traditional Country French.

All *Dassant* products are certified kosher, use only natural ingredients, and contain no artificial flavors or oils. Nutritional information is provided with each mix.

Goldrush Matzoh Balls

Guaranteed the lightest matzoh balls you'll ever eat, they're lightened with Goldrush Gluten, a neutral item that does not have to be kosher.

Mix matzoh meal and gluten together in a large bowl. Combine in a 2-cup glass measure the water, eggs, oil, salt, and pepper. Whisk together then stir into the matzoh mixture. Stir well, cover the bowl, and refrigerate an hour or longer. Drop tablespoon portions into 1½ quarts of boiling chicken broth or water. Turn heat down to a simmer and cook 20 minutes. Enjoy.

1 cup less 1½ tablespoons matzoh meal

1½ tablespoons Goldrush gluten

¾ cup water

4 large eggs

⅓ cup soy or canola oil

1 teaspoon salt (optional)

dash of black pepper

CAL-GAR CORP.

3 Fern Court
Flanders, NJ 07836

CHECKS OR MONEY
ORDERS ONLY

CALL FOR CATALOG

PHONE: 201-691-2928

FAX: 201-691-0963

MINIMUM ORDER: No

Linda Eckhardt's 1995 Guide to America's Best Foods

GOLDRUSH SOURDOUGH STARTERS AND MIXES

If you've been to San Francisco, you know how good the sourdough bread is. Even the airport's filled with the aroma of that luscious sour bite. And, if you've ever attempted to make sourdough starter at home, you know how difficult it seems.

Like putting the genie in the bottle, the Cal-Gar company has finally put San Francisco's Goldrush sourdough starter into a powdered form and offered it for sale. Your best bet is a crock called the Starter Kit. It has everything you need to begin real sourdough bread making.

In addition, you can order a line of first quality mixes that will make Betty Crocker take a hike: pancake and waffle mix, lemon pound cake mix, multi-grain pancake and muffin mix. Bran muffin, cornbread, beer bread, and bread machine mixes—they offer them all and all are spiked with San Francisco's sourdough starter. A new product from Goldrush is Gluten, a neutral wheat product that makes yeast breads rise higher. A tablespoon of gluten added for every cup of heavy flour, such as rye, will guarantee a better texture to the finished bread.

Even though we've all made fun of "just-add-water" mixes in the past because they just tasted like the box they came in, you can't say that about Goldrush mixes. They're free of chemical additives, made with best quality flours and meals, and are kosher.

STONE-GROUND FLOURS AND MEALS

BRUMWELL FLOUR MILL

c/o Schanz Furniture
Highway 6
South Amana, IA 52334

CREDIT CARDS: **Yes**

CALL FOR CATALOG

RETAIL STORE: **In the furniture store**

PHONE: **319-622-3455**

MINIMUM ORDER: **No**

Call up Verna at the furniture factory and she'll not only send you out a catalog listing their reproductions of fine antique furniture that they make to order, but she'll look on the shelf in the back of the showroom and pick out the stone-ground Brumwell's flours to send you.

Graham flour, whole wheat, rye meal and flour, yellow corn meal, plus a bunch of mixes made from stone-ground flours and meals: buckwheat pancakes, oatmeal cookies, corn bread, seven-grain bread mix, dill bread, old-fashioned white bread mix, and 100% stone-ground whole wheat mix.

The Brumwell brothers, Norman and Vernon, learned their trade from their daddy. Until recently, they powered their grinding stones with a 1949 Buick engine. But business has been brisk and now they've been able to replace it with a nice, quiet electric motor. Brumwell's prices are modest and you can order all these products far fresher than any you'd ever be able to get in a store.

We are simply wild about Brumwell's buckwheat pancakes. Made from their mix, you get light, flavorful, nutty cakes that don't bear any resemblance to the slate roofing tiles usually palmed off as buckwheat cakes. The Brumwell's oatmeal cookie mix will make your kids dash home from school. The point is the Brumwells ship the stuff out as soon as they grind it. It's fresh, fresh, fresh. And don't forget about that furniture. Want a four-poster bed? An antique dining room table? The Amana craftsmen will make that for you too.

Bread and Breakfast

17

BUTTE CREEK MILL

P.O. Box 561
Eagle Point, OR 97524

CREDIT CARDS: Yes

CALL FOR CATALOG

RETAIL STORE: Call for directions

PHONE: 503-826-3531

MINIMUM ORDER: No

STONE-GROUND FLOURS, MEALS AND MIXES

Using a method developed by the Egyptians 5,000 years ago, Peter and Cora Crandall stone-grind a dozen different grains using waterpower from Little Butte Creek diverted through a millrace that activates a turbine that turns the wheels that slowly turn the 1400-pound millstones against one another to grind the whole grains into flour.

In addition to flours, meals, and cracked grains, you can order outstanding 10-grain cereal, Scottish oatmeal, and grain and nut cereals. One product line the Crandalls seem to have perfected is mixes. Their bran muffin mix makes a dense, sweet, nutty, dark muffin aromatic with the scent of whole grains. This muffin mix is used by many bed-and-breakfast places up and down our coast. They also make a fine cornbread mix that begins with their germ-in stone-ground cornmeal.

The mill is a great tourist destination stop for visitors to Southern Oregon. Not 20 minutes off of I-5, the mill has been in continuous operation since the late nineteenth century and is quite a step back into our own pioneer period. It is listed on the National Register of Historic Places. Their country store has a wide selection of natural food products in addition to their own.

BUTTE CREEK MILL

EST. 1872

Linda Eckhardt's 1995 Guide to America's Best Foods

18

Cora Crandall's Old World Rye Bread

In a large bowl, combine the flours, salt and yeast. Stir to mix. In a quart glass measure, combine molasses, warm water, and shortening. Heat in the microwave set at 100% until the shortening melts, about 45 seconds. Place half the flour mixture in a food processor fitted with the steel blade. Add half the liquid through the feed tube with the motor running. Process until the dough forms a ball that rides the blade around. Process 60 seconds.

Remove that half of the dough. Add remaining flour mixture to the workbowl fitted with the steel blade. Again, with the motor running, pour the liquid through the tube and process until you have a dough ball. Process 60 seconds.

Combine the dough balls on a lightly floured ball. Sprinkle the caraway seeds over the top and knead in by hand. The dough should be soft, smooth, and elastic. Place in a barely greased bowl, cover and let it rise until nearly doubled in bulk, about 1 hour. Punch down, and let it rise again. The third time, divide the dough into two pieces and form each into a loaf. Place the bread in pans you've spritzed with cooking spray to rise a final time.

Meanwhile, preheat the oven to 350°F. Bake the bread in the preheated oven for about 30 minutes, or until done. Cool on a rack.

3 cups stone-ground rye flour

3¾ cups stone-ground whole wheat flour

3 teaspoons salt

3 tablespoons 50% faster active dry yeast

¾ cup molasses

2¼ cups warm water

1½ tablespoons shortening

3 tablespoons caraway seeds

Bread and Breakfast

CAFE BEAUJOLAIS

P.O. Box 730
Mendocino, CA 95460

〰〰〰〰〰〰〰〰

CREDIT CARDS: Yes

CALL FOR CATALOG

RETAIL STORE: Call for directions

PHONE: 707-937-0443

FAX: 707-937-3656

MINIMUM ORDER: No

BAKING BY THE BOOK

Margaret Fox is an extraordinary cook and innkeeper. She has a successful bakery, restaurant and garden in this seaside resort and not too long ago married Chris Kump, an equally gifted chef, and son of reknowned cooking school director, Peter Kump.

Besides memorable breakfasts, they offer peaceful lunches and staggeringly good dinners. If you're in the California northcoast area, a stop here is a must.

Margaret has written a pair of good cookbooks, one called *Cafe Beaujolais* and one called *Morning Food*. Order from the bakery and Margaret will autograph them.

We are fiends for Margaret's Pan Forte, a medieval confection solid with nuts and candied citrus peels that kept the Crusaders up and running in their search for infidels. I dare say the infidels enjoyed the same thing—since the recipe is purely Mediterranean. Never mind your politics. Order Margaret's version and you're set to start out on your own crusade.

Also excellent are Margaret's waffle and pancake mix, her homemade cashew granola, her pear barbecue sauce and her black-as-sin hot chocolate mix. We ordered the Breakfast Sampler which came in a wicker basket and held not only the waffle mix and hot chocolate mix, but also coffee beans, red raspberry jam, an autographed copy of her book, and a couple of glass mugs. Theoretically, we were planning to use these for hostess gifts, but we couldn't resist. We made our own B&B breakfast right here at home. Yum.

Linda Eckhardt's 1995 Guide to America's Best Foods

GREAT TASTING ORGANIC GRAIN PANCAKE MIX

GRAIN WAVES BAKING PRODUCTS

Rt. 1, Box 298
Hereford, TX 79045

CHECKS OR MONEY
ORDERS ONLY

CALL FOR CATALOG

PHONE: 800-530-4743

MINIMUM ORDER: No

We weren't going to put this company in. It's just one person really, trying to sell organic pancake mix and still not willing to give up her day job in an accountant's office. Seemed like that was just too small. But then, we made the pancakes.

There really is a difference in the taste. It must be the water. Now you wonder why I say this. I grew up in Hereford, Texas, and I know that the water there is the best in the world and when Frank Ford began growing organic grains and selling them, nobody could believe the taste was so much better, let alone the nutrition.

So, now we have a light, fluffy baking mix that only requires of the cook an egg and some water to make perfect pancakes. I tell you, perfect. Order them in those coffee-type sacks. Get a half dozen. You'll use them. I promise. And think nothing of the fact that the company's so small it's little more than a phone number.

HAZELNUT HEAVEN

CRABTREE & CRABTREE, LTD.

89618 Armitage Road
Eugene, OR 97401

CHECKS OR MONEY
ORDERS ONLY

CALL FOR CATALOG

PHONE: 800-944-0153
503-687-6575

MINIMUM ORDER: No

The aroma in this house this morning is absolutely divine. It's the scent of roasted hazelnuts and it emanates from the waffle iron. I'm making hazelnut waffles using Crabtree and Crabtree's mix that calls for nothing more than oil, water and egg to complete. These waffles are light, crisp, and heavily scented with Oregon's own favorite nut. I did find I needed to add a bit more water than the label called for. Probably because it's so dry in my house the flour dried out. When you mix these waffles, just make sure they're thin and soupy before you pour this heavenly batter into your waffle iron.

These folks make other great hazelnut products. Biscotti, hazelnut clusters, an Italian style milk chocolate-hazelnut spread that I just eat out of the jar. They call it *Gianduia*. They also sell a scone mix that's chock full of hazelnuts. The plain truth is that all Crabtree and Crabtree's roasted hazelnut products are addictive. I can't think of having houseguests without their waffles. Don't start this stuff unless you're prepared to order and reorder.

21

Daddy's Corn Bread

Preheat the oven to 500°F. Place 3 tablespoons bacon grease in a 10-inch cast iron skillet and heat until almost smoking over the burner. Meanwhile, mix cornmeal, flour, salt, soda, baking powder, and sugar. Add buttermilk and stir well. Stir in egg. Pour hot grease into batter and completely mix. Pour batter back into the skillet and pop it into the preheated oven. Bake until the top looks dull, no more than 10 minutes or so. Turn on the broiler and brown the top a minute or so. Serve immediately in wedges with lots of butter.

For Mexican corn bread, add 4 slices thin cooked bacon in which you've browned 2 tablespoons chopped onion and bell or jalapeno pepper. Hotcha! That's good.

3 tablespoons bacon grease

1 cup Indian cornmeal

½ cup all-purpose flour

½ teaspoon each: salt, soda, baking powder

1 tablespoon sugar

1 cup buttermilk

1 large egg

SAGEBRUSH MILLS, INC.

Route 3, Box 11
Floydada, TX 79235

CREDIT CARDS: Yes

CALL FOR ORDER SHEET

PHONE: 806-983-2527

FAX: 806-983-3406

MINIMUM ORDER: Yes

Linda Eckhardt's 1995 Guide to America's Best Foods

HEIRLOOM CORN

The Carthel family raises corn on the Texas high plains. They also raise a little wheat. Lately, they've gotten interested in heirloom corn varieties and are now making a cornmeal from colorful Indian corn. They stone-grind it and ship it out in one-pound textile-covered bags. The cornmeal is interesting to look at—having a pepper-and-salt appearance and even more interesting taste, being exceptionally "corny". We adore it for Daddy's Corn Bread which is Texas style, not sweet, and seasoned with flavorful bacon grease.

The Carthels sell the Indian corn meal in caselots through the mail, or in one-pound packs in a gift pack along with one-pound packs of yellow cornmeal, fish fry meal, and organic wheat flour. This is what wheat and corn products are supposed to taste like. I recommend them without reservation.

Sagebrush Mills

Stone Ground

Indian Cornmeal

100% NATURAL
WHOLE GRAIN GOODNESS
NO PRESERVATIVES
REFRIGERATION OR FREEZING RECOMMENDED

NET WT. 16 OZ. (1 LB.)

STONE-GROUND CORNMEAL

KENYON'S CORN MEAL CO.

Box 221, Usquepaugh
West Kingston, RI
02892

S tone-ground corn on native granite in a little old grist mill store just off I-95 in busy Rhode Island makes for a product that will give you great jonny cakes or corn bread. You can make traditional Rhode Island clam cakes using Kenyon's meal. All it takes is some meal and some clams. Before long, you'll be eating Rhode Island-style fritters.

The village of Usquepaugh is worth a side trip off the freeway. It's quaint, the Queen's River flows through the middle of town, and you can see for yourself the power of water as it turns the enormous millstones to make meals and flours. Visit the mill, built in 1886 after the original one from 1711 was destroyed. Go on weekends during the summer, and weekdays from June to December. Other times, they'll take your group through. All you need to do is call.

Order jonny cake meal, yellow cornmeal, real stone-ground rye, whole wheat or graham flours, pancake mixes, and corn bread and brown bread mixes.

CREDIT CARDS: Yes

CALL FOR ORDER SHEET

PHONE: 806-983-2527

FAX: 806-983-3406

MINIMUM ORDER: Yes

HOPPIN' JOHN'S GRITS AND HAM

HOPPIN' JOHN'S

30 Pinckney St.
Charleston, SC 29401

J ohn Martin Taylor is the expert on Southeastern U.S. cooking. He runs a restaurant, store, and mail order business from whence he sells all things genuinely Southern. Want a great cookbook that truly represents the South? Buy his own *Hoppin' John's New South* or *Lowcountry* cookbooks. Want advice about other books? Call him up and ask.

John also offers honest-to-god Southern grits, cornmeal and corn flour. He has the products ground to his specifications at the Logan Turnpike Farm in north Georgia and people who know their grits say that for a real Southern taste, this is it. Make Lowcountry Shrimp and Grits with Skillet Cornbread using these corn products and you'll be whistling *Dixie*.

You can order a Wallace Edwards country ham from John and the copper pot to cook it in. Ask John to put you on the mailing list for his *Educated Palate Newsletter*. It's a good review of what's new in the cooking world.

CREDIT CARDS: Yes

CALL FOR CATALOG

RETAIL STORE: Yes

PHONE: 803-577-6404

FAX: 803-577-6932

MINIMUM ORDER: No

Bread and Breakfast

GRAY'S GRIST MILL

P.O. Box 422
Adamsville, RI 02801

CREDIT CARDS: **Yes**

CALL FOR CATALOG

RETAIL STORE: **Call for directions**

PHONE: **508-636-6075**

MINIMUM ORDER: **No**

*Linda
Eckhardt's
1995
Guide to
America's
Best Foods*

STONE-GROUND JONNY CAKE MEAL

Gray's Grist Mill has been operating since 1717 if you can imagine that. Needless to say, it's been through an owner or two, the latest of whom is Ralph Guild, a New York City businessman who summered in Westport Harbor 25 years before moving down to making the grinding of flours and meals his full-time occupation.

The granite stones that crush and grind the corn and wheat are new. They were put in to replace the old ones. New in 1878 that is. The mill's claim to fame is jonny cake meal. For those of you who haven't had the pleasure, this is Rhode Island's claim to culinary fame. A kind of corn bread that's particularly sweet and delicious because it's made with stone-ground meal. They make a fine polenta-grind cornmeal as well.

Gray's also sells New England brown bread and muffin mixtures of corn, wheat and rye. For pancakes, they sell a fine mix that starts with stone-ground flour.

Their whole wheat and rye flours are incomparable. For serious bakers, this place is a must. You get fresh, fine textured flours that will make the flavor of your homemade bread infinitely better.

The grinding stones are powered by a 1946 Dodge Truck engine, still putting along after they took it out of a Cain's Mayonnaise delivery truck. They began using the truck after the pond dried up, making water power unreliable. They simply parked the truck under the floorboards of the mill and let 'er rip.

Visit the mill and they'll show you the whole operation. It's fun to see.

NEW AGE MIXES FROM
STONE-GROUND FLOURS AND MEALS

THE FOWLER'S MILLING CO.

12500 Fowler's Mill Road
Chardon, OH 44024

I n the just-add-water sweepstakes, enter Fowler's Mill as a finalist. Stone-grinding local grains and seeds in a 159-year-old grist mill, Rick Erickson and the people at Fowler's are combining the best of the old and the new. Beginning with fresh stone-ground flours and meals, they've invented new-age mixes that taste better than grocery-store box mixes, are just as easy to make and are better for you.

Pancake mix, buckwheat pancake mix (my favorite), whole wheat pancake and cornmeal pancake mixes are all splendid. They also offer muffin mixes from buttermilk-blueberry to corn muffins that have a wonderful fresh taste.

Also available are mixes for shortcake, cobbler, chocolate chip cookies, and a raft of other local Ohio products you can pick up at the old mill store—worth a stop if you're nearby—or get through the mail.

CREDIT CARDS: **Yes**

CALL FOR CATALOG

RETAIL STORE: **Call for directions**

PHONE: **800-321-2024**

FAX: **216-286-4076**

MINIMUM ORDER: **No**

YOUR BLUE HEAVEN

BLUE HEAVEN CORN PRODUCTS NATURAL CHOICES, INC.

2101 Commercial, NE
Albuquerque, NM 87102

R oss Edwards, who started this outfit, calls blue corn pancakes "Blue Heaven." Actually, the first time you see blue corn products, you may be a little disappointed. The corn kernels themselves are a deep bluish purple and the ground corn flour is a lovely shade of lavender, but the cooked cakes are golden on the outside, but shirtboard gray inside. Oh well, you get used to it.

And the important thing is that they taste great: corny, sweet, complex. Ross's product line includes heavenly blue tortilla chips, whole kernel popcorn, regular and fine-grind cornmeal and flour, pancake and waffle mix—and it's all organically grown. You can even buy *atole* here. Basically, it's a Hopi food, where ground cornmeal is boiled with water and sweetener into a cream of wheat consistency. The Hopis call it "strong food," Indian Chicken Soup, Pueblo Penicillin. At a hospital in Gallup, *atole* is given to patients who have refused to eat anything else. It makes them better. Try it for your breakfast. It may make you better too.

CREDIT CARDS: **Yes**

CALL FOR CATALOG

RETAIL STORE: **Yes**

PHONE: **505-242-3494**

FAX: **505-242-3839**

MINIMUM ORDER: **No**

Bread and Breakfast

New Mexico Stuffed Turkey

makes 8–10 servings

Remove excess fat from the turkey and discard fat. Pat the bird dry. Lay it on a rack, breast side up. Stir together the cornmeal, cayenne, pepper, and salt. Coat all sides of the bird with this mixture. Cover and set aside on the countertop. Preheat the oven to 500°F.

In a large bowl, combine cornmeal, flour, chile powder, parmesan, and salt. Toss to mix, then in a 2-cup glass measure stir together the honey, milk, egg, and oil. Pour this liquid into the cornmeal mixture and stir to mix. Fold in jalapeno, onion, and corn.

Lightly grease a 10-inch black skillet and add corn bread stuffing mixture to the skillet. Bake in the hot oven until the top is dull-looking and the corn bread is cooked through, about 15 minutes. Turn corn bread out onto the counter and break it into pieces. Stuff it into the cavity of the turkey. Stuff any remaining portion into the neck cavity. Pour a cup of chicken broth into each cavity. Tie the turkey legs together with cotton string, then place the bird in the hot oven.

Roast 20 minutes, then turn the oven down to 325°F and continue to roast until the bird reaches an internal temperature of 175°F, the juices run clear, and the joint moves freely, about 3 hours. Cool 10 minutes before carving.

1 10–12 lb. turkey

1 cup blue or yellow cornmeal

1 tablespoon cayenne pepper

1 teaspoon salt

½ teaspoon black pepper

Stuffing:

¾ cup blue or yellow cornmeal

¾ cup whole wheat flour

1 tablespoon baking powder

2 teaspoons chile powder (or to taste)

3 tablespoons freshly grated parmesan cheese

1½ teaspoons salt

2 tablespoons mild honey

⅔ cup skim milk

1 egg

2 tablespoons olive oil

1 fresh jalapeno, seeded and minced (or to taste)

1 cup minced purple onion

1 cup corn kernels (fresh, frozen, or canned and drained)

1 14½ oz. can chicken broth OR 2 cups homemade broth

Linda Eckhardt's 1995 Guide to America's Best Foods

GRANOLAS AND CEREALS.

OATS. A grain which in England is generally given to horses, but in Scotland supports the people.

—SAMUEL JOHNSON, *Dictionary*, 1755

CHRISTINE AND ROB'S

41103 Stayton Scio
Road
Stayton, OR 97383

~~~~~~~~~~~~~~~~~

CREDIT CARDS: Yes

CALL FOR CATALOG

PHONE: 503-769-2993

FAX: 503-769-2993

MINIMUM ORDER: Yes

OREGON OATMEAL

Just to show how much we're into comfort foods these days, Christine and Rob Bartell took a top prize at New York's fancy food show with their Oregon old-fashioned oatmeal. This is the thick cut, slow-roasted old-fashioned kind like your mother's grandmother made. It will keep you going all day. It's that good. Arnold Schwartzenegger is said to take it with him everywhere.

Another winner in the "add water and cook" category, the Bartells also make a superb oatmeal cookie mix. That's really all you do. Add water, mix and drop dough on a cookie sheet, then bake. The cookies are aromatic with oats and cinnamon. They're crumbly, rich, and delicious.

We took their pancake mix and marionberry syrup on a camping trip and not only did we adore them for breakfast, we found they were quite satisfying for dinner the day we didn't catch one damn trout.

The Bartells make the oatmeal in northeastern Oregon in a place they call "Oatmeal Central." They're living, running proof that the stuff is good for you and we can attest to the fact that it also tastes great. Christine sends out a newsletter with every order and in it are recipes she's gotten back from satisfied customers. We tried the granola recipe that begins with thick-cut oats. We think you'll like it as much as we did.

MICHAELENE'S GOURMET GRANOLA

7415 Deer Forest Ct.
Clarkston, MI 48348

~~~~~~~~~~~~~~~~~

CHECKS OR MONEY
ORDERS ONLY

CALL FOR CATALOG

PHONE: 313-625-0156

FAX: 313-625-8521

MINIMUM ORDER: Yes

NO FAT CHANCE GRANOLA

Granola is not just granola. Michaelene Hearn mixes up a no fat granola she calls No Fat Chance that you simply can't quit eating. She also makes irresistible Cherry Almond Crunch, No Sugar Nutty Raisin and a Granola Cookie with Dried Cherries. Her granola looks like chunky rocks and tastes so good you could eat it right out of the bag.

Looks like a commuter's breakfast to me. Get on the train. Eat it out of the sack.

Michaelene Hearn started her business with fifty bucks worth of ingredients and a quirky idea that she could make a better granola. Some nine flavors later, Michaelene is still stirring and baking up granolas to beat the band. One of her newest hits is Rainforest Naturals, a tropical style granola using whole nuts and tropical fruit additions. Looks like a winner

Kiawah Granola

(From John Cuff, Executive Chef, Kiawah Island Inn, Charleston, South Carolina)

Combine brown sugar, molasses, honey, cold water, oil, and cinnamon in a small saucepan and raise to a boil. Set aside.

Meanwhile, preheat the oven to 325°F. Combine in a large bowl the oatmeal with raisins, currants, walnuts, pecans, almonds, coconut, sunflower seeds, and oat bran. Drizzle the syrup over and stir thoroughly. Lay out in thin layers on baking sheets. Bake until toasted, stirring every ten minutes, for about 40 minutes. Store in a tin.

½ cup firm pack light brown sugar

¼ cup unsulfured molasses

¼ cup mild honey

¼ cup cold water

2 tablespoons vegetable oil

2 teaspoons cinnamon

3 cups oatmeal—Christine & Rob's

½ cup raisins

½ cup currants

¼ cup walnuts, coarsely chopped

½ cup pecans, coarsely chopped

½ cup almonds, unblanched, coarsely chopped

⅓ cup coconut, unsweetened

⅓ cup Sunflower seeds

½ cup oat bran

YANKEE GRANOLA

Deb's granola is pure yankee ingenuity. Without raisins or dried fruits to disguise the flavor, it's chock full of crisp toasted almonds and four organic grains. Slow-roasted with pure Vermont maple syrup for extra crunch and premium flavor, it's—of course—all natural and made with no added preservatives.

We don't bother eating it in a bowl with milk. We just eat it out of the bag for a snack. Or throw it into pancakes for a little zip. Jay, our son, puts it on ice cream. And yesterday, I topped a fall Apple Crisp with this instead of plain oatmeal. It was heaven.

If you're in New England, make a detour to Debra Stark's store. Not only does she sell granola but a whole raft of other well-flavored, nutritious "natural" foods.

THE NATURAL GOURMET

98 Commonweath Ave.
Concord, MA 07573

CREDIT CARDS: **Yes**

CALL FOR CATALOG

RETAIL STORE: **Yes**

PHONE: **800-542-2898**
508-371-7573

FAX: **508-287-4212**

MINIMUM ORDER: **No**

WHOLLY COW
FOODS

37700 HWY 101 South
Cloverdale, OR 97112

xxxxxxxxxxxxxxxx

CREDIT CARDS: Yes

CALL FOR CATALOG

RETAIL STORE: Located in
the Hudson House Bed
& Breakfast

PHONE: 503-392-4277

MINIMUM ORDER: No

BED AND BREAKFAST CUISINE

Anne and Steve Kulju run a bed and breakfast in a 1906 house about two hours south of Portland and just three miles away from the beach. They've developed an awesome reputation for the food and their breakfasts have become a legend. Dutch pancakes, crepes, British bangers, Tillamook cheese, fresh fruits, and always a bowl of their own hand-blended natural granola.

Well, you can guess how this story goes. So many people wanted a doggie bag of the granola to go they figured they might as well bag it up and sell it. So they came up with packaging that looks like it comes from Wisconsin—all black and white cow spots—and they began marketing their fabulous Blackberry Hazelnut cereal. It's made from a blend of grains and spiked with local dried blackberries and local hazelnuts. It's great to eat right out of the box or pour milk over it. Yum. Later, they expanded to make Vanilla Raisin with Walnut granola, and Cranberry Pecan granola. All are as fresh as if you'd made them yourself.

They also sell fine quality cocoa mixes, flavored with cinnamon and hazelnut or almond and butter pecan, and a granola bar mix that makes Apple Cinnamon granola bars you'll love.

*Linda
Eckhardt's
1995
Guide to
America's
Best Foods*

30

FRESH FRUIT AND BERRY JAMS, MARMALADES, CONSERVES, AND CRYSTAL JELLIES.

Come and get one in the yarbles, if you have any yarbles, you eunuch jelly thou!

—MALCOLM MCDOWELL to a rival gang leader in
A Clockwork Orange, 1971

SARABETH'S KITCHEN

169 West 78th St.
New York, NY 10024

CREDIT CARDS: Yes

CALL FOR CATALOG

RETAIL STORE: 3
  restaurants located in
  the New York area

PHONE: 800-552-5267
  212-580-8335

FAX: 212-362-0043

MINIMUM ORDER: No

GREAT JAMS AND GOOD FOODS

Somewhere around 1980, Sarabeth Levine inveigled her aunt into giving her a 200-year-old family recipe for orange-apricot marmalade. She invested a hundred bucks in fruit, sugar, and jars and began making jam in her New York apartment. It was an easy sell to Bloomies, Macy's, and various gourmet shops within walking distance to her place. All it took was one taste. Colored like a good Tequila Sunrise, sweet and sharp with citrus shards, this puts both orange marmalade and apricot jam in the shade. Cooked in small batches, barely stirred, the fruit remains distinct, the color bright, and the flavor intense.

Today, Sarabeth Levine, who started her working life as a dental assistant, owns three homey neighborhood restaurants and a bakery. In a commercial kitchen, she makes nine jam flavors punningly named: Plum Loco, Apricadabra, Rosy Cheeks, Cranberry Relish, Chunky Apple Butter, Lemon-Pear Butter, Cherry-Plum, Strawberry-Peach, and the original Orange-Apricot. Each comes in a mason jar with a flat and lid and is as carefully made as if it were done in your own kitchen. Sarabeth's preserves contain no additives, fillers, or preservatives. She also offers her Morning Crunch Granola in a pound package. It's fresh-tasting and includes oats, almonds, sunflower seeds, raisins, honey, coconut, maple syrup, and bran.

Stop by Sarabeth's at the Whitney Museum or at 423 Amsterdam at 80th on the West side, or 1295 Madison at 92nd on the East. After a bit of Sarabeth's divine Morning Crunch Granola, some preserves on bread, and a cup of tea, you'll be ready for another day of New York sightseeing. *The New York Times* called Sarabeth's one of the nine best places to take guests for brunch. We couldn't agree more. The last time we tried it, we ordered "Goldie Lox," scrambled eggs with salmon and cream cheese. It was to die for.

Since we were on the East side, we remembered we were close to the best cookbook store in the U.S. of A., Kitchen Arts and Letters. We stopped in Nach Waxman's shop after our visit to Sarabeth's and picked out an armful of cookbooks. We're blaming Sarabeth Levine and her good brunch. It made us want to hit the kitchen at a dead run. Or maybe just an armchair for a good read.

Linda
Eckhardt's
1995
Guide to
America's
Best Foods

Sarabeth Levine's Chicken Breasts with Marmalade

makes 4 servings in an hour

Sauté mushrooms and onion in the butter. Season with salt and pepper and set aside. Combine teriyaki sauce, water, and marmalade and set aside. Cut chicken breasts in half and place in electric skillet or frying pan. Pour liquid ingredients over the chicken and cover, then cook at 325°F. (medium heat) turning from time to time, until done, about 20 minutes. Add vegetables, cover and heat about 5 minutes. Serve over rice or couscous.

4 large brown mushrooms

½ cup finely chopped onion

1 tablespoon butter

salt and pepper to taste

¼ cup teriyaki sauce

¼ cup water

⅛ cup Sarabeth's Orange Apricot Marmalade

4 boneless, skinless chicken breasts

GOD BLESS THE WILD PLUM

Thanks to Darrell Corti, I tracked down this hidden, wild plum winery that makes a line of products so exotic and desirable that we think of them as one of our Top Ten. Located in the top northeastern corner of California near the Oregon border, John and Joanne Stringer make a variety of products from the little wild plums that grow so well in the mountains there. Visit and you'll see wild, craggy mountains on one side and Goose Lake on the other. It's all clean air and clean water up here. We know why. Almost no people. Plenty of deer, geese and ducks, as well as the American Bald Eagle, various swans and other wild things pass through here. Fortunately for us, the Stringers have managed to bottle one of them: wild plums.

One of Nature's rarest fruits, it makes a dessert wine so good we can hardly bring ourselves to swallow it, a syrup that turns pancakes into a symphony, and jam that makes your toast stand up and salute. Actually, the jam is too good for toast. It's best reserved as a garnish to pheasant or grouse, or perhaps to transform your Thanksgiving Turkey.

If you want to make a gift to someone that they'll never forget, make it a wild plum product from Stringer's. And if you're thinking of a bird watching trip to this hidden corner of California, stop by the Stringer's place. They don't get much company. They like it. You'll like it too.

STRINGER'S ORCHARD

Box 191
New Pine Creek, OR 97635

CREDIT CARDS: Yes

CALL FOR CATALOG

RETAIL STORE: Call for directions

PHONE: 916-946-4112

MINIMUM ORDER: No

Bread and Breakfast

GREEN BRIAR JAM KITCHEN

6 Discovery Hill Road
East Sandwich, MA
02537

CREDIT CARDS: **Yes**

CALL FOR CATALOG

RETAIL STORE: **Call for directions**

PHONE: **508-888-6870**

MINIMUM ORDER: **No**

SUN-COOKED JAMS

In the old days, when the ripening of fruits and berries coincided with the hottest days of the summer and the home cook was least likely to want to stoke the woodstove all day, sun cooking was a practical solution. Today, in the face of electric stoves and air conditioners, sun cooking is almost a lost art. Almost, however, save for the good ladies of the Thornton Burgess society, who still use the hot New England summer sun to cook the strawberry jam they make to support their nature center.

Jam made thusly begins by barely heating berries and sugar syrup on the stove, then pouring them into wide flat pans, which are then placed on wooden racks to catch the hot southern exposure for two or three days. What you get is whole fruit suspended in clear, ruby-colored syrup so perfect you'll want to spoon it over gelato for dessert. Or you may even want to eat it out of the jar just plain. The berries taste fresh and are crisp and never mushy.

Visit the kitchen and you'll glimpse a Cape Cod tradition since 1903. It's a working museum that gives you a look at what kitchen chores were like before the modern age.

Jams, jellies, and marmalades are available in a half dozen flavors, including apricot, ginger-rhubarb, plum, raspberry and strawberry. They also offer old-fashioned bread and butter pickles as well as a dozen other pickles and relishes, and a group of cranberry products, including excellent cranberry marmalade and a cranberry-orange-pineapple relish to die for.

Linda Eckhardt's 1995 Guide to America's Best Foods

### Shaker Applesauce	*2 lbs. apples, peeled and sliced* *2 cups boiled cider*

Add apple slices to the cider. Simmer on low heat until the apples are tender and coated. Do not stir too much. You'll have a powerful apple flavor here.

ALL FRUIT PRESERVES

WAX ORCHARDS

22744 Wax Orchards Rd. SW
Vashon Island, WA 98070

If you've never tasted preserves sweetened with concentrated fruit juices and nothing else, you don't know what you're missing. Forget the added nutritional value of such preserves, we like them for the taste. We're not even against sugar, we're just for flavor.

Wax has been making these fine preserves for years for those who want natural foods, for diabetics, and for those who simply value the products for the taste. Strawberry, Raspberry, Peach and Blueberry Fruit Fancifuls offer only 7 calories per teaspoon, and act as a ½ fruit for a 4 teaspoon serving on the Weight Watchers exchange.

Their Apple Butter is the perfect breadfellow. It's also a good glaze for angel food cake. Only 7 calories per teaspoon, it tastes like an apple collapsed into a spoon.

Their most remarkable new product is Classic Fudge Sweet. Nothing more than cocoa powder and pineapple juice, it's a dense, sweet chocolate fudge sauce you can top fat-free cookies with or angel food cake. Heck, we love it on Haagen Dazs. It just plain tastes great.

CREDIT CARDS: **Yes**

CALL FOR CATALOG

RETAIL STORE: **Call for directions**

PHONE: **800-634-6132**

FAX: **206-463-9731**

MINIMUM ORDER: **No**

AN APPLE A DAY

WOOD'S CIDER MILL

RD 2 Box 477
Springfield, VT 05156

One of the best-tasting jellies to come by our focus group comes in an innocuous little jar with a pale label that doesn't even hint at the exceptional good taste awaiting inside. Willis and Tina Wood follow a family tradition that began in 1882 when the family added a cider mill to the farm they'd been operating since 1798.

In continuous operation since by one family, they press apples in the fall and boil them down to make cider syrup, cider jelly, and boiled cider, an old-fashioned cooking ingredient that peps up apple sauce, makes a ham festive, or lifts mincemeat into the heavens.

CREDIT CARDS: **Yes**

CALL FOR CATALOG

RETAIL STORE: **Call for directions**

PHONE: **802-263-5547**

MINIMUM ORDER: **Yes**

But back to the jelly. It's crystal clear, it's a dark amber color, and the taste explodes with the goodness of apples. The cider jelly is made from nothing but apples. It takes one gallon of pure apple cider to evaporate down to a 20-oz. jar of jelly. All that's lost is the steam. All that remains is apple goodness.

OLD TIME TEXAS CAFE

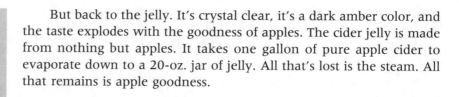

WUNSCHE BROS.
P.O. Box 952
Spring, TX 77383

CREDIT CARDS: **Yes**

CALL FOR CATALOG

RETAIL STORE: **Call for directions**

PHONE: **800-582-5832**
   713-355-5858

FAX: **713-353-4465**

MINIMUM ORDER: **No**

The Wunsche Brothers Saloon celebrated its 90th anniversary this year. You can still get handmade hamburgers here, and country fried foods including sausage sauerkraut balls, sausage crumb salad, and a terrific beer bread. Just north of Houston, it's a respite from the anthill that is the Houston freeway system.

A visit here is like stepping back to some old German grandmother's Texas table. Bonnie and Clyde ate here. Lots of Texas dignitaries have eaten or drunk here. Now you can go for a chicken fried steak and a tall tale or two. It's that sort of place.

When Scott and Brenda Mitchell bought the place in 1982, they added a country store and started making and selling heirloom jellies: Mesquite Bean, Mayhaw, Elderberry and Wild Sloe Plum. These jellies are a sure representation of just exactly what the Texas pioneers had to work with in the way of sweet goods: a sack of sugar and whatever they could pick.

If you visit the Wunsche Saloon do not fail to order yourself up a piece of that Pecan Buttermilk Pie. It's not to be missed. If you can't get in, order by mail their Chocolate Whiskey Cake—it kept us alive during one long rainy camping weekend in Oregon, their jelly gift box, or their cookbook, which has valuable recipes for Dewberry Bread, Smothered Liver, Fried Catfish and Bass, and those infamous Sausage Sauerkraut Balls.

Linda Eckhardt's 1995 Guide to America's Best Foods

WILD AND LOCAL SOUTH DAKOTA JAMS

BLACK HILLS BREAD SPREADS

Rt. 1, Box 214a
Spearfish, SD 57783

CHECKS OR MONEY
  ORDERS ONLY

CALL FOR CATALOG

RETAIL STORE: **Call for
  directions to the ranch**

PHONE: 605-642-4154

MINIMUM ORDER: 3 jars

On a working ranch everybody works, and Sallie Nicholas does her part on her family's Bear Ridge Ranch by making and selling jams, jellies, and fresh horseradish. She picks wild chokeberries, gooseberries and buffaloberries, and makes them into crystal clear delicate jams.

She also makes organic jams using domestic strawberries, rhubarb, peaches, and blueberries. She makes a lovely Peach Apple jam and a jam from Wild Sarvis berries that she fills out with local blueberries.

Her horseradish is made from the whole root dug up right on the ranch. It's the pure stuff. You mix it with mayo or beets to make relishes with that good fresh horseradish taste.

If you're looking for a place for a guided hunt for deer, turkey, or elk, her husband and son will take you a-horseback on their big ranch and you'll get your limit. While you're there you'll see their llamas, their Gallaway Cattle, and whatever else they've decided to branch out into. This is what it means to keep the family farm going today. Even though the place has been in the family since 1900, they have to keep moving ahead. Meanwhile, you'll find Sallie out in the bushes picking wild berries to make more luscious jams.

*Bread and
Breakfast*

A Proper Texas Chicken Fried Steak

makes 4 servings in 45 minutes

1 round steak, ¼-inch
  thick, about 1½ lbs.

Texas Traditions Hot Salt

¾ cup flour

1 large egg

2 tablespoons milk

cooking oil

Pound the round steak with the side of a saucer until it flattens out and is tenderized. Trim away and discard fat. Discard the bone. Cut into four serving sizes. Sprinkle generously with the Hot Salt.

Place flour in a pie plate. Whip egg and milk together in another pie plate until lemony. Tear a sheet of waxed paper and put it beside the stove. Dredge the meat in the flour, then in the egg mixture then again in the flour mixture and lay aside on the wax paper while you preheat the skillet.

Heat about 1-inch of cooking oil in a 10-inch black cast iron skillet over medium high heat. Don't add meat until oil is so hot that when you flick water into the skillet with your fingertips it bounces out, screaming in protest. Slip the meat pieces into hot oil and cook until meat is golden on both sides, turning once. Now turn the fire down, add about 1 tablespoon of water, cover, and steam 5 minutes. Remove to paper towels to drain. Serve with milk gravy.

TEXAS TRADITIONS

Rt. 1, Box 123B
Georgetown, TX 78626

CREDIT CARDS: Yes

CALL FOR CATALOG

PHONE: 800-547-7062
    512-863-7291

FAX: 512-869-6212

MINIMUM ORDER: No

TRADITIONAL TEXAS JAMS

On a little farm, outside Georgetown, Texas, a home business began in the kitchen. Beginning with her grandmother's recipes, Dianne Howard began putting up crystal clear jellies and fresh fruity jams. They stir the jams by hand, hand-processing every single one. What you get is home cooking—without having to wash the dishes.

Dianne's partner, Sue Burton, calls their original recipes "culinary folk art," and so they are. No artificial preservatives, no food coloring, but wait until you see the dazzling, ruby clear Prickly Pear Cactus jelly. Or try the amber-colored Mesquite Bean jelly. Both are made with the same wild things the Texas settlers could pick from the hardscrabble soil. Both just beg for a biscuit. The mesquite bean flavor is delicate and lemony and also makes a terrific glaze for poultry.

They also make a fine Jalapeno Pepper jelly tempered with the addition of sweet bells and apple cider vinegar. We're crazy for the Red Chile Pepper jelly that's terrific on cream cheese.

Texas Traditions also hand-blends Texas-style dry seasoning blends: blackening herbs, seasoning salt, apple potpourri, and sampler baskets. Their Hot Salt, a mixture of salt, pepper, garlic, jalapeno, chile pepper, and onion powder is all you need to properly season a Texas Chicken Fried Steak.

Texas Milk Gravy Like Mama Used to Make

After the chicken fried steaks are cooked and waiting on the paper towels, pour out all but 2 tablespoons of oil from the skillet. Leave any pan drippings in the skillet. Now stir in flour and cook and stir over medium heat to make a golden roux. Season with Hot Salt and pour in the milk, stirring all the while. Patiently stir it until it bubbles and thickens. Taste and adjust seasonings. Make a pool of the gravy and put the steak in it to serve.

2 tablespoons oil from the skillet

2 tablespoons all purpose flour

Hot Salt to taste

1½ cups milk

HILL COUNTRY PEACHES

Fredericksburg is a town that's a tourist treasure for those visiting Austin, Houston, or San Antonio. The whole town's like a museum and the kid who waits on you at the gas station is as likely to have a thick German accent as not. It's that old country.

And the town is known for growing peaches. All around in the stony limestone hills are luxurious peach orchards—and lately, vineyard grapes have sprung up everywhere. Das Peach Haus is a cute little cottage that sells the provender of these local products.

From the fabulous Gillespie County peaches, they make peach butter—dark and spicy like grandmother made, old-fashioned peach preserves, and peach honey—a fruit syrup for pancakes or French toast.

From some of the vineyards—Fischer and Wieser—they've made wine jellies, runny and not too stiff with pectin, but redolent of the

DAS PEACH HAUS

Rt. 3, Box 118
Fredericksburg, TX 78624

CREDIT CARDS: **Yes**

CALL FOR CATALOG

RETAIL STORE: **Call for directions**

PHONE: **800-447-8707 210-997-7194**

FAX: 210-997-6172

MINIMUM ORDER: **No**

robust Texas grapes. We were particularly taken with an onion jelly made with those sweet Texas 1015 onions that are as good as Vidalias.

If you're looking for something totally Texas and off-the-wall, try Cactus jelly which the *Texas Monthly* says tastes like Martian bubble gum. Actually, I was thinking it was more like Venus. But what the hey. It's rare. It's from Texas. It can't be all bad.

OREGON WILD BERRY JAMS

I f there's one thing Oregon's known for it's the berries. Problem is, they're so fragile, they don't ship. So unless you're here during the evanescent harvest, you'll never know the pure luxury that those of us who live here enjoy every summer.

Unless you order wild berry jams and syrups. Stan Ecaas is making divine products using Oregon's best wild berries. I can't begin to tell you how glad I am that he's scratching his arms up in the briar patch to pick these berries so I don't have to do it. He makes spoon jams and syrups and puts them up in handsome hex jars or old-fashioned bail jars. If you want one present this year for yourself that says Oregon, this is it.

Available in wild blackberry, wild huckleberry, wild chokecherry, wild elderberry, American Indian jelly made from Oregon Grape and Salal, marionberry, and raspberry, as well as syrups: wild evergreen blackberry, chokecherry, and huckleberry.

We went camping this summer and served this syrup over pancakes we'd made over an open fire. It was a spiritual experience, let me tell you. These are great products.

OREGON WILD BERRIES

77129 Watach Drive
Clatskanie, OR 97016

CHECKS OR MONEY ORDERS ONLY

CALL FOR CATALOG

RETAIL STORE:: **Call for directions**

PHONE: 503-728-3742

MINIMUM ORDER: **No**

BERRY JAMS AND JELLIES

MAURY ISLAND FARM

P.O. Box L
Vashon, WA 98070

Not only can you buy the best-quality red currant jelly you ever tried from these berry farmers, but they're always coming up with new flavors. Try red currants and raspberries in a preserve that's deep and rich and glazes a lamb to perfection. Among their other good slow-cooked, open-kettle-style preserves are boysenberry, black currant, apricot-orange, seedless raspberry currant, bittersweet blend orange marmalade, heavenly gooseberry, lemon marmalade, and red raspberry jam and jelly.

For a nice gift send out the miniature gift box. An assortment of 10 tiny, 1½-oz. jars is reasonably priced and would be welcomed by your mother if she lives alone. Or anybody's mother who lives alone. They also offer gift boxes with scone or biscuit mixes and a variety of their hand-stirred jams.

All their flavors are rich and fruity without being too "jelled" by added pectins. We like them.

CREDIT CARDS: Yes

CALL FOR CATALOG

RETAIL STORE: Call for directions

**PHONE: 800-356-5880
206-463-9659**

FAX: 206-463-6868

MINIMUM ORDER: No

SMALL BATCH JAMS

MAD RIVER FARM

P.O. Box 155
Arcata, CA 95521

Susan Anderson stirs up North California fruits and berries into some astonishingly good jams. Her Dune preserves made with local wild berries—blackberries, strawberries, and blueberries—are not to be missed. Equally good are the wild huckleberries stirred into jam. She also makes a great apricot from California's best. She makes preserves and jams with whatever's in season, in small batches, and inventing flavors as we speak. Just this week somebody brought her a big batch of rhubarb so she mixed it with some strawberries and voila: Strawberry Rhubarb jam. Just like home cooking.

Additionally, Susan's made some good mixes: pancake, cocoa and scones. The Buckwheat Buttermilk Pancake mix is our favorite.

CHECKS OR MONEY ORDERS ONLY

CALL FOR CATALOG

RETAIL STORE: Call for directions

PHONE: 707-822-0248

FAX: 707-822-4441

MINIMUM ORDER: No

Bread and Breakfast

HOT DAMN JAM
814 Jefferson
Eugene, OR 97402

CHECKS OR MONEY
ORDERS ONLY

CALL FOR CATALOG

PHONE: 800-743-1084
        503-344-1184

MINIMUM ORDER: **No**

HOT DAM THAT'S JAM

Colleen Rudd and Kathy Reich are whipping up a bunch of hot jams using Oregon fruits and their own sophisticated palates for a guide. Think about perfect Oregon strawberries blended with a premium rum and what you get is called Strawberry Daiquiri. A batch of scones, a cup of tea. It's Oregon style high tea—hot dam.

Apricot Amaretto captures the rich tree-ripened flavor of local apricots then pumps that flavor with almond essence of amaretto. Try a duck glazed with their Brandied Plum Sauce and you'll be saying "Hot Dam!" yourself. Choose Raspberry Cassis, Tequila Toe-mato and Gooseberry Goldwasser—a German herbal-orange, liqueur-laced jam containing edible 22-karat gold flakes. Glaze your Christmas goose and you've got a 22-karat celebration. Every product is packed with flavor. They've invented fifteen flavors so far. Call and ask what's new.

GOURMET GIFTS
P.O. Box 1302
Hood River, OR 97031

CHECKS OR MONEY
ORDERS ONLY

CALL FOR CATALOG

PHONE: 503-352-6996

MINIMUM ORDER: **No**

OREGON GRAPE AND ELDERBERRY JELLY

Cheri Paasch puts up Oregon's fruits and berries in good looking hex jars and doesn't muck them up with a bunch of extraneous stuff. The result is the flavor of Oregon: pure, simple, and sweet.

Choose Wild Oregon Grape jelly or Elderberry jelly for two, exclusive-to-Oregon tastes. Also divine are Hazelnut Apple butter, Marionberry or Boysenberry jam, Peach butter, and a variety of fruit syrups: apple, peach, bing cherry, cascade blackberry, and huckleberry.

We particularly recommend the huckleberry products, both syrup and jam. If you've ever gone to the trouble of picking these pesky little berries, you'll appreciate the fact that Cheri's done it for you. The fruit is hard to come by. The syrup and jam are both tart and sweet. Yum.

Goldwasser Holiday Goose

Use this recipe with wild goose or domestic. Either way, you'll find braising brings out the best flavor, lessens the chance of drying the bird out and yet renders away the most fat so that the end result is a tender, flavorful bird. Gild the lily at the end with 22-karat flecked Goldwasser and gooseberry jam and the result is a glistening golden bird fit for any celebration.

makes 8-10 servings in 3 hours

Preheat the oven to 500°F. Season the cavity of the goose with salt and pepper. Pat the goose dry with paper toweling, then set the bird, breast up, on a rack in a roasting pan with a tight-fitting lid. Brown the goose without the lid in the hot oven about 20 minutes. Turn it a time or two to make the color even. Now salt and pepper the bird, place it breast up on the rack and turn the oven down to 325°F. and let the bird continue to roast while you make the braising liquid.

In a large skillet over medium high heat, heat oil or rendered goose fat from the roasting pan and brown together the goose neck, gizzard and heart that you've coarsely chopped, along with sliced onions and carrots. Sprinkle the mixture with sugar and cook until the onions and carrots are caramelized. Stir in the flour and continue to cook while the flour browns. Add stock and stir vigorously to make a thin sauce. Pour this sauce into the roaster under the bird. Add wine. Cover the roaster and let the goose cook until done, about 2½ hours.

The goose is done when the drumsticks move slightly in their sockets and the juices run pale yellow instead of pink. Lift off goose fat. You may save it for cooking or discard.

Heat the jam in the microwave about 30 seconds so that it will pour, then glaze the bird with it and replace in the oven, uncovered. Roast 10-15 minutes until the glaze sets. Remove to a serving platter and keep warm.

Skim all the fat from the roaster and boil down the liquid until its thick enough to coat a spoon. Correct seasoning with salt and pepper. Stir in the port and simmer a moment. Strain the sauce into a gravy boat. You'll have at least a quart of sauce.

Serve the goose with a purée of potatoes and rutabagas, and steamed Brussels sprouts, cinnamon-spiced apple sauce, a glass of champagne, and a loaf of rustic bread. It's Thanksgiving.

1 goose, about 9 lbs., plucked, scrubbed, and drained

goose neck, gizzard and heart, coarsely chopped

salt and freshly milled black pepper

1 large yellow onion, peeled and sliced thin

1 medium carrot, scraped and sliced thin

1 teaspoon granulated sugar

4 tablespoons rendered goose fat or cooking oil

6 tablespoons all purpose flour

1 quart chicken broth

3 cups dry white vermouth or wine

½ cup port wine

1 8-oz. jar Gooseberry Goldwasser jam

GOOD STUFF OF
TEXAS

27 Cheska Hollow
Beaumont, TX 77706

~~~~~~~~~~~~~~

CREDIT CARDS: Yes

CALL FOR CATALOG

RETAIL STORE: Open by
appointment—love to
show people around

PHONE: 409-898-2710
409-246-3276

MINIMUM ORDER: $15

ESSENCE OF
OREGON

P.O. Box 4189
Salem, OR 97302

~~~~~~~~~~~~~~

CREDIT CARDS: Yes

CALL FOR CATALOG

PHONE: 800-392-9106
503-399-7965

MINIMUM ORDER: $50

*Linda
Eckhardt's
1995
Guide to
America's
Best Foods*

MAYHAW, MUSCADINE JELLY

Ann Ethridge cooks in a log cabin way out on her farm in the deep piney woods of Southeast Texas near Kountze. The kitchen was built in 1900 and, like Topsy, has grown until it's so big now she can cater parties for 75 people out there. Every addition is also log so the integrity of the pioneer kitchen has been maintained.

Ann's a great cook and has been putting up the provender of Texas for a good number of years. She makes a Mayhaw jelly that's tart, sweet, and fully flavored with the sweet wild little fruit that's native to the south. She also makes Muscadine jelly from the wild grapes of Texas. This flavor is wild and wooly and makes a great glaze for a pheasant.

She also makes Huckleberry jam, Blackberry and Blueberry jams and jelly, a Blueberry topping, and the ubiquitous Jalapeno jelly.

She has a bunch of genuine Texas gift baskets to choose from. The Grande Basket is shaped like Texas and filled with jams and jellies.

If you're in the Beaumont area and would like to visit the farm, call and make an appointment. It's a beautiful secluded spot and gives you a small taste of what pioneer Texas life was all about.

OREGON BLACKBERRIES

I wish I could take you with me when we go blackberry picking here in the Oregon mountains. You can eat all you want of the sweet, warm, wild berries. Yes, you'll come home with your arms scratched up from reaching in to get that perfect bursting black beauty that's just out of reach, but you won't mind. You won't even mind that your fingers are stained purple forever.

Can't come to Oregon? Pat Scheidt has bottled Oregon and will ship it to you. Jams, syrups, and jellies—all made from the best that Oregon has to offer: Blackberry, Marionberry, Raspberry, Loganberry, Boysenberry and Blueberry. All are put up in various ways. Our personal favorite is the Black-Strawberry jam, an enticing blend of black berries and the delicate little super sweet strawberries that grow in Oregon and are only available fresh about one week a year.

At the age of 62, Pat Scheidt left her position as program coordinator with the Center for Dispute Resolution to make jam. Who could blame her? It's lots more fun to stir up jams than to settle jams. She won an award this year as the "Older Entrepreneur of the Year" from the Oregon Older Worker League. All I know is that her labels are gorgeous, her products as pure as an Oregon stream.

CHERRIES, CHERRIES, CHERRIES

If you're touristing through Michigan during the autumn to see the fall colors, The Cherry Hut is a lunch stop that's been luring the gawkers since 1922. Wanna know how pies are made? Look through the window and watch them whip out those homemade pies. Wanna real middle-America meal? Order a turkey with dressing dinner. Something local? Ask for deep fried whitefish or baked lake trout.

This is an "I Love Lucy" sort of place. And the best thing they do, you can take home or send for. Cherry pies, cherry conserve, cherry preserves, or cherry jelly. These are pure red cherry products made with both sweet and sour cherries, as dazzling a cherry red as you'll ever hope to see and made with Michigan's own cherry crop. Think of this as Michigan Memorabilia. That and a jar of pure red cherry preserves will make your breakfast bright, long after you've let Michigan become nothing more than a memory.

WILD MUSCADINE GRAPES

Muscadine grapes grow wild in the Southeastern United States. A deep purple with a woody and wild taste, they make terrific orange-colored jams and jellies. Aunt Bettie—believe me, you'll want to claim her after you taste these homemade products—makes muscadine jelly with jalapenos as well as muscadine pepper syrup she calls Muscadine Hot Sauce. Additionally, Aunt Bettie puts up garlic jelly, fig preserves, wild blackberry preserves, mayhaw jelly, and yellow squash pickles.

Now this is truly home cooking. She puts her products up in Ball half pints, uses paraffin on the tops, then seals them with flats and lids and finishes the tops with cotton bonnets, either checked, striped, or sometimes lace. Looking over a group of these jars, I feel like I'd just made a trip to my grandmother's cellar.

THE CHERRY HUT

P.O. Box 305
Beulah, MI 49617

CHECKS OR MONEY ORDERS ONLY

RETAIL STORE: Call for directions

PHONE: 616-882-4431

MINIMUM ORDER: No

AUNT BETTIE'S AND UNCLE EARL'S KITCHEN

P.O. Box 1854
Natchez, MS 39120

CHECKS OR MONEY ORDERS ONLY

CALL FOR CATALOG

RETAIL STORE: Call for directions

PHONE: 800-448-8286
318-757-2197

MINIMUM ORDER: 1 case

Aunt Bettie's Deep South Salad

Mix a cup of Muscadine Hot Sauce with ½ cup nonfat yogurt and pour over a bowl of mixed fruit—fresh or canned.

The muscadine is particularly valuable as a meat glaze and can be used to perk up stir fries for people who are trying to heighten flavors without adding fats.

Thanks Aunt Bettie and Uncle Earl. Keep on canning.

BABABERRIES

The sandy hills of East Texas grow a particular raspberry they call the bababerry. It actually came from California where it grew wild, and the starts were brought to Texas by Gertrude Millikan whose Texas grandchildren called her Baba. Get it?

The berry is bright-colored and has a tangy, wild flavor. You can buy the berries fresh in the spring and fall from the Walkers, Lynn or Bob, and the rest of the year content yourself with their frozen puree, their PS sauce, or their outstanding Raspberry Vinaigrette.

The puree can be used to make fat-free sorbet, or a heavenly sauce to serve with peaches, better than French Melba. A kind of Wild Texas Peach Melba. Delicious.

BERRY COUNTRY FARM

P.O. Box 657
Brownsboro, TX 75756

CREDIT CARDS: Yes

CALL FOR CATALOG

RETAIL STORE: Call for directions

PHONE: 903-852-4100

FAX: 903-852-4100

MINIMUM ORDER: $30

Linda Eckhardt's 1995 Guide to America's Best Foods

46

ALL AMERICAN JAMS AND MUSHROOMS

AMERICAN SPOON FOODS

P.O. Box 566
Petoskey, MI 49770

American Spoon Foods takes its name from the characteristic of its all-natural fruit preserves. Unlike mass-produced jam, as stiff as jujubes, American Spoon all-fruit preserves must be "spooned" onto that hot biscuit. But wait until you taste them. They're grand-mother's.

Justin Rashid, a native of voluptuous northern Michigan, began kicking up wild morels and other native comestibles in the seventies. After a brief stint as an actor, he followed in his father's footsteps and opened a country grocery. Then providence, in the form of a vaca-tioning waitress, stepped in and introduced him to New York restau-rateur, Larry Forgione.

In Forgione's restaurant, *An American Place,* with its egg yolk-yel-low walls and its belief in the primacy of native American products, Justin Rashid's Michigan groceries found a home.

Soon the two formed a partnership to produce and sell Michi-gan's goods: mushrooms, cherries, black walnuts, as well as jams like grandma put down in the cellar. Rashid's wife, Kate Marshall, added her low- and no-fat salad dressings called "Dazzlers" and soon Amer-ican Spoon became nationally respected by food opinion makers.

Located in a storefront in the quaint tourist town of Petoskey, where cherry orchards abound and wild berries grow in such profu-sion you couldn't pick them if you had an army to help, American Spoon has become one of the town's tourist draws.

We particularly adore the Red Haven Peach preserves. And I couldn't keep house without their dried red tart cherries. I sprinkle them into muffins, pancakes, and salads made with mesclun greens and finished with one of Kate's salad Dazzlers. Try the raspberry. It's heaven. Forgione's salsas and sophisticated sauces are also recom-mended.

CREDIT CARDS: Yes

CALL FOR CATALOG

RETAIL STORE: Call for directions

PHONE: 800-222-5886

FAX: 616-347-2512

MINIMUM ORDER: $10

Bread and Breakfast

Larry Forgione's Grilled Pork Tenderloin with Michigan Dried Cherries and Cherry Sauce

makes 2 servings in 45 minutes

Have pork at room temperature. Tuck the thin end under and skewer. Brush with oil. Sprinkle with pepper and fennel seed. Grill over medium-hot charcoal to an internal temperature of 140°F. turning several times. Remove to a heated platter, cover and let it rest 8–10 minutes. Slice on the diagonal then fan pieces out over a pool of dried cherry sauce. Garnish with dried red cherries and a sprig of mint.

1 small (9–11 oz.) pork tenderloin
extra virgin olive oil
fresh cracked black pepper
fennel seed
Dried Red Cherry Sauce (recipe follows)

American Spoon Michigan Dried Red Cherry Sauce

Combine cherries, garlic, and wine in a saucepan. Simmer uncovered until reduced by half. Cut butter into pieces and swirl into the sauce. Serve at once.

½ cup dried red tart cherries
1 small head garlic, peeled
⅓ bottle Barolo wine
2 tablespoons unsalted butter

ALASKA WILD BERRY PRODUCTS

528 E. Pioneer Ave.
Homer, AK 99603

CREDIT CARDS: Yes

CALL FOR CATALOG

RETAIL STORE: Yes

PHONE: 907-235-8858

MINIMUM ORDER: No

ALASKA WILD BERRIES

Forty-five years or so ago, Hazel Heath began picking berries ripened by the midnight sun, and turning them into jams she shipped to the lower forty-eight. The business is still housed in a wooden structure that looks like Santa's workshop, complete with not-for-special-effects snow on the ground. If you're in Homer, Alaska, stop by the famous kitchen and taster's table. In back you'll find a Wild Berry picnic park complete with wildflowers and berries of Alaska, an old-fashioned food cache, a working sluice box where you can pan for real Alaskan gold, and the log cabin that served as the original post office for pioneers in Homer.

Order jam and you can choose from rosehips, lingonberries, highbush and lowbush cranberries, wild raspberries, mossberries, and salmonberries. From these they make a variety of pure jellies, jams, and sauces. Write for a complete list of their products.

Honeys, Maple Syrups, and Sugars.

I eat well, and I drink well, and I sleep well, but that's all.

—WILLIAM MORRIS (1834–1896)

MECH APIARIES

P.O. Box 452
Maple Valley, WA
98038

CHECKS OR MONEY
ORDERS ONLY

CALL FOR CATALOG

RETAIL STORE: **Call for
directions**

PHONE: **206-432-3971**

MINIMUM ORDER: **No**

JERECO, INC.

21527 Rich Valley Road
Abingdon, VA 24210

CHECKS OR MONEY
ORDERS ONLY

CALL FOR CATALOG

PHONE: **703-628-3544**

MINIMUM ORDER: **3 Jars**

*Linda
Eckhardt's
1995
Guide to
America's
Best Foods*

EPICURE'S HONEY

And you thought honey was honey. It all depends on the bees and do the Mechs go out of their way to get the best bees to work for them? They do. Driving all over the state of Washington to set out hives, they get some of the most aromatic, individual tasting honeys I've ever put into my mouth.

Choose from wild huckleberry, fireweed, wild blackberry, snowberry, and rare maple blossom. The list keeps changing. Currently they also offer raspberry blossom, wild blackberry, Mt. Rainier fireweed, clover, Washington wildflower and Saldhonig '92, a dark forest honey.

Order three jars at a time. They only charge three or four bucks a jar and believe me, one jar won't be enough.

BLACK WALNUT SYRUP

Virginia's known for its huge black walnut trees. One of their traditional favorite foods is a syrup made from black walnuts that's poured over jonnycakes or biscuits. Jere and Lou Counts have figured out a way to prize the meat from the black walnuts in a way to make it possible to produce this rare exotic product in a big enough volume to sell.

The Counts use their old family recipe to produce this punchy syrup, and you'll find the syrup a rare and exotic addition to the breakfast or tea sideboard. My son pours it over ice cream. It's too exotic for words.

OREGON HONEY

JOANN'S HONEY
3164 Maple Ct.
Reedsport, OR 97467

Joann Olstrom collects honey on Oregon's coast and finds some pure, mild flavors we like for cooking. Coos Bay Wildflower honey is a pale amber color and a perfect addition to homemade granola. She also puts up honey with walnuts, which is an ancient preserving idea Joann's made new again. You can order pure beeswax here, and a Honey Bear.

Want to start your own beekeeping business? Write Joann and she'll send you all the beekeepers' supplies you could ever need.

Joann's Honey Stix are nifty snacks. Clear plastic cannisters full of the stix are great for kids' afterschool snacks and a handy snack for camping trips. Joann calls them Flower Power in a Straw, and says they're easy to carry, a quick energy source, and available in sixteen flavors from wintergreen to grape.

CHECKS OR MONEY ORDERS ONLY

WRITE FOR CATALOG

PHONE: No phone orders

MINIMUM ORDER: $10

NORTHERN CALIFORNIA GRADE A FANCY FLAVORED HONEYS

DELIGHTFUL HONEYS
100 Ericson St., Ste. 155
Arcata, CA 95521

Vickie Luick-Hutt puts up a variety of local honeys. Some she flavors, and some she leaves just the way the bees want them. All are packed in attractive hex jars with good-looking blue labels. Flavors include Orange, Lemon, Cinnamon, Chocolate, Peppermint, Jalapeno, Rose and the new Redwood Spice.

Vickie likes to mix peanut butter with flavored honey, zap it a minute in the microwave then drizzle it on popcorn. Her flavored honeys are also nice to sweeten tea. She uses natural flavors and extracts.

CHECKS OR MONEY ORDERS ONLY

PHONE: 707-826-7037

FAX: 707-822-8982

MINIMUM ORDER: No

**MOONSHINE
TRADING COMPANY**

P.O. Box 896
Winters, CA 95694

CREDIT CARDS: **Yes**

CALL FOR CATALOG

RETAIL STORE: **Call for
directions**

PHONE: 916-753-0601

FAX: 916-753-5301

MINIMUM ORDER: **$20.00**

**MAVERICK
SUGARBUSH**

P.O. Box 99
Sharon, VT 05065

CREDIT CARDS: **Yes**

CALL FOR CATALOG

PHONE: 802-763-8680

FAX: 802-763-8684

MINIMUM ORDER: **No**

*Linda
Eckhardt's
1995
Guide to
America's
Best Foods*

CALIFORNIA HONEY AND APRICOTS

Pure California Sunshine in a jar. That's the honey apricot jam from Moonshine. Combining the best of California honey with legendary California apricots into a new spread that demands good toast. It's honey sweet and fruit tart. Pour it over cream cheese for an apricoty cracker spread. Baste poultry with it and you've got an outstanding California fruity barbecue.

The honeys put out by the Moonshine Trading Company look so enticing, you may just want to feast your eyes on the labels. But do open the jars. They choose honeys flavored from yellow star thistle, sweet clover, sunflower, orange blossom, eucalyptus, black button sage, and Christmasberry. Each honey is distinctive in taste—going, as honeys do, from light to dark in strength and intensity. Our favorite is the eucalyptus. Moonshine also packages splendid Almond Nut butter to go with the honey for your next gourmet picnic.

ORGANIC MAPLE SYRUP

You'd almost buy the maple syrup for the label. Unlike the usual Vermont label, this one is dazzling red, gold, and purple, as modern as the best design, and as enticing as the organic maple syrup inside.

Maverick Sugarbush is at the end of a dirt road outside the village of Sharon, Vermont. With more than 500 acres under management, Anne and Arthur Berndt strive to produce first quality organic maple syrup. You may think all maple syrup is organic, seeing as how they just plug a maple tree then boil the syrup down. But the Berndts go to special lengths to retain the purity of their syrup. They fertilize organically. They defoam organically. What you get is a pure, pure product.

Just this year, they've made a foray into the funny water business. It's so simple. Instead of boiling down the sap to make syrup, they simply pasteurize the sap as it comes from the tree, bottle it, and offer it as a new bottled drink, Vermont Maple-Tapped Sapwater. It's clear, fresh, and only slightly sweet tasting. An old-fashioned elixir you can order by the case during the sugaring off season. It's rare and it's precious. Get your orders in early.

David Marvin's Vermont Spring Chicken

Preheat the oven to 400°F. Butter a shallow baking dish and arrange chicken pieces in the dish, one layer deep. Combine melted butter, maple syrup, lemon zest, salt, pepper, almonds and lemon juice. Pour evenly over the chicken. Roast uncovered 50-60 minutes in the preheated oven. Baste occasionally. Terrific on a bed of aromatic rice.

1 3-lb. chicken, cut into pieces

2 tablespoons melted butter

½ cup maple syrup

½ teaspoon grated lemon zest

1 teaspoon salt

freshly milled black pepper to taste

¼ cup chopped almonds

2 teaspoons lemon juice

VERMONT MAPLE SYRUP

Forester David Marvin comes by his love for maple trees naturally. His father was a botanist who specialized in maple research at the University of Vermont. Dad purchased the original plot of land for Butternut Farm and planted sugarbush maples in the fifties. David now shepherds 600 acres making maple syrup and sugar, growing Christmas trees, cutting spruce for wreaths, and cutting sawlogs, firewood, and pulpwood. In 1983, he was named National Outstanding Tree Farmer of the Year.

You won't see the picturesque buckets on trees here, but rather a spider web of plastic tubing that by gravity and vacuum draws the sap to holding tanks, a system that turns 144,000 gallons of sap into 3600 gallons of pure maple syrup. Buy it in three grades: Fancy, the light amber, delicate-flavored syrup, Grade A medium amber—the most popular, and Grade A dark amber, the most robust that comes only at the end of the season. Do try maple sugar. It looks like fine dust, but is such a concentrated maple taste, you'll want it on your steel-cut oats every morning for breakfast. Ask for a fancy glass container for your syrup. They offer several.

A visit to the farm store is a treat. A two story wooden building set in a field of trees, it's a good tourist stop. You'll be able to buy there not only Butternut's products, but other fine Vermont products including Old Mill Apiaries Fruitful Honey Creme. Available in raspberry, straw-

BUTTERNUT MOUNTAIN FARM
P.O. Box 381
Johnson, VT 05656

CREDIT CARDS: Yes

CALL FOR CATALOG

RETAIL STORE: Call for directions

PHONE: 800-828-2376
802-635-2403

FAX: 802-635-7644

MINIMUM ORDER: No

Bread and Breakfast

berry, blueberry, and cinnamon, this stuff begs for pancakes. And have they got the pancake mix. It's as fine as their very best syrup.

EVERETT AND KATHRYN PALMER

P.O. Box 246
Waisfield, VT 05673

CHECKS OR MONEY
ORDERS ONLY

RETAIL STORE: **Call for directions**

PHONE: 802-496-3696

MINIMUM ORDER: **No**

HANDMADE MAPLE SYRUP

Everett Palmer, hovering around 85, and his wife, Kathryn, a couple of years younger, have been making maple syrup the artful old-fashioned way for all of the 60-plus years of their marriage. According to Everett, whose made a living tapping trees on his 34 acre farm his entire life, they're "too old" to buy the new scientific equipment. This means that Everett Palmer, by himself, cuts, loads, hauls, and stacks 45 cords of wood every year. In the spring, when he can smell it in the air, Everett Palmer straps on snow shoes and slogs through knee-deep snow every day for six weeks, collecting sap from the same trees his grandfather and father before him tapped. For this part of the job, at least, he has the help of his son and three hired hands.

Everett uses his century-old wood-fired evaporator in a sugarhouse that he's never quite gotten around to electrifying. His wife, Kathryn, stands and stirs the boiling sap, holding a spoon up until the golden syrup sheets off just to suit her. Then, the two of them pack 800 gallons of syrup—by hand. Much of it, they sell right out of the sugarhouse to devoted customers who know the product is in short supply and only available as long as the Palmers can keep up the pace of this vigorous outdoor life.

The Palmers maple syrup is the purest ginger ale color, the highest grade. All made by hand in a way that blends art, experience, and craft so subtly it probably never can be passed on to another generation.

PURE CANE SYRUP FROM SOUTH LOUISIANA

It's kind of embarrassing to make a fool of yourself over syrup, but that's exactly what happened when the cans of Steen's syrups came to our house. Like many Southerners before us, my husband Joe and I grew up with pure ribbon cane syrup as a staple in the house. This meant that this kind of syrup was on the table at every meal as surely as salt and pepper. Sometimes we used it for dessert with nothing besides butter and bread. Sometimes we used it for the main course, when we were having French Toast for breakfast—or for supper. Some Southerners just pour Steen's syrup all over everything on their plate. Even on the pork chops and the greens. We do love it so.

Steen's syrup is not the same as "sorghum" or "molasses". It's the result of open kettle cooking of whole sugar cane stalks. Basically, it's the same idea as maple syrup. All they do is boil down the stalks, strain and bottle the stuff. From our point of view, no sissy maple syrup can begin to compare. Make a pecan pie with Steen's syrup and you'll jump to your feet and sing "Dixie." Make molasses cookies with their molasses and you'll weep and wish for your mama.

Steen's makes pure cane syrup, molasses, pure cane vinegar, which is delicious, and industrial strength molasses in 50-gallon drums in case you'd like to sweeten the feed of your own herd of cattle.

If you're in South Louisiana during the fall, stop in and watch them make syrup. Just follow your nose to the mill. The scent of baking sugar cookies will lead you there. It's a patient process, syrup-making. Eight hours of paddling in an open kettle and the hot, molten gold is ready to pour into jars, bottles, and cans. And, as they say, nothing is added, nothing extracted.

Ask, and they'll send you an adorable cookbook and history complete with charming illustrations. It makes me wish for another trip to South Louisiana. I'd really like the chance to shake hands with the best-looking man in South Louisiana, "Ugly" Steen himself, the owner of the syrup mill. *Le bon temps* and all that stuff.

C.S. STEEN SYRUP MILL

119 North Main St.
Abbeville, LA
70511-0339

CREDIT CARDS: **Yes**

CALL FOR CATALOG

RETAIL STORE: **Yes**

PHONE: **318-893-1654**

FAX: **318-893-2478**

MINIMUM ORDER: **Yes**

Bread and Breakfast

55

FINE BUTTERS AND HANDMADE CHEESES.

She ate the poisoned cheese sandwich and turned up her toes.

—JAMES CAGNEY in *Jimmy the Gent,* 1934

CHEESE IS IDEAL

IDEAL CHEESE SHOP
1205 Second Ave.
New York, NY 10021

Ed Edelman is a walking encyclopedia. He knows everything there is to know about cheese and dispenses wisdom and knowledge along with the cheese from his spanking clean cheese shop on Manhattan's upper East side.

The Zagat guide says it's the best cheese store in New York and to my mind, the second best thing about it is that you can order custom cut cheeses from Ed and he'll ship them out.

If you tasted a cheese on your travels and figure you'll never taste it again, think again. Ed Edelman may carry it. France, England, Canada, Holland, Greece, Germany, Norway, Denmark, Belgium, Bulgaria, Ireland, Switzerland, Spain. If it's cheese, Ed's probably got it.

Talking with Ed is an education in itself. He can recommend cheeses to go on your cheese tray. He can tell you what cheeses to cook with. While you've got him, get him to sell you his very own cookbook. It's filled with valuable information.

Think of Ideal Cheese as your source for Asiago, Reggiano, Gorgonzola, and Taleggio. Here's where you can buy Kasserie, Aged Edam and Gouda, Tomme de Savoie, fine Danish Saga, Norway's Gjetost and Switzerland's Raclette. They also have a good selection of low-fat, low-cholesterol cheeses.

Ed also sells patés, mousses, smoked ham, buendnerfleish, olives and gift baskets.

CREDIT CARDS: **Yes**

Send $2 for a Catalog

RETAIL STORE: **1205 Second Ave. between 63rd and 64th**

PHONE: **800-382-0109 212-688-7579**

MINIMUM ORDER: **No**

Bread and Breakfast

**HOUSE OF
WISCONSIN CHEESE**

107 State St.
Madison, WI 53703

CREDIT CARDS: **Yes**

CALL FOR CATALOG

RETAIL STORE: **Yes**

PHONE: **800-955-0238
608-255-5204**

FAX: **608-255-5321**

MINIMUM ORDER: **No**

WISCONSIN CAPITAL CHEESE: MOOVALOUS CHEESE

Located in the capitol city of Madison right on State Street is a good source for Wisconsin's favorite product: cheese. Not only can you buy or order a variety of Wisconsin cheddars, Colbys, bricks, Monterey Jack, Edam, Swiss and summer sausages, but—lo and behold—you can buy an astonishing number of cow souvenirs and Wisconsin collectibles. And let me tell you—if it's from Wisconsin, it will more than likely be black and white—like the cows. They do love their cows in the Moo State.

Visit the State Capital, the State Historical Museum, and the Children's Museum after you've tossed down a few cheese curds from the shop. Then, after you've bought your tee shirt that says "Eat Cheese or Die," and after you've bought your Cheese Baseball Cap and your Cheese Can Cooler, that looks like a giant wedge of cheese with a beer can sticking out of it, know that you can get honest to god Cow-Moo-Flage clothing, right here. Shirts, pants, shoes, cow eggs.

But seriously folks—as if anyone in Wisconsin can be made to be serious—these people are so cheerful you'd think they were full of the bubbly instead of plain old cheese. You can order more than 50 varieties from this complete cheese shop. Mail home a gift of cheese.

*Linda
Eckhardt's
1995
Guide to
America's
Best Foods*

A CASTLE OF CHEESE

MARS CHEESE CASTLE

2800 120th Ave.
Kenosha, WI 53144

Mario Ventura, Sr. and his wife, Martha, bought an old school house in 1946 and converted it to a cheese market. Now the company's a lot bigger. And the little school house has grown turrets and flying pennants. They have everything but the drum rolls. And they do call it a castle.

They call it Mars because that was Mario's childhood nickname. But his hard work and dreams show he was firmly planted on Earth. Now, he sells so much cheddar, he orders it 10 tons at a time.

We got a nice crock of cheddar spread which tasted a lot better than the imitation cheese spread normally packed in crocks. Spread on a cracker, Mars' spreadable cheddar is mouth-watering. A robust, full-flavored cheddar flavor that's hard to quit eating.

In addition to a variety of cheeses—call and inquire—they sell good apple, pumpkin, and apricot butters made in Wisconsin. They also stock a good selection of fine Wisconsin smoked meats including summer sausages, hams, and bacon.

Stop in the castle and you'll be treated to Wisconsin hospitality. They'll make you a sandwich. They'll give you a smile. They may even carry your groceries to the car. This is friendly Wisconsin at its best.

CREDIT CARDS: Yes

CALL FOR CATALOG

RETAIL STORE: Yes

PHONE: 414-859-2244

FAX: 414-859-2230

MINIMUM ORDER: No

Bread and Breakfast

CHECKS OR MONEY
ORDERS ONLY

CALL FOR CATALOG

RETAIL STORE: Call for
directions

PHONE: 216-868-4196

FAX: 216-868-7947

MINIMUM ORDER: No

OHIO CHEESE DELUXE

Phil and Polly Mueller say made with love from Moo to you, and rightly so. Their handmade cheeses are brightly flavored, fresher than fresh, and will live in your memory. They make cheese the old-fashioned way, just like Grandpa Max P. began in 1894, using the German techniques he'd brought over with him from the old country. Now 4th generation cheesemaker Phil R. combines the best of new and old techniques to give us exceptional cheeses.

Particularly good is their 1935 Mellow Cheddar which has an extremely complex taste. They also make a fine Colby and Pepper Jack as well as an interesting line of so-called Light cheeses. They call these Minerva Lace, Cheddarwise, Colbywise, and Farmerwise. Basically, these cheeses have reduced fats and salts yielding about 75 calories per ounce serving, with about 5½ fat grams and 180 mg. sodium.

But for taste, our money's on Buckeye Swiss. Named for the state's motto, "The Buckeye State," this Swiss cheese is among the best we ever tasted anywhere: domestic or imported. It's nutty, smooth, aromatic, and delicious.

They also make fine goat's milk cheddar that's a new twist on an old idea. Using Ohio's bounty, including mushrooms, Chef Milton Awa cooked up this good stuff at the Ohio State Fair and they were lining up around the block for a taste.

Linda
Eckhardt's
1995
Guide to
America's
Best Foods

Minerva's Ohio Strudel with Wild Mushrooms and Goat Cheddar and Madeira Sauce

Preheat the oven to 350°F. Sauté in butter the mushrooms and shallots adding garlic as the mixture dries. Add wine and boil down until the mixture is syrupy. Off the heat, add herbs and goat cheese.

Place 3 phyllo sheets on each half of a parchment paperlined sheet pan. Brush with 2 teaspoons of butter. Place half the mushroom mixture along each of the long sides of phyllo. Roll each strudel tightly, taking care not to tear the phyllo. Brush with remaining butter and mark 5 portions on each strudel roll.

Bake in preheated oven 10 minutes or until golden brown. Serve with Madeira Sauce, sour cream, mushroom caps, and watercress.

To make the Madeira Sauce, boil consomme and wine down to ½ cup.

1½ tablespoons butter

1¼ lbs. Wild Ohio mushrooms, assorted, sliced

3 tablespoons shallots, minced

1 tablespoon minced garlic

½ cup Ohio white wine

¼ cup Minerva Maid Raw Goat Milk Cheddar, shredded

2 tablespoons EACH: parsley, chives, chervil, tarragon, chopped

6 phyllo sheets

1½ tablespoons butter

1¾ cups Madeira sauce (see below)

¼ cup sour cream

10 mushroom caps, sauteed in butter

1 bunch watercress

Madeira Sauce:

1¾ cups jus de Veau Lie OR canned beef consomme

¼ cup Madeira wine

MOUSEHOUSE
CHEESEHAUS

Jct I-90 and Hwy 19
P.O. Box 527
Windsor, WI 53598

CREDIT CARDS: Yes

CALL FOR CATALOG

RETAIL STORE: Yes

PHONE: 800-526-6873
   698-846-4455

MINIMUM ORDER: No

BEST QUALITY WISCONSIN CHEESES

Order from the Mousehouse and you know you're getting cheese that's been made in a small Wisconsin cheese factory. No big commodity cheeses are sold here. Art and Carmen Sobczak and their son, Tony, carefully scrutinize from among the ka-zillions of cheeses made in Wisconsin and choose only the best to sell in their store. They handpick, cut, wrap, and wax cheeses made in the state. Some of the cheeses are aged over five years to bring them to their peak of perfection.

Mousehouse Jack is soft and buttery—a great cooking and eating cheese. But perhaps their best are the cheddars. *Wine and Spirits* magazine called their aged cheddar "excruciatingly delicious," and went on to describe the flavor of a three-year-old cheddar as "deeply nutty with a beguiling crumble and grapefruity aroma."

Here's a source for some of Wisconsin's German-style sausages too. And Limburger for those who'd like to try Wisconsin's "Bachelor Cheese." Wisconsin-made parmesan, romano and fine quality asiago are also found here. If you're in the Madison area, take the kids out to see the Mousehouse. They'll spot it first. There's a big mouse eating a wedge of cheddar mounted on the roof. And the sign on the Swiss-style building says, Cheese—Gifts—Liquor—Beer. Wisconsin souvenirs are available here. Read C-O-W in every form and fashion. They also offer maple syrup, honey, and jams. Open every day but Christmas, the Mousehouse is a good stop on a Wisconsin vacation. And they're so helpful on the phone, they'll make a custom gift basket for you and even make good suggestions for what you should include.

*Linda
Eckhardt's
1995
Guide to
America's
Best Foods*

Wisconsin Great Greek Salad

2 main dish servings

Tear romaine leaves into bite-sized pieces and place in a large salad bowl. Add cucumber half-moons, radish slices, and diced onions and olives. Toss.

Whisk together the vinaigrette, beginning by mulling together vinegar with salt, pepper, and oregano. Whisk in oil, then pour over the lettuce mixture and toss to mix.

Divide the lettuce between two dinner plates. Top each serving with tomato wedges, crumbled Wisconsin feta cheese, and a generous grating of fresh pepper. Garnish with additional fresh oregano leaves and serve at once.

1 head Romaine lettuce, outer 6 leaves discarded

1 medium cucumber, peeled, deseeded, and sliced

6 radishes, scrubbed and sliced thin

4 green onions and tops, cut into fine dice

12 large Kalamata olives

2 medium tomatoes, cut into 8 wedges

¼ lb. Wisconsin Feta cheese, rinsed, drained, and crumbled

Oregano Vinaigrette:

¼ cup red wine vinegar

salt and freshly milled black pepper to taste

2 teaspoons fresh oregano (OR 1 tsp. dried)

¼ cup olive oil

Bread and Breakfast

**HERKIMER FAMILY
TREASURE HOUSE**

Upper Otsego St.,
Rt. 51
Ilion, NY 13357

CHECKS OR MONEY
ORDERS ONLY

CALL FOR CATALOG

RETAIL STORE: Yes

PHONE: 315-895-7832

FAX: 315-895-4664

MINIMUM ORDER: No

NEW YORK CHEDDAR

The elements in Herkimer County are pure serendipity: climate, soil, grass, and cattle. Add to that English immigrants who settled the country and brought their craft for making cheddar along, and something good was bound to happen. It did. This area produces some of America's finest cheddars. Visit the Herkimer's place and you can buy the best of New York's cheddars as well as some antiques if you're in the market. Open weekdays 9–5, and Saturdays from 11–3. Sunday, they're open by chance or by appointment. Just give a call to Mrs. B.

The Sheldon Basloe family has been making and selling New York-style cheddars since 1949. Just this year, Mr. B. will be inducted into the USDA Hall of Fame for his innovative work with cheeses. For not only has he made and sold fine white and yellow cheddars, he's developed and perfected cheese spreads that come in crocks that are absolutely divine. He also made the first commercial cheese balls. He'd go around to three or four grocery stores in his hometown, picking up nuts, then he and the wife and kids would sit around cracking nuts to roll the cheese balls in.

He also invented a cheddar fudge. This sounds bad but tastes good, since the cheese substitutes for the milk and butter you'd normally find in the product and the cheddar gives the sweet fudge a nice bite. We also really like his new mustard cheddar, which is a natural for hot dogs but also a good spread on top of finer sausages.

**HARMAN'S CHEESE
AND COUNTRY
STORE**

Route 117
Sugar Hill, NH 03585

CHECKS OR MONEY
ORDERS ONLY

CALL FOR CATALOG

RETAIL STORE: Yes

PHONE: 603-823-8000

MINIMUM ORDER: No

FINE AGED CHEDDAR

In the far north country of New Hampshire sits Harman's in a town so small you don't need directions to find the store. The owners live upstairs. The products they sell are few, carefully chosen, and as pure as a New England winter. For example, a two-year-old cheddar that is rich, crumbly, looks like butter, and is sharp but never bitter. This same cheddar is folded into *Sandeman Oporto* (port), then laced with Courvoisier Napoleon brandy to make a cocktail spread with a light texture and a sharp aftertaste. You can shop by mail from this little country store for a small collection of hard-to-find, pure, top-quality New England delicacies. Ask for Maxine. That's Maxine Aldrich, who started working here in 1974 and bought the business from Harman's estate.

Following the food philosophy of the Harmans, Maxine stocks best-quality maple syrup, Atlantic blue crab claws, dried soldier beans, local honey, kipper fillets, and New England common crackers.

CHEDDAR AND PEACE OF MIND

SHELBURNE FARMS
Shelburne, VT 05482

CREDIT CARDS: **Yes**

CALL FOR CATALOG

RETAIL STORE: **Call for directions**

PHONE: **802-985-8686**

FAX: **802-985-8123**

MINIMUM ORDER: **No**

The Shelburne Farms were the Utopian dream of Dr. William Seward Webb who bought up 30 small farms and hired Frederick Law Olmsted—who designed Central Park—to do the grounds. He employed Robert Robertson, a New York architect, to design buildings that resemble English country houses. Actually, it looks like an American's idea of what he'd like his castle to be. Located on the shores of Lake Champlain, Shelburne Farms is listed on the National Register of Historic Places. Only 3 miles away is the Shelburne Museum, with the country's foremost collection of Americana.

Now Shelburne is a nonprofit educational organization for farm and garden concerns. It's also an inn and a restaurant with a formidable reputation for fine food. School children are shepherded through here and taught about the good green earth. They offer five tours a day from Memorial Day to mid-October. It's still a Utopian place. And quite worth a visit.

Home to many cultural events and concerts, Shelburne is a place where you can go to rest, to sleep, to eat, to listen to music, to learn about agriculture, or just to walk on bucolic grounds. Bring your children to the children's farmyard. You and the kids can even learn to milk a cow.

Order cheese from their on-site facility—the new vat holds 7,000 gallons of milk from their herd of brown Swiss cows—and you'll be delighted. In this cheddar plant they make the cheese several ways, but control the process from the brown Swiss cows up—the feed, the handling of milk, and the processing of cheese. It's all done here under strict controls. Aged six-months to two-years, the black-waxed raw milk cheddar comes in medium, sharp, and extra sharp, as well as smoked. This cheese meets the standards for first quality cheddar: it's crumbly, rich, and sharp-flavored. Shelbourne also makes bread to accompany the cheese. Other Vermont products are available here: cob-smoked Vermont hams, maple syrup, honey mustard, and various jams and preserves.

Bread and Breakfast

Vermont Cheese Pudding

Preheat the oven to 325°F. Cut crusts from bread then dip the bread slices in butter. Completely line a 2-quart soufflé dish with buttered bread. Whisk together cream, eggs, port, Worcestershire, mustard, cheese, salt, pepper, and paprika. Pour into the dish and place it in a pan of hot water that comes ¾ of the way up the sides of the dish. Bake on the middle rack of the oven until the top puffs and is brown, about 1 hour. The pudding is done when a knife inserted in the middle comes out clean. Cool on a rack 10 minutes before spooning onto plates for serving.

8 slices French bread

¼ lb. butter, melted

3 cups half-and-half

3 eggs

¼ cup port

1 teaspoon Worcestershire Sauce

1 teaspoon Dijon mustard

½ lb. sharp cheddar, grated

salt, pepper, and paprika to taste.

SUGARBUSH FARM

RR 1, Box 568
High Pasture Road
Woodstock, VT 05091

CREDIT CARDS: Yes

CALL FOR CATALOG

RETAIL STORE: Call for directions

PHONE: 800-281-1757

FAX: 802-457-3269

MINIMUM ORDER: No

Linda Eckhardt's 1995 Guide to America's Best Foods

MAPLE SMOKED VERMONT CHEDDARS

Smooth, sharp, crumbly—a cheese to remember. That's what you'll find from Sugarbush. And they handwrap the cheese in foil and three coats of red, cream or black wax. If I had one cheese I'd want to tuck into a picnic basket to go along with a loaf of dark bread, this would be it.

A small, old-fashioned kind of business, Sugarbush ships orders the same day they get them. And it's been a family business since 1945. Betsy Luce's daddy, Jack Ayres, started the business, aging and smoking cheddars he bought from small cheese factories in Vermont.

Gourmet magazine says of the Luce's cheese, "one of the most dependable places in America in which to find assertive yet richly mellow cheddar." Amen to that. The Ayres-Luces also tap maple trees and make syrup, maple sugar, cream, and a melt-in-your-mouth maple sugar bonbon in the shape of a maple leaf. You get good, personal service here, and superior Vermont products.

CARR VALLEY CHEDDAR

CARR VALLEY CHEESE COMPANY

S 3797 County G
La Valle, WI 53941

O ne hundred years of experience pays off. You can taste handmade cheddar and cheese curds made in small batches and cut to order for you from the Carr Valley people. They make rind-ripened cheeses that are dipped in wax and left to age on special wooden racks in climate-controlled rooms.

Order curds for the squeaky fresh taste of baby cheddar, or get medium, mild, or sharp cheddar aged from 1 to 3½ years. If you've never tasted cheddar that's been aged three years, I urge you to order this. It's a rare and wonderful experience.

They also make and sell low-fat cheddar, smoked cheddar, a 5½ lb. wheel of cheddar, Colby, Guernsey (2-color cheddar), Monterey Jack, Pepper Jack, Vegie Jack, and Sid's Dariworld—a new variety of nutty-flavored Swiss style cheese they just invented.

You can also get a variety of other Wisconsin products: jams, jellies, honey, butters, mustards, and sausages.

CREDIT CARDS: Yes

CALL FOR CATALOG

RETAIL STORE: Call for directions

PHONE: 608-986-2781

MINIMUM ORDER: No

FRESH MADE MOZZARELLA AND GOAT CHEESE

MOZZARELLA COMPANY

2944 Elm St.
Dallas, TX 75226

W hen Paula Lambert returned to Dallas after living in Italy she missed fresh mozzarella. So, in true Texas fashion, she just started making it herself. That was 1982. She was a hit with the cooks and food critics from the moment she began selling her handmade cheeses. Her cheeses are all handmade in the European manner without added preservatives. She now sells an impressive list of cow's milk, goat's milk, and sheep's milk cheeses.

Paula Lambert just can't quit winning prizes. Her exquisite cheeses have been taking home the blue ribbons since she started in business. Latest in a long line of winners is her Scamorza, a handformed, low-moisture mozzarella that won a blue ribbon in the Pasta Filata Category of the prestigious American Cheese Society Contest.

Also winning in the same contest were her Queso Blanco with Chiles and Epazote, a fresh moist disc of Mexican-

CREDIT CARDS: Yes

CALL FOR CATALOG

RETAIL STORE: Yes

PHONE: 800-798-2954
214-741-4072

FAX: 214-741-4076

MINIMUM ORDER: No

style cheese that begs for an enchilada. This is a smooth, melting cheese that will not "grease out" like American cheddars or Longhorn.

Her Texas Goat cheese is a fresh, moist, creamy chevre in the classic style of French cheeses. Her Montasio, Goat's Milk Caciotta, and fresh ricotta won gold medals at the American Dairy Goat Association Cheese-Judging Contest in Madison, Wisconsin.

She deserves all this praise. Paula Lambert is exacting, scientific, and artful in her production of cheeses. Order from her and you're assured of getting a first quality cheese.

SWISS STYLE RAW GOAT'S MILK CHEESES

For a mild, white, firm goat's milk cheese particularly suited to cooking, Mt. Capra makes an elastic-curd cheese they call Cascadian and a more crumbly, dry, sharp type they call Mt. Capra Natural. The latter comes with or without caraway seeds.

Most interesting is their own version of *gjetost*, known as Viking Brown Whey cheese. It's a rich, caramel brown, melts on the tongue, and has the complex taste of caramels, but without the sugar. Popular with runners, it's high in potassium, phosphorus, and carbohydrates. It's made from skim milk and is low in fat.

MT. CAPRA CHEESE
279 S.W. 9th St.
Chehalis, WA 98532

CREDIT CARDS: Yes

CALL FOR CATALOG

PHONE: 206-748-4224

MINIMUM ORDER: No

Linda
Eckhardt's
1995
Guide to
America's
Best Foods

68

ORGANIC GOATS

BRIER RUN FARM

HC 32 Box 73
Birch River, WV 26610

CREDIT CARDS: **Yes**

CALL FOR CATALOG

PHONE: **304-649-2975**

MINIMUM ORDER: **$25**

Greg and Verena Seva got into the cheese business because they felt sorry for a goat. They'd bought this lush, West Virginia farm covered in hardwoods and rhododendrons. They bought the goat for milk, penning it up in a handmade enclosure they'd made of saplings. Squeaky the goat cried like a baby all night long. She was lonely. So, Greg and Verena bought her some pals.

Before long, they were awash in goat's milk. With some help from the West Virginia Agricultural people, they began making fresh goat cheese. They are strict about everything being organic—the feed, the surroundings. The cheese is pure, splendid, unspoiled. That's because the Sevas' goats get lots of exercise on the steep West Virginia hillsides, and they get lots of good organic hay to eat to supplement their diet of briers and herbs that are on the land. The result is perfect cheese.

In the seventeen years since the Sevas first set foot in West Virginia, they've expanded to make many fine fresh goat cheeses. Quark, a low-fat, no-salt cheese, that's a lot like sour cream, is great with fruit or as a substitute for sour cream or mayonnaise. They also make Fromage Blanc, Chabis, Banon, Pyramid, Crottin, Buche, and Chevre. You can order the finish you'd like on your cheese. Specify from these choices: black pepper, Italian herb, thyme, basil, herbs de Provence, garlic and herb, dill seed, lemon thyme, hot pepper, rosemary, savory, lemon pepper, and Oriental mix. This is extravagantly good cheese available at ridiculously low prices.

Bread and Breakfast

CORRALITOS CHEESE COMPANY

2909-D Freedom Blvd.
Watsonville, CA 95076

~~~~~~~~~~~~~~~~~~~~~

CHECKS OR MONEY
ORDERS ONLY

CALL FOR CATALOG

PHONE: 408-722-1821

FAX: 408-722-7680

MINIMUM ORDER: $12 plus
   shipping

GOOD GOAT CHEESE

You want to talk about building a business from the ground up. Johanne Christmas has built this goat cheese business from the grass up. She breeds and raises the goats, she milks them, and she makes the cheese. She sells it at local farmer's markets in Monterey, Santa Cruz, and Los Altos. Sundays she goes to Salinas. Johanne can practically look at a round of her own lily white goat cheese and tell you what the goat had for dinner the night before. She's that careful.

As a result, she's had high praise for her fresh chevre. She's won prizes from Goat Cheese Makers' contests, but more importantly, she's built a devoted clientele who wait for her to show up at the farmer's markets.

Johanne's a farm girl who grew up in the country. She suggested buying the first goat because the Christmas family had an abundance of poison oak on the place and she knew goats could clean that up in a hurry. It came as a surprise dividend that their first goat turned out to be such a milk factory on four legs. Before long, the Christmas family was in the cheese business. Like it or not.

Now, her most popular product is a fresh herb and garlic cheese with a pesto and tomato swirl closing in fast. As for us, we like the simplest, plain fresh chevre smeared onto a piece of French Farmstead bread with a fresh pear for lunch. What more could you ask?

SADIE KENDALL CHEESE

P.O. Box 686
Atascadero, CA 93423

~~~~~~~~~~~~~~~~~~~~~

CREDIT CARDS: Yes

CALL FOR CATALOG

PHONE: 805-466-7252

MINIMUM ORDER: No

GREAT HANDMADE GOAT CHEESES

Sadie Kendall is the kind of food expert you can trust. She's a trained dairy scientist, with an interest in and respect for traditional methods of her craft as well. She's blended art and science to raise fresh goat cheeses to new heights. She also makes the finest butter in America and a *creme fraiche* you cannot duplicate at home.

Sadie Kendall's Chevrefeuille is as good as any in France. It is hand-dipped and double cream, making it delightful when young, and even more complex when mature. Her pure goat's milk Camembert, Chevre Sec, Chevre Frais, and Chevredoux, made with half goat's milk and half cow's milk, are equally subtle and authoritative.

For the serious cook, chocolatier, and baker, Sadie Kendall's butter, always in short supply, is the only unsalted, ripened cream butter available in the U.S. that isn't imported. Her *creme fraiche* is thick enough to float a silver spoon. Ask for her cookbook. It's a treasure.

*Linda
Eckhardt's
1995
Guide to
America's
Best Foods*

DRY GRATING JACK CHEESE

VELLA CHEESE COMPANY

315 Second St. East
P.O. Box 191
Sonoma, CA 95476-0191

One day I sat on the airplane coming home beside a courtly 95-year-old with a pink box of cookies on his lap. It was Mr. Tom Vella, who'd started out this cheese business in the teeth of the depression. He was on his way to Oregon to see about his other business—The Rogue Valley Creamery—that makes Oregon Blue and Cheddar. Mr. Vella still works every day. It must be all that good cheese. With a few cookies Mama throws in for the trip.

Vella's Dry Jack is now made by Ignazio Vella, the son and heir, who's made a great business of the labor-intensive Dry Jack. It's formed in muslin sacks, brined, coated, oiled and re-oiled, then cured until it achieves a nutty-sweet, medium cure, Parmesan-like California original taste. It's rare and wonderful. I keep a wheel of it on hand at all times. It's coated with cocoa and is such a beautiful thing to look at I can hardly bear to grate it. But oh, that lovely taste. Last year, this tiny creamery earned a gold medal at a World Cheese contest for this rare cheese. Some thought it was a Basque Pyrenees product from the appearance, but then when they tasted it they knew it was better. It won out over thirteen mostly European hard cheeses. No wonder.

Ig also makes other fine California cheeses, including Bear Flag high-moisture Jack, sometimes shot through with garlic or peppers. This cheese is mild and creamy, never nondescript. He makes a wild and wooly cheddar he's justly proud of, and a raw milk cheddar that is staggeringly good.

If you're planning a wine-tasting tour of the area, stop in the creamery and pick up fresh cheese and bread. You'll love it. The building itself is worth the stop. A stone-quarried building made with local stone, it's an architectural wonder in shaky, earthquakey California.

CREDIT CARDS: Yes

CALL FOR CATALOG

RETAIL STORE: Yes

PHONE: 800-848-0505
707-938-3232

MINIMUM ORDER: No

Bread and Breakfast

GETHSEMANI FARMS, INC.

3642 Monks Road
Trappist, KY
40051-6102

~~~~~~~~~~~~

CREDIT CARDS: Yes

CALL FOR CATALOG

PHONE: 502-549-3117

FAX: 502-549-8281

MINIMUM ORDER: No

TRAPPIST CHEESES AND FRUITCAKES

The Trappists have operated this farm in Kentucky since 1848 and support themselves by the manufacture of cheese, fruitcakes, and fudge. The cheese has become the official White House cheese and is served at state dinners—through Republican and Democratic administrations. Regardless of the politics, they all agree this cheese is the best. Last time I spoke with the Brothers, they'd just shipped off seven big wheels for the Washington Big Wheels.

And no wonder. Taste this cheese and you'll never forget it. A semisoft cow's milk in the same family with Havarti, it is one of the most enticing we've tasted out of literally hundreds of wheels that have rolled through this office. This is no pale, sissy cheese, but an iron fist in a velvet glove. The mild (young) cheese has an identity, and the aged version has enough authority to tell you to sit down and button your lip. I love these cheeses. Use them from the beginning of the meal to the end. Whether for hors d'oeurves or dessert, this cheese is memorable.

And in that same punchy spirit, the brothers have begun making fine, homestyle fudge that's loaded with Kentucky bourbon and nuts. I predict this product will have a long and happy life in their line. They also make a fine quality fruitcake.

HAWTHORNE VALLEY FARM

Rt. 2, Box 225 A
Ghent, NY 12075

~~~~~~~~~~~~

CHECKS OR MONEY
ORDERS ONLY

CALL FOR CATALOG

RETAIL STORE: Call for
directions

PHONE: 518-672-7500

FAX: 518-672-4887

MINIMUM ORDER: Yes

SWISS CHEESE AND FARM BREAD

Handmade Swiss-style Alpine cheese from Hawthorne Valley Farm is strong enough to make you pay attention, and their dense loaf of sourdough rye is as good as any *bauerbrots,* or farm bread from Switzerland or Germany. This is honest food, prepared in an honest way, and from an outfit whose philosophy even extends to shipping their fine products with a bill—"confident" you will pay promptly.

Christoph Meier is the visionary farmer who operates this combination farm/school under the aegis of the Rudolf Steiner Farming and Gardening Association. He uses biodynamic farming methods that guarantee that this raw milk cheese is perfectly pure. It's graded from mild to sharp but the mild is sharp enough to satisfy American sissies. He taught Edi Griffiths to make cheese, and she's developed a love for the rhythms of rural life and a substantial forearm from hoisting heavy slabs of cheese in the painstaking, labor-intensive method demanded by this Swiss process.

OREGON BLUE

ROGUE RIVER VALLEY CREAMERY

311 N. Front
Central Point, OR
97505

CREDIT CARDS: Yes

CALL FOR CATALOG

RETAIL STORE: Yes

PHONE: 503-664-2233

MINIMUM ORDER: No

In the heart of the depression, an Italian cheesemaker named Tom Vella from California's Napa Valley kept hearing from his old country relatives that the country was about to go to war. He looked around and said to himself that there weren't enough cows in the California Bay area to keep them in cheese should their population increase by a bunch of soldiers. And so he heard about a little creamery in Oregon that was about to go under.

Ignazio Vella's father left his wife and several children and took the train from San Francisco to Medford, Oregon. From there he hired a taxi to drive him to the unimposing little concrete block creamery in nearby Central Point. Before long, he'd bought out the former owner, gotten himself a contract with Kraft, and was cranking out cheddar to keep the soldiers in cheese.

Then, in the Fifties, after his original cheese business took off, he and his wife went to France for a little vacation. They went to the Roquefort area and he struck up a friendship with the Italian cheesemakers who were running the Roquefort cheese place. Somehow, it reminded Tom of Oregon. The rocks, the grass, the water. He came home, added a man-made concrete cave to his building and they've been making Oregon Blue Cheese there ever since. And they use the original Roquefort seed that old Mr. Vella brought over then, along with new seed from France.

Mr. Vella is nearly 96-years-old, and his son Ig Vella runs the business. This cheese is something. I recommend it. And if you're ever in the Rogue Valley stop in. But look carefully. It's easy to miss it. The Vellas do not go in for fancy remodeling jobs. But you can take the kids and peer in the windows and watch the big stainless vats fill up with milk. Watch the cheesemakers as they cheddar, and then cut the cheese. Be sure and buy a bag of fresh curds. They're delicious. And just breathe in that luscious cheesy smell and be grateful the Vellas' Italian relatives warned them about that war.

Bread and Breakfast

MAYTAG DAIRY FARMS

P.O. Box 806
Newton, IA 50208

CREDIT CARDS: **Yes**

CALL FOR CATALOG

RETAIL STORE: **Call for directions**

PHONE: **800-247-2458 (Nationwide)**
800-258-2437 (Iowa)

FAX: **515-792-1567**

MINIMUM ORDER: **No**

MONASTERY COUNTRY CHEESE

Our Lady of Angels Monastery
Rt. 2 Box 288A
Crozet, VA 22932

CHECKS OR MONEY ORDERS ONLY

CALL FOR CATALOG

PHONE: **804-823-1452**

FAX: **804-823-6379**

MINIMUM ORDER: **No**

*Linda
Eckhardt's
1995
Guide to
America's
Best Foods*

MAYTAG BLUE CHEESE

No, this cheese isn't shook up in a washing machine and yes, it is the same family. The Maytag farm was originally the plaything of a washing machine heir who took to cows more than to laundry. But once he was out of the picture, the grandchildren said, "Well, we eight make this thing pay off, or we dump it." They decided to make cheese.

At various times, Maytag cheese has been called the best American Blue on the market. At other times, it has been called the world's best Blue. So much for excess. This is a good, reliable product that comes to you with the same kind of backing as the washer that never needs repairs. You won't complain about this cheese. It's the real thing. Maytag cheese is aged a full six months and this gives character to its taste. Maytag melts on the tongue and is assertive, full, and piquant. With a Comice pear and port for dessert, it's to die for.

GOD-BLESSED GOUDA

The Good Sisters of Our Lady of Angels support themselves by producing a fine quality Gouda cheese. They begin with good Guernsey milk, handmake the cheese the traditional way, then dip it in gleaming red wax, and set it aside on wooden racks to cool and cure in their Cheese Curing room.

A glorious, mellow-flavored, two-pound Gouda comes postpaid and is modest—to say the least—in price. Better you should order the five-pound wheel. It keeps well, and after you serve it a time or two with your own homemade (or bought from the best bakery you know) Farmstead bread, you'll want it as a standard item in your larder.

These are Cistercian nuns, more familiarly known as Trappistines. Their monastic life is patterned after the Rule of St. Benedict which requires the monks to "live by the work of their hands." We can thank God they picked Gouda as a craft to master. We're all blessed as a result.

Sally Jackson's Fresh Pasta with Sheeps' Cheese and Bacon

makes 4 servings in 20 minutes

Cook pasta al dente and drain. Meanwhile, cook bacon, then crumble. Toss hot pasta with bacon, cheeses, and sour cream. Serve immediately.

¾ lb. fresh fettucine

3 strips bacon, cooked, drained and crumbled

4 ozs. feta cheese, crumbled

4 ozs. sheeps' or goat cheese

½ cup light sour cream

AGED SHEEPS' CHEESE

Sally and Roger Jackson produce sheeps' cheeses of extreme delicacy and subtlety. They grow their own hay. They care for their animals' needs with the care most people reserve for children. In addition to fresh sheeps' cheeses, they carefully make soft and semihard goat cheeses plain or with herbs, semihard cow cheeses plain or with herbs, and a soft sheeps' cheese packed in olive oil. The Jacksons will even custom-make a five-pound wheel of cheese for you, marbling goat and cow cheeses with your choice of herbs. We particularly recommend the small sheeps' milk cheese, aged with a thickish dark rind, with a creamy interior, and a grassy-tangy flavor.

SALLY JACKSON CHEESE CO.

Star Rt. Box 106
Oroville, WA 98844

CHECKS OR MONEY ORDERS ONLY

WRITE FOR CATALOG

PHONE: Unlisted. Mail orders only please.

MINIMUM ORDER: No

Bread and Breakfast

PLEASANT VALLEY DAIRY, INC.

6804 Kickerville Road
Ferndale, WA 98248

CHECKS OR MONEY
ORDERS ONLY

RETAIL STORE: Call for
directions

PHONE: 206-366-5398

MINIMUM ORDER: No

DUTCH-STYLE GOUDA

Dutch-style Gouda—smooth, subtle, and nutlike—makes a fine beginning or ending to a meal with fresh fruit. George and Dolores Train, who have been in the dairy business a good while, make a Gouda from their own cows' milk. They control every step of the procedure and do not bleach, color, or chemically treat the milk or cheese. Each wheel is hand-dipped in wax, dated by hand, and left to age at least 60 days. The cheese is made with natural calf rennet which makes a better quality aged cheese. They also have a Farmstead cheese that's pale, sharp, and smooth, a cousin to cheddar.

If you're in Washington state between Blaine and Bellingham, and would like to see a bucolic scene more vivid than any calendar— dazzling green, undulating hills, spotted cows, brilliant blue sky, clean air, barn—stop by any day but Sunday and look around the Train's farm. Their "on-farm" shop is open 6 days, never on Sunday, July through December. The rest of the year it's only open on Saturdays.

FARMER'S MARKET

Mushrooms, and organic produce, delivered dewy fresh to your door. Exotic fruits and vegetables, herbs, sweet onions and garlic. Citrus, apples, and pears by the box. Sulfur-free dried fruits, sun-dried tomatoes, peppers, and apples. Nuts galore.

"She should be thinking of higher things. Nothing could be higher than food,'' said Leah.

—IVY COMPTON-BURNETT (1892–1969)

MUSHROOMS AND ORGANIC PRODUCE, DELIVERED DEWY FRESH TO YOUR DOOR.

Give me neither poverty nor riches; feed me with food convenient for me.

—PROVERBS 30:8

MUSHROOMS FRESH AND DRIED FROM AROUND THE WORLD TO YOU

AUX DELICES DES BOIS

4 Leonard St.
New York, NY 10013

CREDIT CARDS: **Yes**

CALL FOR CATALOG

RETAIL STORE: **In Tribeca**

PHONE: **212-334-1230**

FAX: **212-334-1231**

MINIMUM ORDER: **$15**

You want to talk about a luxury. The day I opened a great big box filled to the brim with fresh chanterelles, soft tangerine-colored, aromatic with the woods, and fresh as if I'd just picked them myself, that, my friends, is luxury.

Aux Delices De Bois, "Delicacies of the Woods," has been providing fresh mushrooms from around the world to the finest restaurants and grocers, as well as other fresh produce and dried delectables. Amy and Thierry Farges now sell retail. If you're in the Tribeca section of Manhattan, stop in the store. They love to talk mushrooms. The aroma of mushrooms may make you swoon. Go ahead. It's normal when confronted with such splendor.

Prices are reasonable and the choices are staggering. But the most dazzling possibility is a conversation with Mr. Farges, who hails from the Perigord region of France. Want to know your mushrooms? Talk with Thierry. "Mushrooms are mysterious," he told *New York Times* reporter Michael T. Kaufman. "They grow in dark places. There are millions of types and some are dangerous. They have very different tastes, different as apples and bananas, which after all, are both fruits. They are subtle."

Choices vary with the season and the weather but may include morels, white trumpets, black trumpets, enoki, oysters, hen-of-the-woods, wine caps, lactaires, matsutakes, lobsters, bluefoot, procinis, portobellos, and porcini. Besides these, a vast assortment of dried mushrooms and mushroom paraphernalia are available, as well as fresh fiddlehead ferns in season, sea beans, ramps, white asparagus, pea shoots, sunflower sprouts, cavaillon melons from Provence, and organic wild rice. Recently, Thierry even got a stash of stinging nettles which he assures us are not only edible but desirable.

Gift packs from *Aux Delices* are unique. A mushroom-of-the-month club, a mushroom assortment, a mushroom garden, a vacation larder for you to take to the cabin—even funky French socks embroidered with toadstools. If it starts with mush and ends with room, you'll find it here.

Farmer's Market

DIAMOND ORGANICS

P.O. Box 2159
Freedom, CA 95019

CREDIT CARDS: Yes

CALL FOR CATALOG

PHONE: 800-922-2396
408-763-1993

FAX: 408-763-1993

MINIMUM ORDER: No

FRESH ORGANIC VEGETABLES TO YOUR DOOR

One of the most thrilling packages to be delivered out of the UPS man's hands was the big box of fresh, dewy-ripe and perfect organic vegetables from Diamond Organics. Jasch Hamilton lives in the heart of a great growing area on the central California coast where terrific produce can be grown nearly year round. He cuts to order and ships the same day.

There are people who fill out Jasch's fax order form and stick it in the fax machine to him every week. They get a package of fresh organic produce to use weekly.

Besides the usual lettuces, mesclun, and other good stuff you'd expect, Jasch is an excellent source for exotics like burdock root, ginger root, baby bok choi, frisse, cherimoya, Fuji apples, edible flowers, and the great-tasting, organically grown potatoes, carrots, beets, and onions.

They ship these veggies as far away as the Virgin Islands. It all gets there in fresher condition than you'd ever see in a roadside fruit stand or a grocery store. This stuff is great.

If you want to try them for a week or so, ask for the Sampler. I got a bag of mesclun salad mix, a bunch of Siberian kale, two mixed specialty lettuces, Bibb and Green Oak Leaf, a bunch of Opal basil, a bunch of scallions, a bag of green and golden zucchini, a bulb of garlic, a bag of red new potatoes, corn on the cob, and some fruit: oranges, plums, pears, nectarines, peaches, tomatoes, and grapes. The sampler will be tailored to give you the best of what's available the week you ask for it. And, in case you don't know what to do with all that great produce, Jasch will send along serving suggestions and a simple recipe or two to get you started. Such a deal. Great, good, healthy food and recipes for how to use it.

*Linda
Eckhardt's
1995
Guide to
America's
Best Foods*

Exotic Fruits and Vegetables, Herbs, Sweet Onions, and Garlic.

A solid man of Boston. A comfortable man, with dividends, and first salmon and the green peas.

—HENRY LONGFELLOW (1807–1882)

FRIEDA'S RARE &
EXOTIC FOODS

P.O. Box 58488
Los Angeles, CA 90058

CREDIT CARDS: Yes

CALL FOR CATALOG

PHONE: 800-241-1771
213-627-2981

FAX: 213-741-9443

MINIMUM ORDER: No

EXOTIC FRESH FRUITS AND VEGETABLES BY MAIL

Frieda Caplan is the produce maven who brought kiwis to America. Beginning in Los Angeles' tough produce row, Frieda quickly figured out she'd have to carve out her own niche in the cutthroat produce biz. She did. Now, you'll see Frieda's groupings of exotic fresh and dried products from around the world in most grocery store produce departments.

She also sells products directly by mail. A couple of weeks ago I needed Cactus fruits for a Mexican food spread I was working on. One phone call to Frieda's and two days later the fruits arrived, tucked in her signature lavender paper and nestled in a foam nest so each one was perfect.

Order such items as an exotic dried mushroom basket complete with chanterelles, porcinis, oyster mushrooms, and morels. Or how about a New Zealand basket with fresh kiwis, passion fruit, horned melon, pepino, feijoas, tamarillos, asian pears, and kiwi jam?

Frieda's always known that the secret to expanding the cook's repertoire is to teach the cook how to use new and exotic fruit. Recipes are always included.

If you're looking for something rare in the produce department and you can't find it, give Frieda a call. More than likely, she has it and can send it to you. Service here is terrific.

HICKINS
MOUNTAIN
MOWINGS FARM
AND GREENHOUSE

RFD 1 Black Mountain
Road, Box 293
Brattleboro, VT 05301

CHECKS OR MONEY
ORDERS ONLY

CALL FOR CATALOG

RETAIL STORE: Call for
directions

PHONE: 802-254-2146

MINIMUM ORDER: No

VERMONT GARDEN GOOD

Frank Hickin, according to the *Brattleboro Reformer*, can "work up a missionary zeal about a carrot." Frank and his wife, Mary, love to grow things. They generally produce more than 100 varieties, from traditional garden offerings and fresh herbs to the new gourmet baby vegetables. If you're looking for radicchio or lemon cukes, or any one of 25 varieties of lettuce, call up Frank Hickin. He's probably got it in the ground. In addition, they make their own maple syrup, sell Vermont cheeses, salami, Vermont apples, and raspberries—both red and black-purple, amber and yellow. Plus jams, jellies, and a dazzling array of pickles. Choose from dill, maple icicle, maple mustard crock pickles, splendid dilly snow peas, dilled fiddle heads, and dilled asparagus tips. If you're travelling through New England, the Hickin's farm is a good stop for a picnic and supplies and a taste of the beautiful Vermont countryside.

FRESH ARTICHOKES

GIANT ARTICHOKE
11241 Merritt St.
Castroville, CA 05012

CREDIT CARDS: Yes

CALL FOR CATALOG

PHONE: 408-633-2778

MINIMUM ORDER: No

You want to talk about big and beautiful. Just wait until you open up a great big box filled with gorgeous green globe artichokes from the very heart of America's artichoke fields. Available from March to May, these California beauties are shipped in a ventilated box. Once you get them home, all you have to do is sprinkle them with water, bag 'em in plastic, and refrigerate. They'll keep two to three weeks this way.

Boil, steam or microwave them and be prepared for a sumptuous dinner. And to think, an artichoke—even a big one—only has 25 calories and no fat at all.

You can order artichokes any way you want them. Get the #1 Pack and you'll get a specific number of the size you want for just over fifty bucks: 160 extra small bite-sized ones, 60 smalls, 45 mediums, 30 medium-larges, or 24 humongous artichokes.

Order them packed in jars and marinated, either whole, the crowns, or hearts only. Or order the #2 Fresh Pack, which is half the volume of the #1, but just as delicious.

FRESH ASPARAGUS

MISTER SPEAR, INC.
P.O. Box 1528
Stockton, CA 95201

CREDIT CARDS: Yes

CALL FOR CATALOG

PHONE: 800-677-7327
209-464-5365

FAX: 209-464-3846

MINIMUM ORDER: No

You want asparagus? Mr. Spear will give you asparagus. Thick as your thumb and tender as love, these asparagus are grown in California's central valley. Available in both green and white varieties, this is as good as it gets. Available during spring, this asparagus is worth the wait and will make any of that stuff you've bought in the grocery store pale by comparison.

Chip Arnett, who runs this place, also sells jumbo green artichokes in April, garden ripe tomatoes in August, and flavorful Fuji apples in December. He'll even put in your personal card with the order if you'd like. This is your farm connection for the best-from-California San Joaquin Valley produce.

We agree with *Money* magazine. They said Mr. Spear's giant artichokes, some weighing a pound each, are a great value. When we opened our box of those perfectly fresh, perfectly huge beasts, we had to agree. Each one fed two people, with the heart left over for cold soup the next day. What a treat.

But the best is still the asparagus, available from mid-April to

*Farmer's
Market*

early June. You'll get 7½ lbs., about 50 spears. For the ultimate luxury, serve lunch that's nothing but a mound of perfectly steamed asparagus with a choice of sauces: hollandaise, melted butter with pine nuts, or a light lemon vinaigrette. A loaf of perfect bread. Skip the wine, it tastes odd with asparagus. Gelato for dessert. A lovely lunch.

PICKLED BEANS

WICKLUND FARMS

3959 Maple Island
   Farm Rd.
Springfield, OR 97477

CHECKS OR MONEY
   ORDERS ONLY

CALL FOR CATALOG

PHONE: 503-747-5998

FAX: 503-747-7299

MINIMUM ORDER: 1 case

Larry Wicklund figured there had to be a better Bloody Mary and he finally discovered the answer was in the beans. Larry grows and harvests acres of Blue Lake beans that he then pickles and packs whole in glorious clear glass jars. At first, he just sold the pickled beans to be used the way you'd use any pickle. But when he stuck one in a Bloody Mary and made a Bean Swizzle Stick out of it, he was in business.

Stop in any bar in the Northwest, order a Bloody Mary, and you'll probably get one of Larry's beans. They're great to eat by themselves, but they're dynamite in a Bloody Mary.

BLACK-EYED PEAS

PEAS ON EARTH

225 South Prairieville
Athens, TX 75751

CREDIT CARDS: Yes

CALL FOR CATALOG

PHONE: 800-767-PEAS
   903-677-1639

FAX: 903-677-1555

MINIMUM ORDER: No

You knew a bowl of steaming black-eyed peas and hot cornbread would bring you good fortune and prosperity, didn't you? Provided you ate it on New Year's Day. That's an old Southern tradition that Mary Lou Williams hopes to build a year-round business on.

She's custom-canning black-eyed peas and selling them with a package of Texas-style corn bread mix. It's a good idea to eat them anytime you feel your luck needs changing. Beats the heck out of playing the lottery. Don't you agree?

And if you're in the neighborhood of Athens, Texas during the summer, stop in for the Black-Eyed Pea Festival. It's an event you won't want to miss. Call the Chamber of Commerce for details.

Persillade	¼ cup finely chopped garlic
Mix garlic and parsley then sauté in a touch of olive oil until the garlic is beginning to brown. Whisk it off the fire and use it to top steamed veggies, a chicken breast, or a grilled lamb chop.	¼ cup finely chopped Italian parsley leaves

GARLIC ANY WAY YOU WANT IT

THE GARLIC SURVIVAL COMPANY
1094-A50 Revere Ave.
San Francisco, CA
94124

Walt McBride is a stockbroker turned garlic peddler who backed into the business because he just plain loved garlic. Living close to Gilroy, the Garlic capital of the world, he learned there is more to the stinky lily than a braid.

Not only can you buy premium quality garlic in several varieties from Walt, but the ubiquitous braids, a garlic pesto, an exotic garlic-pepper blend, a garlic powder 'n spice, and a ceramic garlic holder to keep the bulb fresh without refrigeration.

Walt also makes and sells GarliQue Sauce—a barbecue sauce for garlic nuts. His salesto—a cross between salsa and pesto, is good not only as a dip, but is terrific when tossed with pasta. And it's got enough of a garlic hit that you're safe from the vampires for days.

Order from Walt and you'll know, from the aroma, when your package arrives. Even your mailman may swoon. If you order only one item, you should order Walt's crushed garlic in a jar. This is the single most important prepared food product I've found in years to speed up cooking. Who cares how many cloves of garlic a recipe calls for? A little spoon of crushed garlic in the sauce and the recipe sings. I love this stuff.

CREDIT CARDS: Yes

CALL FOR CATALOG

PHONE: 800-342-7542
415-822-7112

FAX: 415-822-6224

MINIMUM ORDER: No

Farmer's Market

THE PICKLED
GARLIC COMPANY

1118 Del Monte
P.O. Box 846
Pacific Grove, CA 93950

CREDIT CARDS: Yes

CALL FOR CATALOG

PHONE: 800-775-9788
   (Nationwide)
   408-373-8660
   (California)

FAX: 408-655-8876

MINIMUM ORDER: 1 case

PICKLED GARLIC

A t last. Garlic you don't have to peel before you use it. Ken Knapp, a kindly looking guy in Clark Kent glasses, took his old family recipe for pickled garlic and began making it for sale. Now, I'm hooked. Garlic that's been pickled retains all the good garlic flavor but seems to lose the burn of the fresh product. Plus it's just so *there*. I find myself using six cloves instead of two and the recipes are the better for it.

Ken, 69, began pickling garlic for the Gilroy Garlic Festival, using his sister's recipe. The people at the festival just snapped it up. Then, he took it to a local farmer's market and taught people they could eat a clove of garlic like an almond or olive. Good taste and no bite.

You may see Ken at food festivals around the country. You'll know him when you see him. He's the guy with the headpiece that's shaped like a white head of garlic. What a guy.

Order pickled garlic in the original flavor, jalapeno, red chili, lemon dill, or smoke flavor. Then, next time you have people over for drinks, put out a bowl of drained pickled garlic cloves alongside the almonds and the olives. You'll be surprised. So will your guests.

MCFADDEN FARM
Potter Valley, CA 95468

CREDIT CARDS: Yes

CALL FOR CATALOG

PHONE: 800-549-8230
   707-743-1122

FAX: 707-743-1126

MINIMUM ORDER: No

ORGANIC HERBS

I n case you hadn't heard, whenever you buy a little bottle of imported dried herbs you may be taking home more than you bargained for: pesticides, herbicides, desiccated insects, and dirt. Want pure herbs? Buy a locally made organic product.

Guinness McFadden saw the light way back in 1970 when he graduated from Stanford School of Business and bought up a 500-acre farm in the Mendocino area. He's turned that plot of ground into a virtual cottage industry.

Growing there now are certified organic herbs that he puts up in clean glass jars, sun-dried tomatoes, and certified organic heirloom beans including black turtle, French navy, Swedish brown, Jacob's Cattle, European Soldier, Flageolet, Speckled, Bayou, and pink beans.

Also available from McFadden are garlic braids, bay leaf wreaths, and wild rice. These products are all grown and processed on the farm from the planting to the braiding. And he guarantees it.

Guinness McFadden grows grapes, he grows beans. He shifts gears every chance he gets. He learned a long time ago, "a future of

*Linda
Eckhardt's
1995
Guide to
America's
Best Foods*

offices and corporations didn't feel good to me." He's kept his life interesting and he brings interesting products to the market. And they're all packaged in a distinctive, clean-looking pack with a quail on the label. You'll like them.

HERBS AND HERB TEAS

The Shakers have been growing and foraging herbs for 150 years in their southwestern Maine, 1700-acre plot. Besides herbal teas—originally used as curatives—they mix culinary herbs into some surprisingly fresh-tasting blends.

Naturally, they offer individual herbs including chervil, rosemary, basil, and the other herbs you'd expect out of any respectable backyard herb garden. What's surprising are the bursts of flavor you can get from marigold blossoms, rose hips, and coriander.

They also sell herb vinegars, a fir balsam pillow, tea strainers made from wicker, and glass jars filled with potpourri or herb mixtures with such enticing names as Woods Mixture.

Nine Shakers living at the community are responsible for cultivating, harvesting, foraging, drying, and mixing the herbs and teas. The quality of these products is impeccable. Packed in reusable tins, you can reorder herbs and teas in polybags. We particularly recommend the rose water made from their own roses, and the potpourri which will make your house smell like a home. Their bouquet garni is generous, aromatic, and fresh-smelling—a must for any one who uses Julia Child's original cookbooks for fine French cooking. I do wonder if I ordered a fir balsam pillow, if I'd sleep better at night. Sounds like it's worth a try.

Drive south of the town of Poland Spring to visit the Shaker Society. Visit their museum and learn all about Shaker life. The store and museum are open from May to December. Sign up early for workshops on special days. Basketmaking is taught on July 4th. Quilting's taught on Labor Day and weaving on Columbus Day. Call for a complete list of the workshops the Shakers offer. They're held from March to October in the 1821 Sister's Shop, and cover subjects from doll making to herb planting. If you'd like a tour of the herb garden, call for an appointment. If you're interested in using herbs for medicinal or culinary purposes, we recommend a trip through their complete book section. A visit here is like a step back in time. We recommend it for stress reduction.

UNITED SOCIETY OF SHAKERS

Sabbathday Lake,
RR #1 Box 640
Poland Spring, ME
  04274

CHECKS OR MONEY
  ORDERS ONLY

CALL FOR CATALOG

RETAIL STORE: **Call for directions**

PHONE: **207-926-4597**

MINIMUM ORDER: **No**

*Farmer's
Market*

Bland Farms West Indies Onion Salad

makes 4 servings

Place half the chopped onions in a bowl. Add crabmeat and season to taste with salt and pepper. Add remaining onion. Pour oil over the salad, then vinegar and finally, ice water. Toss slightly. Cover and marinate at least four hours before serving. Garnish with chopped red and yellow bell peppers.

1 large Vidalia onion, finely chopped

1 pound fresh crabmeat

salt and pepper to taste

½ cup vegetable oil

½ cup cider vinegar

½ cup ice water

red and yellow bell pepper for garnish

BLAND FARMS

P.O. Box 506, Rt. 4, Hwy 169
Glennville, GA
   30427-0506

CREDIT CARDS: Yes

CALL FOR CATALOG

RETAIL STORE: Call for directions

PHONE: 800-843-2542

FAX: 912-654-4280

MINIMUM ORDER: No

Linda Eckhardt's 1995 Guide to America's Best Foods

KNOWING YOUR ONIONS

R aymond and Ruby Jean Bland began farming more than fifty years ago. But not until their boy Delbert, 27, loaded up a bunch of Vidalias (vy-DALE-yuhs) in 1984 and offered them to every produce manager he could buttonhole, did the notion of this sweeter-than-an-orange onion begin to take hold. Now, you see them in fancy restaurants everywhere during their brief evanescent season in early summer.

With 12½ percent sugar, these onions can indeed be eaten like an apple. And, as a bonus, they're now grown for sale during two brief seasons, spring and fall. Using Grandma Ruby Jean's recipes, the Blands now sell onion relish, pickled onions, and other products from quiches to breads.

People do seem to get addicted to them. One New York lawyer was more excited about his 50 lb. bag of Vidalia onions than who'd just been appointed to the supreme court. He joins the group of Vidalia fanatics who wait for the crop to come in. Don't order these onions unless you're prepared to become an onion fiend.

WALLA WALLA ONIONS

Order 20 pounds of Walla Walla sweets from the Children's Home Society before August 1, and not only do you get a box of excellent onions, but you will have donated to a worthwhile charity that aids family support and foster care programs in the Northwest. These are those wonderful onions so sweet you can eat them like an apple—just like Errol Flynn did, playing General Custer in the 1941 film, "They Died With Their Boots On."

CHILDREN'S HOME SOCIETY

405 Denny Bldg.
Walla Walla, WA 99362

CREDIT CARDS: **Yes**

PHONE: **509-529-2130**

MINIMUM ORDER: **20 lbs.**

OLD TIME FRESH SAUERKRAUT

Virgil Morse began making sauerkraut in 1918. Later his son, then his widow, took over the business. Through two world wars, economic ups and downs, men on the moon—whatever, the Morses have kept on shaving off Maine grown cabbage to make an authentic German style sauerkraut.

If the only sauerkraut you ever ate came out of a can at the supermarket, you don't really know what sauerkraut tastes like. Morse's is crisp, salty, sour, sweet, crunchy, and mouthwatering. It's delicious just eaten out of the jar. It's heavenly in a variety of made products.

They also make and sell other genuine Yankee inventions: Their Maple Baked Beans with Pork are what the pork-and-beans people aspire to. Rich, smoky, sweet, and full of nutrition, these beans are a main dish. They also prepare home-style pickled beets just like my grandmother made, and a spikey beet relish that's so good I keep sneaking into the refrigerator for a taste. They also make and sell several kinds of mustard.

Visit the plant and you'll see long-time workers cleaning cabbage—up to 3,000 pounds a day. Buy some baked beans, a loaf of homemade bread, and a bucket of sauerkraut. Go have yourself a picnic. There's a nice gravel pit next door. And some parks down the road a piece. Ask.

MORSE'S SAUERKRAUT

3856 Washington Road
Waldoboro, ME 04572

CREDIT CARDS: **Yes**

CALL FOR CATALOG

RETAIL STORE: **Call for directions**

PHONE: **207-832-5569**

MINIMUM ORDER: **5 pounds of sauerkraut.**

Farmer's Market

German Chocolate Sauerkraut Cake

makes one 8 × 12-inch sheet cake

Preheat the oven to 350°F. Coat with cooking spray a glass baking pan about 8 × 12-inches. Generously dust the pan with cocoa and set aside.

Fit the steel blade in the food processor bowl then add butter and sugar. Process 30 seconds or until thoroughly creamed. Add vanilla and eggs through the feed tube and continue to process until the mixture is light.

Sift together the cocoa, baking powder, salt, soda, and flour. Open the food processor lid and arrange the dry ingredients evenly over the egg butter mixture. Pulse to mix. Now add water and sauerkraut and barely pulse, no more than 8–10 times to mix. Turn it into the prepared pan and bake in the preheated oven until the top springs back at the touch, about 30 minutes. Frost with Cocoa Buttercream.

½ cup butter

1½ cups sugar

2 teaspoons vanilla

3 large eggs

½ cup Dutch process cocoa

1 teaspoon baking powder

½ teaspoon salt

1 teaspoon soda

2¼ cups sifted cake flour

1 cup water

⅔ cup drained, rinsed, and chopped sauerkraut

Cocoa Buttercream

In the food processor fitted with the steel blade, combine cocoa, salt, and sugar. Pulse to mix. Add butter and vanilla through the feed tube and process 20 seconds, then with the motor running, add the whipping cream through the feed tube and continue to process until mixture is well-blended. Spread on top cooled cake.

¾ cup Dutch process cocoa

a pinch salt

2 cups confectioners' sugar

½ cup butter

1 teaspoon vanilla

¾ cup whipping cream

CITRUS, APPLES, AND PEARS BY THE BOX.

―――――――――――――――――

Oh, Beaulah . . . peel me a grape.

―MAE WEST to her maid in *I'm No Angel*, 1933

PITTMAN AND
DAVIS, INC.

P.O. Box 532227
Harlingen, TX
78553-2227

CREDIT CARDS: Yes

CALL FOR CATALOG

PHONE: 210-423-2154

FAX: 800-289-7829

MINIMUM ORDER: No

TEXAS PINKS AND ORANGES

About the same time Harry and David were tramping through New York offices trying to drum up orders for pears (see page TK)—during the Depression when all orchards were suffering—Frank Davis, Sr. and Howard Pittman were trying to figure out how to stay alive in Texas' Rio Grande Valley. They'd been shipping vegetables by railway express but about the time of the great Depression, roads got better and orders got worse. They were really at their wits' end. Mrs. Davis, who worked as a proofreader, making sure orders were properly addressed, came up with the idea of concentrating on gift baskets and Christmas orders. Mrs. Davis was right. Soon, they were out of the vegetable business altogether.

During the harvest from November through April, Frank Davis ships Ruby Red grapefruit from south Texas and from Florida. If you're looking for fresh, healthful gifts or a treat for yourself at the most reasonable price, these are the people to call.

One interesting thing about Pittman and Davis. They still do business the old-fashioned way. You can order Christmas fruit and pay in January. It's just a little thing, but it makes them people I just plain like.

RED COOPER

Rt. 3, Box 10
Alamo, TX 78516

CREDIT CARDS: Yes

CALL FOR CATALOG

PHONE: 800-876-4733

MINIMUM ORDER: No

ORANGE SWEET GRAPEFRUIT

If you never tasted a grapefruit so sweet that the juice ran down your arm and made it sticky, then you've never tasted a Red Cooper grapefruit. They're a rare hybrid, grown here only and available for a brief four-month period, beginning about the Christmas season. But they grow real big and you may find yourself, as we did, eating the darned things like a giant orange.

Red is a small citrus farmer and lets the grapefruit ripen on the tree before its handpicked and packed. The color of the flesh of this grapefruit is a kind of intense salmon pink, and it's stable and will keep in your refrigerator a good long while.

Red's Fruit-of-the-Month Club is a little different from those of the big boys. You get grapefruit every month for four months, then it quits. You'll be hanging on the mailbox, waiting for Christmas to come again.

Linda Eckhardt's 1995 Guide to America's Best Foods

TEXAS ORANGES AND GRAPEFRUITS

REED LANG FARMS
P.O. Box 219
Rio Hondo, TX 78583

When my mother was growing up on a panhandle Texas ranch in the early part of this century, the greatest Christmas gift came by train from the Valley: a box of oranges and a box of grapefruits fresh off the farm. Those ranch families jumped on boxes of fresh fruit. It was the only fresh fruit they got all winter. We still don't think it's Christmas without oranges and grapefruits from the Valley.

Reed Lang and his wife, Violet, have owned and operated this farm since the early fifties. Grapefruit and avocados have been shipped from these very trees since 1917. This family farm has been recommending citrus "three times a day" since before the Great War. As Reed says, "Place your orders from the quiet comfort of your home." He guarantees your satisfaction.

The Langs also farm cotton, corn, milo, and sugarcane. It takes that kind of diversity to survive. In 1989, every single grapefruit tree they had froze in an unseasonable cold snap. They didn't blink. They replanted and now the baby trees are turning out quite satisfactory fruit.

This is a small family run business. You'll get personal service. It's nice.

CREDIT CARDS: **Yes**

CALL FOR CATALOG

RETAIL STORE: **Call for directions**

PHONE: **210-748-2354**

FAX: **210-748-2888**

MINIMUM ORDER: **No**

Farmer's Market

93

BLUE HERON FRUIT SHIPPERS

3221 Bay Shore Drive
Sarasota, FL 34234-5725

~~~~~~~~~~~~~~~~~

CREDIT CARDS: Yes

CALL FOR CATALOG

PHONE: 800-237-3920
813-355-6946

FAX: 813-351-2061

MINIMUM ORDER: No

FLORIDA ORANGES AND GRAPEFRUITS

You may already know that an orange is not always an orange, and a grapefruit can be one of many things. But for the pick of the crop, you have to order direct from the orchard.

Blue Heron ships out only the best of the season's crop: ruby red grapefruit bursting with flavor and navel oranges they call their ambassadors of the Florida sun. They even offer a Tropical Paradise box that includes both oranges and grapefruits along with sugarcane, Caribbean pineapples, coconuts, and zesty limes.

Most of their products are available November through January, but they also offer Temple oranges in February, Valencias from March to May, and Honeybell Tangelos only in January. Not only that, but from October to May, they'll ship fresh stone crab claws. And here's your source for smoked Florida alligator tail. Farm-raised, they make a great business gift.

Blue Heron is so good at mail order—they've been at this since 1946—that they even ship overseas. Here's a place to get your Peace Corps' kid a box of fruit for Christmas.

CUSHMAN'S FRUIT CO., INC.

3325 Forest Hill Blvd.
West Palm Beach, FL 33406

~~~~~~~~~~~~~~~~~

CREDIT CARDS: Yes

CALL FOR CATALOG

PHONE: 407-965-3535

FAX: 407-965-7263

MINIMUM ORDER: No

CHRISTMAS GRAPEFRUIT

It wouldn't be Christmas without a box of Cushman fruit. That's what I keep hearing from New York friends. They're talking about a venerable old fruit packer from South Florida that's been shipping oranges, grapefruits and their own Honey Bells to customers for years. Honey bells are particularly rare and interesting. A January-only citrus grown only in Florida, these bright orange fruits are dripping with sweetness and have a taste all their own that's a cross between an orange and a tangerine.

The Palm Beach Deluxe is a good gift box that includes oranges, grapefruits, coconut chocolate patties, a half-pound of paper shell pecans, and a half-pound of their own fruit-filled orange marmalade.

Cushman has its own fruit-of-the-month plan, including King George peaches in September and Florida mangos in August. Yum.

*Linda
Eckhardt's
1995
Guide to
America's
Best Foods*

94

PEACHES LIKE MAMA USED TO PUT UP

SHAWNEE CANNING COMPANY

P.O. Box 657
Cross Junction, VA
22625

CHECKS OR MONEY ORDERS ONLY

CALL FOR CATALOG

RETAIL STORE: **Call for directions**

PHONE: 703-888-3429

MINIMUM ORDER: **No**

And you thought a can of peaches was just a can of peaches. That's because you never cranked open the can opener on a can of Shawnee hand-peeled peaches. They look like the ones you get in the grocery store, but that's before you taste them. These peaches are steamed to lift off the peel and packed either without sugar, or in heavy syrup. As for me, I want a case of them in the basement at all times.

George and Damaris Whitacre have raised Red Haven, Glow Haven, and Loring peaches along with a variety of apples on this Virginia farm since the late depression days. Now, their son William Lee and his wife JoAnne run the business. But they still can peaches "the way Grandma did." And boy do they taste like it.

Besides peaches, the Shawnee Canners put up apple sauce, syrup, butter, and cider. They'll send you some just-picked Virginia apples in the fall and winter. Choose what you like: McIntosh, Jonathon, Golden Delicious, Red Delicious, Rome Beauties, or Yorks.

You can still buy old-fashioned Virginia products from them: smoked or sugar-cured hams, stone-ground flours, honeys, jellies, and preserves. This is old-fashioned country preserving. My favorite gift pack is the one they call the Bread Basket. It is indeed just that— a good looking bread basket filled with three jars of preserves: strawberry, peach, and plum. All you provide is the bread. Want a custom-designed gift basket? Just ask. They'll mix and match it just to suit you. They keep a little farm store open at the Shawnee Springs Market. It's just 10 miles north of Winchester on Highway 522 North. Watch for the signs. You can't miss it. Even if it is almost to West Virginia.

Farmer's Market

95

HARRY AND DAVID
P.O. Box 712
Medford, OR 97501

CREDIT CARDS: **Yes**

CALL FOR CATALOG

RETAIL STORE: **Call for directions**

PHONE: **800-547-3033**

FAX: **800-648-6640**

MINIMUM ORDER: **No**

ORCHARDS
441 South Fir
Medford, OR 97501

CREDIT CARDS: **Yes**

CALL FOR CATALOG

RETAIL STORE: **Call for directions**

PHONE: **800-955-6569**

FAX: **503-776-3222**

MINIMUM ORDER: **No**

*Linda
Eckhardt's
1995
Guide to
America's
Best Foods*

FRUIT-OF-THE-MONTH BEGINS WITH COMICE PEARS

Harry and David wrote the book on the shipping of perishable fruit. They developed a drop-ship system that means your order is filled from a regional warehouse and gets to you within a couple of days. The pear is one fruit that is never allowed to ripen on the tree, so it is ideal for shipping. Picking, packing, and shipping are an absolute science with these pear growers. Reliability is their middle name. Since starting in the heart of the Depression as a mail-order shipper of pears, Harry and David has grown to include seasonal fruits, exotic fruits, vegetables, and plants, all of which are offered in a variety of gift packs and Fruit-of-the-Month Clubs: for three, five, eight, or twelve months. I still think fresh fruit is the best business gift I know of. Want somebody to remember you all year long? Send little surprises throughout the year—like a box of fresh peaches in August that they can dive right into. Believe me, when it comes time to place an order, they'll think about you.

PEARS AND APPLES

So you want fresh pears for Christmas? Here's a terrific packing plant right in the Rogue Valley that offers best quality comice pears in a variety of good-looking packs. They also offer local and Washington apples packed with the pears and a variety of candies, almonds, and pistachios.

Their Fruit-of-the-Month Club offers first quality fruit up to twelve times a year. Pears, then apples, oranges, grapefruits, kiwis, pineapples, bing cherries, plums, nectarines, fabulous 49'er peaches, grapes, and finally, buttery Bosc pears.

Call for a catalog and see all their choices. Everything is guaranteed fresh and flavorful.

Jim Fobel's Jig Saw Pears with Custard Sauce

serves 6

Combine water, juices, optional bourbon, and sugar in a microwave safe casserole dish and microwave at 100% power 3 minutes. Stir to completely dissolve the sugar.

Peel the pears carefully, leaving stem ends intact. Cut the bottoms off so that the pears will stand flat. Now stand the pears in the dish and spoon hot syrup over the pears. Cover and microwave at 100% power for 10 minutes. Remove the cover and spoon syrup over the pears again. Allow them to cool to room temperature then cover and refrigerate until serving time.

Carefully cut cooked and cooled pears in half in a zig-zag pattern. Remove the core of the pears with a melon baller and stuff each core with two walnut halves. Put the pears back together into a zig-zag.

Stand each pear on a dessert plate in a pool of custard sauce. If you've got some mint leaves, add a sprig of mint to the top of each pear.

½ cup water

½ cup apple juice or bourbon

¼ cup lemon juice

½ cup brown sugar

6 large, firm, ripe pears

6 walnuts, cracked and halved

Custard Sauce:

makes 2 cups

Place milk in a 2-cup glass measure and heat in the microwave at 100% for 3 minutes. Meanwhile, whisk egg yolks in a large microwave safe bowl until foamy. Add sugar by the tablespoon full and continue whisking a couple of minutes until the mixture is smooth.

Use a wooden spoon to stir hot milk into the egg mixture taking care not to foam the sauce. Now, replace in the microwave and heat at 70% power for 1 minute. Stir. Now, continue to heat, stirring and checking at 15 second intervals until the sauce coats the back of a spoon so that when you draw your finger across it, you'll see a light creamy layer that holds its shape. When you're stirring the sauce, look at it closely. You do not want it to boil, or it will curdle the egg yolks. What you want is for it to thicken around the edges, barely bubbling. If you see steam rising, stop. The sauce is just hot enough.

Finish the sauce off the heat by beating in butter and flavorings, if you wish. Sometimes, I just leave it as is, the pure vanilla taste being enough. Store in the refrigerator, covered, in a clean jar for several days.

1½ cups milk

6 large egg yolks

⅔ cup sugar

1 tablespoon vanilla

3 tablespoons butter or margarine, optional

2 tablespoons rum, liqueur or brandy, optional

SULFUR-FREE DRIED FRUITS, SUN-DRIED TOMATOES, PEPPERS, AND APPLES. NUTS GALORE.

It's certain that fine women eat crazy salad with their meat.

—WILLIAM YEATS (1865–1939)

DRIED FRUITS AND NUTS

TIMBER CREST FARMS
4791 Dry Creek Rd.
Healdsburg, CA 95448

CREDIT CARDS: **Yes**

CALL FOR CATALOG

RETAIL STORE: **Call for directions**

PHONE: 707-433-8251

FAX: 707-433-8255

MINIMUM ORDER: **Yes**

Rancher Waltenspiel looks a good bit like the man in "American Gothic" and when you look into his tanned, creased face, you know he didn't get into farming as a tax dodge. He and his wife, Ruth, own an orchard 75 miles north of San Francisco, where they grow and dry a variety of fruits and nuts. Many Waltenspiel products are organic, and all are free of added sugar, sulfur dioxide, or other preservatives. They allow apricots, pears, and peaches to ripen completely before drying. What you get is intense flavor.

Order dried tomatoes, dried tomato tapenade, or, our favorite, a product Ruth Waltenspiel developed that she calls "Season It." A blend of dried tomato bits, Parmesan cheese, onions, garlic, basil, parsley, and diced red bell peppers, it's a great sprinkle for salads and pasta and will make a canned soup come alive.

Ruth's developed a dozen or more dried tomato products that can be made into sauces and spreads. She even offers a sun-dried tomato cookbook. It's everything you ever wanted to know about the use of dried tomatoes.

WANNA DATE?

SPHINX DATE RANCH
3039 N. Scottsdale Rd.
Scottsdale, AZ 85257

CREDIT CARDS: **Yes**

CALL FOR CATALOG

RETAIL STORE: **Yes**

PHONE: 602-941-2261

FAX: 602-941-1840

MINIMUM ORDER: **No**

Farmer's Market

Drive out to Scottsdale from Phoenix and you'll find one of the old farm houses now houses a "date ranch." Now, this isn't where you can go to fix up your love life, but it is a place where you can satisfy your need for sweets. Sphinx dates are grown around here and are huge, moist, and sweet. Eat them plain or try them in a Sweet Date Shake. Or maybe in some date bread, made on the spot. The Scottsdale Date Ranch offers not only their own dates in the store, but a lot of other Southwestern stuff: cactus candies and jellies and citrus packs.

We are crazy for the Date Pecan Pie and highly recommend it. Take the kids here and show them the real date palms growing outside in the yard. This new "old farm" isn't where the Date Ranch began. Actually, they started out in a roadside stand in a grove of date palms planted in Phoenix in 1917. Eventually, the housing developments overtook that grove and the ranch had to move.

Here's your source for the Cadillac of dates, the black Medjool. Like owner Rick Heetland says, "Dates are the fruit of the Southwest. They're fresh, they're different, and they're delicious."

THE GIRDLED GRAPE RAISIN CO.

P.O. Box 345
Sultana, CA 93666

CREDIT CARDS: **Yes**

CALL FOR CATALOG

RETAIL STORE: **Call for directions**

PHONE: **209-626-4094**

FAX: **209-626-4902**

MINIMUM ORDER: **No**

RAISINS RAISINS RAISINS

In the heart of the grape-raisin country, sits a little country store with an attitude. Showing humorous raisins in corsets, they've made a good business by girdling their own grapes. The store sells a full line of raisin products made with locally grown product. The notion of the girdle is more than a joke, however, A ring is cut around the grapevine to produce a larger grape. This makes plumper, larger, more flavorful raisins than you can buy from the big commercial packers. These raisins have a real raisin flavor and—of course—require no artificial preservatives or sweeteners.

Buy raisins plain, or mixed with walnuts, or covered with chocolate or yogurt. They also offer local almonds sliced, slivered, and whole, and locally grown walnuts and pecans.

L'ESPRIT DE CAMPAGNE

P.O. Box 3130
Winchester, VA 22604

CHECKS OR MONEY ORDERS ONLY

CALL FOR CATALOG

PHONE: **703-955-1014**

FAX: **703-955-1018**

MINIMUM ORDER: **No**

VIRGINIA DRIED TOMATOES

The hot Virginia sun grows great tomatoes and Joy Lokey both dries and packages them in oil. She also dries Virginia apples and cherries. Her dried tomatoes julienne in extra virgin olive oil would be fine for a pasta sauce—as is. Her minced tomatoes in oil are just the ticket to top a focaccia or a pizza.

One of the best products Joy makes comes from the scraps. Nothing but sprinkles of dried tomatoes she blends with other herbs and spices, it makes for a handy soup pepper-upper and a way to give your supper a lift. I couldn't live without this stuff.

All of Joy's tomato products are bursting with flavor and came out on top in a taste test conducted by the finicky *New York Times* food section.

DRIED TOMATOES, PEPPERS, AND APPLES

JUST TOMATOES
P.O. Box 807
Westley, CA 95387

CREDIT CARDS: Yes

CALL FOR CATALOG

RETAIL STORE: Call for directions

PHONE: 800-537-1985

FAX: 800-537-1986

MINIMUM ORDER: No

Karen Cox took along her favorite snack to an art workshop at Yosemite: glorious home-dried red pinwheel wafers of tomato, and the other artists in her group got more excited about the garlic-olive oil scented bites than the subject they were supposed to be painting. When they asked her what she called them, she replied, "Just tomatoes."

Combining her artist's eye, her marketing skills, and the tomatoes from her central valley family farm, Karen Cox soon had a business. Her husband made a Rube Goldberg dehydrator on the farm his family's owned for four generations and now the Coxes not only dry tomatoes—two tons a day from July to September—but also bell peppers, apples, persimmons, and mixed fruits.

Without adding salt, sulfur, or sweeteners, they've created products that are bursting with flavor. We are wild for Karen's mayo suggestions: a few of her dried tomatoes and bell peppers tossed into mayonnaise with some lemon juice, chives, and black pepper to taste. As a finish for grilled fish, this is superb. Karen's written two terrific little cookbooks that tell you how to use these products. Ask for them. You'll like the recipes, you'll like the art.

The Coxes welcome visitors to the family farm. Come and watch them dry tomatoes.

FRESH ALMONDS FROM THE ORCHARD

LUKES ALMOND ACRES
11281 South Lac Jac
Reedley, CA 93654

CHECKS OR MONEY ORDERS ONLY

CALL FOR CATALOG

RETAIL STORE: Yes

PHONE: 209-638-3483

FAX: 209-637-7788

MINIMUM ORDER: No

This is real simple. The Neresians grow almonds on their Reedley Orchard property. They sell the almonds right off the farm and love to visit with people who are scouring the countryside on weekends away from the cities.

Their almonds are simply fresh and wonderful. They make almond butter that puts peanut butter in the shade. If you visit the farm in the summer, you'll see the family with a few helpers sorting, drying, and weighing nuts for packaging. They farm just 20 acres of almonds but let me tell you, that acreage produces a boatload of nuts, about 15 tons to be exact—and all delicious.

From the farm, they also sell dried California fruits, and chocolate and yogurt covered nuts and raisins. Barbara Neresian oversees every mail order and happily customizes orders to suit.

How to Make Almond Paste

In the work bowl of a food processor, fitted with the steel blade, add almonds. Process to a fine powder, by pulsing. Add sugar, egg whites, and extract. Process until smooth, scraping the sides of the bowl every 10 seconds or so. Turn out onto plastic wrap and form a log. Wrap tightly and refrigerate at least 24 hours. Use in place of commercial almond paste in any recipe.

2 cups (about 10 ozs.) blanched whole or slivered almonds

1½ cups confectioners' sugar

2 large egg whites

1 teaspoon almond extract

1 teaspoon rose water (optional)

NUNES FARMS
P.O. Box 311
Newman, CA 95360

CREDIT CARDS: Yes

CALL FOR CATALOG

RETAIL STORE: Call for directions

PHONE: 800-255-1641
209-862-3033

FAX: 209-862-1038

MINIMUM ORDER: No

Linda Eckhardt's 1995 Guide to America's Best Foods

ALMONDS EVERY WAY

Maureen Nunes not only sells her family's almonds in the shell, but also offers them blanched, roasted, chopped, roasted, and salted, or in an almond toffee crunch. For heavy-duty bakers, this would be a good source for nonpareil supreme blanched almonds that still taste like something when you use them in baked goods.

Perhaps the best news from Nunes Farms is that they offer premium tree-ripened stone fruits, handpicked from their own farm. You won't find anything even close in the grocery store. Tender white juicy peaches, giant sun-ripened apricots, and nectarines as sweet as sugar. Call and ask how Mother Nature's doing and when the fruit will be perfect. They won't air freight it to you a day before the fruit is completely ripe and perfect.

OREGON HAZELNUTS: JUMBOS AND EXTRA LARGE

Here's a short and sweet product list. Hazelnuts. But these are the Oregon Orchard Jumbos and Extra Large hazelnut kernels so prized by bakers and holiday cooks. They come raw or dry roasted and are, of course, shelled.

HAZY GROVE NUTS
P.O. Box 25753
Portland, OR 97201

CREDIT CARDS: **Yes**

CALL FOR CATALOG

PHONE: **800-574-NUTS**
  503-244-0593

MINIMUM ORDER: **No**

OREGON HAZELNUTS

Hazelnuts are Oregon's state nut. Now I know that all states have their own nut, but Oregon claims this one. Known to some as filberts, they're the most desirable cooking nut known to French cooking. You can get first-quality mammoth hazelnuts right out of the orchard here. Also available are bakers' packs of broken nuts suitable for candy and cake baking. Marlyce Tolvstad and her partner, Mary Mills Weil, also produce and sell a good number of fine hazelnut products: hazelnut butter, chocolate hazelnut butter, mocha hazelnut butter, and walnut hazelnut butter. These butters come creamy and crunchy.

For ardent bakers, their most desirable product is still the whole-roasted *skinned* hazelnuts. No more rolling the damn things in a tea towel to knock the husks off. These come in vacuum packed tins from two lbs. up to 32 lbs. For the serious and the insane Christmas bakers.

DUNDEE ORCHARDS
P.O. Box 327
Dundee, OR 97115

CREDIT CARDS: **Yes**

CALL FOR CATALOG

PHONE: **503-538-8105**

FAX: **503-538-8105**

MINIMUM ORDER: **No**

Farmer's Market

PRIESTER'S PECANS

227 Old Fort Drive
Fort Deposit, AL 36032

~~~~~~~~~~~~~~~~

CREDIT CARDS: Yes

CALL FOR CATALOG

RETAIL STORE: Yes

PHONE: 800-277-3226
205-227-8355

FAX: 205-227-4294

MINIMUM ORDER: No

BEST QUALITY MAMMOTH PECANS

Priester's motto is "Home of the Southern Kernel and Southern Hospitality." Amen to that. These pecans are mammoth, dripping in nut oil and fresh as spring. Visit the store and you'll want to buy them in all their permutations. If the taste doesn't get you, the Southern hospitality will.

See them making peanut brittle in huge copper cauldrons. Watch the expert cooks cutting up candy. Try free samples of whatever they're cooking. See them hand-dip chocolates and pull brittle. I dare you to resist buying up a boatload of this stuff. It's that good. In an old-fashioned, calories-be-damned way. Eat it up.

A big 1 lb. 8 oz. tin of mammoth pecan halves is about the most luxurious present you could ever offer to a Southerner. Especially if that Southerner's been exiled to the North or West. Of course you may witness an adult who's breaking down crying. Don't worry about it. Those are tears of joy. And soon that person may be humming "Dixie." Run and rent "Gone with the Wind." It's that kind of experience. I love this place.

SAN SABA PECAN, INC.

2803 West Wallace
San Saba, TX 76877

~~~~~~~~~~~~~~~~

CREDIT CARDS: Yes

CALL FOR CATALOG

RETAIL STORE: Yes

PHONE: 800-621-8121
915-372-5727

FAX: 915-327-5729

MINIMUM ORDER: No

*Linda
Eckhardt's
1995
Guide to
America's
Best Foods*

TRUE TEXAS PECANS

We've been ordering pecans from this outfit ever since the time we lived in the hill country area of Texas. San Saba calls itself the pecan capital of the world, and rightly so. Native Texas pecan trees bend low over both the Colorado and San Saba rivers here. Buddy Adams, who owns this pecan-shelling business, read an account of the Texas Rangers camping out on local river banks who picked enough pecans to last the troops the whole winter.

You can get enough to last you the winter too. All you have to do is decide how you want them. We generally get some in the shell, some shelled, and—just for our own secret pleasure—in a tin packed with pralines. The smooth, sticky kind of pralines that you think about all year, until the next time you get a box from San Saba Pecan.

Stop by the plant and you may notice the sign still says San Saba Hide and Pecan. That's because the original business also dealt with sheep and mohair hides—San Saba's other claim to fame. There's nothing more fun than walking through the cool, dank warehouse looking into gunny sacks full of dusty pecans. You can choose your favorite from five or six varieties. The hybrid paper shell pecans, rich and oily, include Stewarts—our pecan of choice.

When buying pecans in the shell, look for smooth, clean shells with no splits or cracks.

If you choose shelled halves, look for plump nutmeats uniform in color and size and a bright golden shade.

Pecan pieces are the most economical buy and suitable for most cooking.

•A pound of pecans in the shell yields about 2¼ cups pecan nutmeat.

•4 ounces of shelled pecans equals a cup.

Store pecans away from onions, oranges or other odor-emitting products.

•In the pantry no longer than 3 months
•In the refrigerator up to 6 months
•In the freezer up to 2 years

MACADAMIA NUTS FROM HAWAII

Here they are, genuine macadamia nuts straight from Hawaii, in four-ounce to fifteen-ounce packages. They also come chocolate-covered, in cookies, candies, and confections. Available roasted and salted, or dry-roast salted, or roasted and unsalted. This is the mother lode for macadamias. How do you want them? Give them a call.

MAC FARMS OF HAWAII
3615 Harding St., Ste. 207
Honolulu, HI 96816

CREDIT CARDS: **Yes**

CALL FOR CATALOG

RETAIL STORE: **Call for directions**

PHONE: **808-737-0645**

FAX: **808-734-4675**

MINIMUM ORDER: **No**

Farmer's Market

In the Sierra Nut House newsletter, sent out with all orders and affectionately known as *Nutsy News Notes,* you can learn arcane facts about nuts and find recipes and tips for the latest in food trends. For example:

•Sunflower seeds contain 2½ and 4½ times as much potassium as bananas and oranges respectively.

•According to current research studies, vitamin-E-rich nuts lower cholesterol levels and the three nuts most effective are walnuts, pecans, and almonds.

•Pumpkin seeds are rich in magnesium and may help keep the prostate healthy.

•Ever wonder why some pistachios are dyed red? Inferior quality pistachios, or ones held in storage too long, develop dark spots on the normally light-colored shell. When this happens, they're dipped in a salty red dye.

SIERRA NUT HOUSE

3034 E. Sierra
Fresno, CA 93710

CREDIT CARDS: Yes

CALL FOR CATALOG

RETAIL STORE: Yes

PHONE: 800-397-6887
209-299-8131

FAX: 209-299-7683

MINIMUM ORDER: No

*Linda
Eckhardt's
1995
Guide to
America's
Best Foods*

NUTS TO YOU

If you like nuts, you'll love this place. We took some of their trail mix on a campout and couldn't stay out of it. We ate it all the first day. It was that fresh and good. And for dinner, doing our Sierra campout up right, we dined on Mama Sorrenti's Minestrone soup that I'd made from a Sierra Nut mix. This soup was delicious. It even looked good in the package: pasta shells, kidney beans, limas, dehydrated potatoes, cabbage, onions, carrots, celery, bell peppers, tomatoes, and garlic. I did dress it up a bit with fresh tomatoes from the garden. But, even as is, the soup is terrific. Healthy, with no chemical additives, and better the second day than the first. Ideal for campouts. They call these products Sierra Bean Bags and they come in several flavors: black bean chili, pasta e fagioli, and French-style chicken with beans. Each one's better than the last.

Jo Ann Sorrenti Arvanigian and her husband, Richard, began this business out of their family's almond ranch near Fresno in 1969. Besides almonds, trail mix, and bean bags, they ship tons of Hollister apricots and prunes. These are the dried fruits that drip with flavor and are rich in color and nutrition. The kind you can't stop eating.

Now they have a shop in Aptos right on the tourist route. Stop in and you'll see baskets dangling from the ceiling, glass cannisters filled with nuts, coffee beans, candy, and ingredients to make the most of California's generous provender. They sell wine; they make gift baskets. They make candy—almond bark. They do a whole line of grains. If there's something exotic you've been looking for—call them up. Or go see them in Fresno or Aptos.

MISSOURI PECANS

Pecans grow in the Midwest as well as the South, and Mary Ann Byrd sells Missouri pecans from her little roadside store. The pecans are long, sweet, and meaty. You can get them cracked, shelled, or in the shell. The Byrd's store is easy to find if you're in the neighborhood. Mary Ann says they're just down the road from the ranch where the pecans are grown. Not far from Kansas City on Highway 52 between Butler, Missouri and Trading Post, Kansas.

Order by mail and you'll get a recipe brochure with authentic recipes for Earthquake Cake—yes, they do have earthquakes in Missouri, Coke Salad, and Pecan Pumpkin pies, among other things.

SOUTHERN FRUITS AND FANCY PECANS

An institution in the South, Callaway Gardens began as a roadside fruit stand and now has grown to include resorts, gardens, golf course, etc. But their real claim to fame are pecans and jams, as well as other deep south country foods. Order country-cured hams, muscadine jellies, preserves and sauces, pear and fig preserves, good Speckled Heart stone-ground grits and corn meal, as well as a raft of other southern products.

The original fruit stand was built in 1952 with eighteen-inch thick walls of stone quarried at Blue Springs, Georgia. Notice the hand-hewn beams and slate roof. It's worth a visit just for the view. Look out over Georgia's good green hills. Before you're through, you may want to join the Callaway Gardens as a member. Then you'll get a quarterly newsletter, advance notice of their many workshops, discount privileges, and a whole lot more. Particularly recommended is the Azalea Festival that occurs in late March and early April when the flowers burst into bloom. Lots of entertainment, fine southern food, and fun for the family is yours. Go.

BYRD'S PECANS
Rt. 3, Box 196
Butler, MO 64730

CHECKS OR MONEY ORDERS ONLY

CALL FOR CATALOG

RETAIL STORE: Call for directions

PHONE: 816-679-5583

MINIMUM ORDER: No

CALLAWAY GARDENS
P.O. Box 2000
Pine Mountain, GA 31822-2000

CREDIT CARDS: Yes

CALL FOR CATALOG

RETAIL STORE: Call for directions

PHONE: 800-282-8181

MINIMUM ORDER: No

Farmer's Market

SUNNYLAND FARMS, INC.

Wilson Road at
   Pecan City
P.O. Box 8200
Albany, GA 31706-8200

~~~~~~~~~~~~~~~~~

CREDIT CARDS: Yes

CALL FOR CATALOG

RETAIL STORE: Call for
   directions

PHONE: 912-883-3085

FAX: 912-432-1358

MINIMUM ORDER: No

GEORGIA PECANS

You knew Georgia grew great peaches, but don't forget the pecans. Huge, meaty, full of aromatic oils, these pecans are almost too good for Pecan pie, but not quite. Harry and Jane Willson have a thriving mail order business in pecans—in lots of different shapes and sizes.

Order pecans plain and fancy. Desirables or Schleys, by the box or by the tin. In the shell or out. Halved or in pieces. The Willsons— who freely admit to "being nuts"—have been processing pecans for 45 years and are the Southeast coast experts on the mail order of these products.

One way we like to see these pecans packed are in "jiffy gifts." These are clear plastic containers about the size of coffee sacks, decorated with bells and holly. They make a handy on-the-spot gift for people at the office, your kid's teacher, the mail person, and the guy who reads the meter.

The Willsons have expanded and now offer California colossal pistachios, salted and toasted and sold in a big tin or box. They also sell jumbo cashews from Southern India, and Macadamias from Hawaii. For special orders, ask to speak to Jane Willson. She'll help.

Besides these basic nut packs, they offer nutty fruit cakes, candy, brittle, and a variety of first quality dried fruits: Calimyrna figs, pears, dates, Mission figs and Extra-Fancy apricots. Call for a catalog. There's too much good stuff to name.

*Linda
Eckhardt's
1995
Guide to
America's
Best Foods*

108

BLACK WALNUTS

If you have ever been so ambitious as to attempt to remove the meat from a black walnut, you will see why this company provides a valuable service. They procure 100 percent Eastern black walnuts, then crack them for you and send them out, shelled, in one-pound packages. The black walnut is one variety that's so pungent, it seems to lose nothing in the shelling—except the yellow stain on your fingers and the curses when you mash your thumb with the hammer.

Also available are fancy native pecan halves and pieces, fancy roasted and salted Mammoth pecan halves, extra large fancy super cashews, California pistachios, fancy macadamia nuts, nonpareil supreme whole almonds, and thin sliced almonds.

If it's nuts you want, this is the place.

MISSOURI DANDY PANTRY
212 Hammons Drive East
Stockton, MO 65785

CREDIT CARDS: **Yes**

CALL FOR CATALOG

RETAIL STORE: **Call for directions**

PHONE: **800-8-PANTRY**

FAX: **417-276-5187**

MINIMUM ORDER: **No**

PASTA, RICE, BEANS, AND BOX DINNERS

Winners in the Just-Add-Water sweepstakes. Imported and domestic durum wheat pastas, both fresh and dried, both plain and flavored, and the sauces and marinaras to accompany them. Best quality wild rices, organic Basmati, Texmati, long and short grain white and brown rices. Tamales, chili, barbecue beans. Brunswick stew and knishes. New Age Box Dinners that combine beans and grains for easy preparation. Heirloom beans, bean mixes, and soup mixes.

Strange to see how a good dinner and feast reconciles everybody.

—SAMUEL PEPYS (1633–1703)

IMPORTED AND DOMESTIC DURUM WHEAT PASTAS, BOTH FRESH AND DRIED, BOTH PLAIN AND FLAVORED, AND THE SAUCES AND MARINARAS TO ACCOMPANY THEM.

Sir we could not have had a better dinner had their been a synod of cooks.

—SAMUEL JOHNSON (1709–1784)

Lemon Pepper Pasta and Seared Scallops with Lemon Vodka Sauce

makes 2 main dish servings

In a small sauté pan over medium high heat, warm the oil and butter until the butter foams, then sauté the scallops until golden on both sides, turning once. Cover and set aside. Keep warm.

Meanwhile, heat water in a medium large sauce pot to a full boil. Drop the fettucine into the boiling water and cook until barely done (2 minutes for fresh pasta; 8 minutes for dried). Drain.

To make the sauce, grate zest and mix with juice and set aside. Boil together the cream and vodka for three minutes, then add lemon juice and zest and boil another minute or until thick.

Toss drained hot pasta with lemon sauce. Divide between two warmed dinner plates. Top with seared scallops. Season lightly with salt. Grate black pepper over all. Top with chives and Parmesan and serve at once.

½ lb. large sea scallops
1 tablespoon olive oil
1 teaspoon butter
12 oz. dried lemon pepper fettucine
3 quarts barely salted water

Lemon Vodka Sauce
juice and zest of 1 lemon
½ cup whipping cream
2 tablespoons vodka
1 tablespoon dried chives
salt and freshly milled black pepper to taste
freshly grated Parmesan for garnish

FRESH PASTA AND SAUCE

Here's another Just-Add-Water winner. In this case, all you do is boil water, drop in first quality pasta, cook until done, then toss with one of these freshly made sauces. It's too easy and it's too good.

The brainchild of Paul Milani, Carol Angell, and Christine Buchholz, Fresh Pasta works on the principle that you want great food, but you don't have time to cook it yourself. They hand blend fresh herbs and other products to create heavenly international sauces that are not only good on pasta, but over a baked potato, on a boboli, or with rice. They make their own pastas as well and offer suggestions for mating up pastas and sauces.

They believe, and rightly so, that pasta can be the beginning of a fast and easy meal. The business began on Martha's Vineyard but grew to a mainland factory and cafe in Northampton. You can still enjoy a quick pasta lunch at their retail store. Take it home or order it in, and you have a no-brainer dinner that will knock your socks off in the time it takes to boil the pasta.

FRESH PASTA COMPANY

Box 37
Northampton, MA
01061

CREDIT CARDS: Yes

CALL FOR CATALOG

RETAIL STORE: Call for directions

PHONE: 413-586-5399
413-586-5875

FAX: 413-586-3715

MINIMUM ORDER: No

Pasta, Rice, Beans, and Box Dinners

Some of our favorite sauces include: Buttery Asiago and Almonds (staggering), Creamy Cajun, Walnut Ricotta, Salsa Verde, Roasted Red Pepper, Pesto, Satay Teriyaki, Curry, Gorgonzola, and Champagne—made with champagne, butter and tomatoes. Yum.

GASTON DUPRE
7904 Hopi Place
Tampa, FL 33634

CHECKS OR MONEY
ORDERS ONLY

CALL FOR CATALOG

PHONE: 800-937-9445
813-885-9445

FAX: 813-886-1314

MINIMUM ORDER: **No**

SPECIALTY PASTA

Gaston Dupre has carved out a niche in the market by making brightly-flavored and colored pastas. After twelve years of innovations, and thirty-two flavors, this company is well respected in the field for producing a product that not only looks good, but tastes good as well.

This pasta is hand rolled, not extruded, until every bit of flavor is ready to burst in your mouth. It's the same principle as making bread. By kneading the dough, the gluten develops and you get a full-flavored result. Then, the pasta is slow-dried so that the flavor is not lost, as it is in big factories where pastas are super-heated and microwaved into submission.

In fact, this pasta really stands out in the Just-Add-Water sweepstakes, because the pasta tastes so good, after you've boiled it, about all you need are a few drops of good olive oil to complete. No need to refrigerate—this is instant dinner at the ready.

Excellent flavors include Tex-Mex, Chinese Spice, Teriyaki, Thai, Jamaican Spice, Spinach Nutmeg, Lemon Pepper, Garlic Parsley, Confetti, Tomato Basil, Tarragon Chives, Wild Mushroom, and Whole Wheat. These pastas are so colorful, ranging in shades from bright red to cinnamon-colored to a nearly black one. They're made without eggs or salt and with 100 percent Durum flour and 100 percent natural veggies. They cut them in both fettucini and angel hair widths. All you have to do is boil the stuff 3–4 minutes and dinner's served.

*Linda
Eckhardt's
1995
Guide to
America's
Best Foods*

114

HANDMADE FRESH RAVIOLI

RAVIOLISMO
1318 N. Peak St.
Dallas, TX 75204

CREDIT CARDS: **Yes**

CALL FOR CATALOG

RETAIL STORE: **Yes**

PHONE: **800-80-PASTA**

MINIMUM ORDER: **3 Dozen**

Philip Civello and his sister Chena have been making fine fresh ravioli for upscale restaurants for more than ten years. They stuff their all-durum wheat ravioli with a variety of fillings, some Italian, some southwestern, and some vegetarian. We like the red bell pepper with basil and the spinach with shrimp. Most popular are the beef with spinach and the ricotta with provolone and romano.

Southwestern flavors include black bean, Paula Lambert's goat cheese with green onions and cilantro, or three cheese with the ubiquitous Texas jalapeno. They also hand-stuff Italian sausage and make a variety of sauces daily to go with their more than 12 flavors of ravioli.

If you've never seen ravioli or sausage being made—take the plunge. It's quite a craft. Visit the factory on weekdays from 9 to 3, just east of downtown Dallas at the corner of Peak and Bryan. It's quite an interesting thing to observe. And if you can think of a great new filling for ravioli, tell Philip and Chena. They're always up for a new idea.

Order ravioli for home use and you get either three dozen or six dozen frozen ravioli which you can store in the freezer until you're ready to use. Then it's easy. Just slip them into boiling water, follow the directions that come with them, and voila. The little pillows are yours.

PASTA POWER AND PUNCHED-UP JELLIES

JUDYTH'S MOUNTAIN
1737 Lorenzen Dr.
San Jose, CA 95124

CREDIT CARDS: **Yes**

CALL FOR CATALOG

PHONE: **408-264-3330**

MINIMUM ORDER: **No**

Mona Onstead wrote the book on making specialty pasta sauces in a jar. For more than ten years she's been blending California products to make pasta sauces with character. We love the California Almond with Leek and Caper sauce. We also adore the Pepper Olive with Walnut sauce. And a dollop of the Cream Garlic Butter with Pesto atop a grilled chicken breast is simply heaven.

Mona figured out a long time ago a way to vacuum seal in the good flavor of butter and fresh herbs to make the most ardent non-cook into a quick gourmet. It's instant joy. She's just invented a new pasta sauce she calls Puttanesca, that's made with Spanish olives and

Pasta, Rice, Beans, and Box Dinners

115

tomatoes, mushrooms, onions, garlic, olive oil, red wine vinegar, and sugar. It's exquisite.

She also makes ginger jelly that's a cousin to pepper jelly, but with an Indian zing. And a curried ginger marinade that contains her famous ginger jelly but will make chicken fly away. Her tart cumin lime marinade is a Cal-Mexican specialty that's highly recommended.

ROMAN TOMATO PESTO

MORNING STAR
Box 748
Mt. Home, ID
  83647-0748

CREDIT CARDS: Yes

CALL FOR CATALOG

PHONE: 208-857-7010

FAX: 208-857-8370

MINIMUM ORDER: Yes

If you ever grew tomatoes in the backyard and dried them yourself, you'll remember this taste. Bursting with flavor, these dried tomatoes are well-blended with olive oil and a variety of other flavors to produce a couple of exquisite home-style tomato products.

Jim Elias buys dried tomatoes from California, New Mexico, and Texas and then creates these mouthwatering products. Roma Tomatoes in pure olive oil with garlic and herbs is just the beginning. His Roman Tomato Pesto is simply to die for. Combining tomatoes with olive oil, sweet basil, Romano and parmesan cheeses, almonds, and herbs, this product yields an intense tomatoey sauce that tossed with pasta makes lunch a banquet. Dropped onto scrambled eggs, it makes breakfast an aria.

GREAT MARINARA

SCHIAVONE'S FOODS, INC.
1907 Tytus Ave.
Middletown, OH 45042

CREDIT CARDS: Yes

CALL FOR CATALOG

RETAIL STORE: Yes

PHONE: 513-422-8650

MINIMUM ORDER: No

Paul Newman can take his spaghetti sauce back to Connecticut. Taste-tested at the *Seattle Times* against Schiavone's, it just didn't make the grade. The Schiavones operate a restaurant in the heart of America: Middletown, Ohio, where they grew up in the bosom of a loving Italian family who spent Sundays eating and arguing and talking all afternoon.

Mama Yolanda invented the sauce and inspired the restaurant. Fifteen years ago, after customers got down on their knees begging, the Schiavone family began canning Mama's sauce. This is not in a jar. It's in a real can. And that's what makes it all the more delightful. Crank the can open and you get a sauce so fresh, aromatic, and garlicky that its aroma rushes up to greet you before you even heat it. The sauce is a deep red color, not too salty, and the thin kind you find at Sunday dinners in real Italian homes. You'll have to buy a case, but you won't mind.

MAMA'S PASTA SAUCE

Patrick Timpone and Jill Ward harvest bushels and bushels of fresh basil to blend with their tomatoes to make a homestyle pasta sauce that's genuinely Italian in taste and texture. Not overly thick or weighted down with tomatoes, this is a light, flavorful pasta sauce that I'm crazy about.

They also make fresh salsa, salsa verde, salsa muy rica, and a Sicilian dressing. Every batch is small enough to be hand-stirred. They buy fresh produce daily and use organic ingredients whenever possible. Their Rose's Muy Rica Salsa has a divine toasty taste because they smoke the tomatoes first over an open wood fire, then add them to extra virgin olive oil, chunks of fresh garlic, fresh onions and herbs, plus a dose of natural vitamin E to keep the sauce fresh. The sauce is then shot through with chipotles for that Mexican smoked jalapeno zing. This stuff is heaven with chips.

The Sicilian dressing is a blend of extra virgin olive oil, fresh squeezed lemon juice, fresh chopped garlic and herbs with spices and more of that natural vitamin E to maintain the freshness of the oil. The gorgeous green color comes from the olive itself. Yum. This dressing tastes as good as it looks.

TIMPONE'S FRESH FOODS

2311-B Thornton Rd.
Austin, TX 78704

CHECKS OR MONEY ORDERS ONLY

CALL FOR CATALOG

PHONE: 800-883-3238
512-442-7772

FAX: 512-443-7773

MINIMUM ORDER: 1 Case

Pasta, Rice, Beans, and Box Dinners

117

BEST QUALITY WILD RICES, ORGANIC BASMATI, TEXMATI, LONG AND SHORT GRAIN WHITE AND BROWN RICES. TAMALES, CHILI, BARBECUE BEANS. BRUNSWICK STEW AND KNISHES.

Soup of the evening, beautiful soup.

—LEWIS CARROLL (1832–1898)

ORGANIC JASMINE AND WILD RICE

ESTUS GOURMET
1555 Park Ave., Unit A
Emeryville, CA 94608

Estus Gourmet sells rice in jars. Not any old rice you understand but premium quality grown-in-California rices—either singly or in blends: Upland wild rice, jasmine, three grain rice (our favorite), calmati, two Indian rice, organic three grain rice, organic wild and brown rice, and premium wild rice.

Along with a jar of good rice, you'll get a recipe card with terrific suggestions for new ways to cook rice. They also sell whole peppercorns—white, green, black, and pink—as well as herbs for the barbecue and *herbes de Provence*.

Tasting these various rices, cooked in a rice cooker and on top of the stove, we became exquisitely aware of the subtle differences in rice. California three grain, for example, after being cooked in water, then sautéed with butter and garlic, smells and tastes like popcorn. Kids love it. The blends are carefully done so that you get a new taste sensation with every one.

Order in 13-oz. plastic jars or in bulk. Don't forget to ask for the recipes.

CREDIT CARDS: Yes

CALL FOR CATALOG

PHONE: 510-653-0496

FAX: 510-530-7428

MINIMUM ORDER: No

WILD RICE AND FRUIT CAKES TOO

ITALIAN BAKERY
205 S. 1st St.
Virginia, MN 55792

Minnesota is known for its wild rice and one of the best places to buy it is a bakery. Located in the heart of the wild rice country, the Italian Bakery sells authentic wild rice in one-, two-, and three-pound packages.

They also sell a Potica—that's a kind of rolled pastry filled with walnuts and brown sugar. Made with butter, whole eggs, honey, lots of walnuts, and pure vanilla, it has no preservatives and is best kept frozen until you're ready to serve.

CREDIT CARDS: No

CALL FOR CATALOG

RETAIL STORE: Yes

PHONE: 800-238-8830
        218-741-3464

FAX: 218-749-6810

MINIMUM ORDER: No

*Pasta, Rice, Beans,
and Box Dinners*

MELTING POT
FOODS

1120 North Linden
Oak Park, IL 60302

CREDIT CARDS: Yes

CALL FOR CATALOG

PHONE: 800-282-8327
  (Simpson & Vail)
  708-956-3340
  (Melting Pot Foods)

FAX: 914-741-6942
  (Simpson & Vail)

MINIMUM ORDER: No

BETTER BEANS AND RICE

O ne more in the Just-Add-Water hall of fame is this line of healthy ethnic foods that begins with couscous or pasta. Attractively packaged in brown, recycled looking boxes, these dinners are to the nineties what Kraft dinners were to the Fifties. A must for every swamped cook who needs to get dinner on the table when she's exhausted.

These dinners taste good—highly flavored, and made with a carefully blended herb mixture. You can choose from grain-based dinners or pasta dinners in several flavors: Wild Mushroom Couscous, Lucky 7 Vegetable, Napoli Mixed Beans and Radiatore, Sicilian Red Lentils and Bow Ties, Pasta e Fagioli, Tuscan White Beans and Spinach Rotini, and Florentine Cranberry Beans and Fusilli.

The beans are precooked then freeze-dried so that when you add boiling water and follow the box directions you get a quick, nutritious, grain or pasta-based dinner in about fifteen minutes. It tastes good. It's good for you. Working families should keep a mixed case on hand for the ultimate in care free dinners.

SORRENTI FAMILY
FARMS

1360 Main St.
Escalon, CA 95320

CREDIT CARDS: Yes

CALL FOR CATALOG

RETAIL STORE: Yes

PHONE: 209-838-1127

FAX: 209-838-7809

MINIMUM ORDER: No

*Linda
Eckhardt's
1995
Guide to
America's
Best Foods*

RITA'S RICE DINNERS IN A BOX

A lfred Sorrenti immigrated from Italy in the early part of the twentieth century to a California coastal valley as gorgeous as you may remember from the movie version of Steinbeck's *East of Eden.* The Sorrentis began growing rice and other crops and now, two generations later, are still farming in the valley outside Escalon.

In 1986, daughter-in-law Rita got the bright idea to package quick rice mixes. She wisely hired a graphic designer to help with the labels and soon, after lots of taste-testing in the farm kitchen, she launched a line of rice products that's gotten rave reviews from specialty foods people.

Besides the taste, the best thing about Rita's box dinners is that they're done in 10 minutes. Choose from Wild Rice Supreme, Italiano, Festiva, Creole, or Milano. Each box combines the Sorrentis own homegrown wild rice with brightly flavored natural seasonings and pasta. We particularly adored their "Mighty Wild Muffins" which require almost no attention and taste crunchy and bright.

THE BEAN QUEENS

MRS. BRITT'S OREGON KITCHEN

P.O. Box 985
Grants Pass, OR 97526

When I first met Jeanette Dickson, she and her partner, Pat Sheets, were mixing beans in the back bedroom of Pat's house. They'd pull out huge gunny sacks of beans and handmix all the beans, then stuff the gunny sacks back into the closet until their next order came in. Now, some seven years later, they have a real warehouse and a real office and a real mailing list of devoted customers.

I count myself on that list. Their original bean mix is made up of a variety of dried beans and a bouquet garni. Cook with a ham hock and it's home at your house tonight.

Also recommended are the minestrone mix, the chili bean mix, the oven-baked beans, and the bean salad. They also offer quick bread mixes for scones in several interesting varieties: oat and hazelnut, Fiesta with red pepper flakes, and Garden Herb with flecks of onion and bell pepper.

We took their Oregon Train Sippin's on a campout with us. It tasted a lot like Tang and one of our group remembered that as a college girl in the Sixties, they mixed hot Tang with tequila for a depth charge drink known to California college students as Poontang. We shot our Sippin's full of Tequila and had a drink to warm the hearts of campers and pioneers alike.

CREDIT CARDS: **Yes**

CALL FOR CATALOG (**$1 charge**)

RETAIL STORE: **Call for directions**

PHONE: **800-323-0566 503-474-3393**

FAX: **503-474-7916**

MINIMUM ORDER: **No**

Pasta, Rice, Beans, and Box Dinners

121

WOODSMAN
ENTERPRISES

P.O. Box 343
Gainesville, VA 22065

CREDIT CARDS: Yes

CALL FOR CATALOG

RETAIL STORE: Call for
directions

PHONE: 703-494-6600

MINIMUM ORDER: No

BEAN SOUPS AND SPICE BLENDS

Dan Eizak and Sumei Ko have a store they call "The Watkins Man" located in historic Occoquan, Virginia, just 10 miles outside the D.C. beltway. The entire town has been declared a national monument and makes a great walking tour for those who've seen enough of their Capital but haven't quite gotten their shopping fix yet.

Dan and Sumei have concocted a range of sugar and salt-free spice blends, as well as half a dozen bean mixes that are quite nice. We particularly liked the Twelve Bean soup mix. Following the directions, we added a ham hock, an onion, a bay leaf, a clove of garlic, and a little can of tomatoes. The resulting soup just begged for a piece of steaming corn bread and a big glass of milk. It made a dandy lunch. One reason it tasted so good was the hand-blended spices they pack with the mixed beans: black pepper, ground mustard, chili powder, and celery seed.

In addition to their own mixes, they offer Benchley tea bags in 30 to 40 flavors, a boat load of coffees, and Made-in-Virginia baskets containing Virginia peanuts, a cider sack, honey, apple butter, and a Virginia state cookie cutter. Other gift baskets are available.

BUCKEYE BEANS &
HERBS, INC.

P.O. Box 28220
Spokane, WA
99228-8220

CREDIT CARDS: Yes

CALL FOR CATALOG

RETAIL STORE: Call for
directions

PHONE: 800-449-2121

FAX: 509-484-5500

MINIMUM ORDER: No

A BOWL OF BEANS

Doug and Jill Smith began mixing beans in their basement 10 years ago, but eventually moved upstairs. Their beans are upstairs kind of products. They don't use MSG in their spice blends. They don't use inferior beans. Just subtle, interesting blends that make for no-brainer dinners you can really sink your teeth in.

We love the Buckeye Bean soup that's a blend of several beans, whole grains, and spices. You add the can of tomatoes and before long, you've got a great tasting, good-looking soup that's good for you besides. They also make a good Barley Beef, Chick-a-doodle that's rice and thyme-scented, a Lentil soup, and a Veggie Bean made with a dozen different beans and zesty spices. Cut up fresh veggies from your garden into their blend—it makes an outstanding soup. There's more than a dozen different bean and grain soup combos to choose from. They're all delicious.

PRAIRIE BEAN MIXES

Pat Palm lives on a ranch east of Cheyenne, Wyoming, near the village of Albin, Wyoming. Go past the cemetery and soon you'll see a sign that says Palm Tree. No, it doesn't mean desert palms, it means three families of Palms who live close to each other: Chuck, Hazel and Carl. The Palms raise wheat and would love to show you around. Call first. They might be in town picking up the mail.

Pioneers lived on beans, and Pat Palm offers not only mixed dried beans, and a lentil mix, but terrific prairie recipes to go along. If you've never tasted food the way our Westering forefathers enjoyed it, now's your chance. Try the 16-Bean mix, the Lentil mix, a Chili Bean mix (our favorite), or a Black Turtle Bean mix.

The herbs and seasonings enclosed with the bean packs are well-balanced and make a homey-tasting bean soup. Pat also sells gourmet popcorn grown in Wyoming, and for those of you who love to bake yeast bread from scratch at home, here's a source for winter wheat. You can grind your own wheat to make flour. Then you can say your homemade bread was truly made from scratch.

GRANDMA PAT'S PRODUCTS

P.O. Box 158
Albin, WY 82050

CREDIT CARDS: No

CALL FOR CATALOG

PHONE: 800-330-1549
307-246-3351

MINIMUM ORDER: No

HEIRLOOM BEANS AND STUFF

Here's a working farm you can take the kids to visit. It's especially recommended around Halloween when you can join their part of Half Moon Bay's Pumpkin Festival. At the ranch you'll see vegetables in the field. Lush, gorgeous vegetables. Visit a barn and let the kids pet honest-to-god farm animals. If there are 15 or more of you, you can arrange a guided tour.

The ranch grows herbs, plants for your garden, and an astounding array of heirloom beans that they dry and offer for sale. They make jams, vinegars, and bean packs. With more than 40 varieties, you can find exotic Rattlesnake beans, Appaloosas, Florida Speckled Butterbeans, Swedish Browns, and many others. There is a 5-pound minimum order.

On your visit to the farm, depending on what's being harvested at the moment, you might be able to buy just-picked ollaliberries, strawberries, raspberries and boysenberries. Garlic, onions, potatoes, sweet potatoes, or carrots. Shallots, ginger, and exotic specialty vegetables are also offered.

PHIPPS RANCH

2700 Pescadero Rd.
P.O. Box 349
Pescadero, CA 94060

CREDIT CARDS: Yes

CALL FOR CATALOG

RETAIL STORE: Call for directions

PHONE: 415-879-0787

MINIMUM ORDER: No

Pasta, Rice, Beans, and Box Dinners

Visit their aviary and see everything from parakeets to cockatiels, lovely finches, and a collection of South American and African birds as well as Australian rosellas. Stroll through the greenhouse and pick out your potted herbs. Buy picnic fixin's and enjoy lunch in an area bordering their berry fields. There's an English garden. There're two creeks. It's too bucolic.

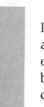

SUSIE Q'S (RIGHETTI SPECIALTIES)

7476 Graciosa Rd.
Santa Maria, CA 93455

~~~~~~~~~~~~~~~~~

CREDIT CARDS: **Yes**

CALL FOR CATALOG

PHONE: 805-937-2402

FAX: 805-937-7243

MINIMUM ORDER: **No**

SANTA MARIA STYLE BARBECUE BEANS

Beans are beans, and barbecue is barbecue—that is, until you get to this central coastal valley town. In Santa Maria, they barbecue steak over oak coals and offer it with a bean dish like no other. They begin with tiny pink beans that are an upscale cousin to the pinto bean. Now, thank goodness, you can order these beans to make your own Santa Maria-style bean dish.

Trust me on this. You'll like it. They call the beans pinquito, and in addition to selling them dried, Susie Q also sells a good dry rub for barbecue, a California style bean seasoning, and big sacks of beans for those who get addicted. Susie Q is also known as Susan Righetti and she freely admits to using her mom's famous recipe for the beans. You can make the beans at home easily, using Susie's dry spice mix, a blending of her herbs and spices.

If you're in the Santa Maria area, stop in and ask around to see where the Santa Maria boys are barbecuing this week. It's worth a stop. Finest steak barbecue, lots of California-style pinquito beans to eat, and usually a hoedown to boot.

VINEGARY FINE MISSOURI BARBECUE

Every region has its specialty and in Missouri, it's vinegary tart barbecue. And in Missouri, they like their beans as well. So an old-time roadside cafe called Zarda put the two together and came up with a fine product they call BBQ Beans. They're smoky, sweet, vinegary good, and dotted with barbecued beef bits. Zarda's ships them out in frozen pints and you can keep them on hand until "Barbecue Desperation" hits you. They're sure to satisfy.

If you're travelling in Missouri, stop in. This is your old-time, Fifties-style place that has everything but carhops. They make barbecue sandwiches here you won't forget.

ZARDA BAR-B-Q & CATERING
214 North, Hwy. 7
Blue Springs, MO 64014

CREDIT CARDS: **Yes**

CALL FOR CATALOG

RETAIL STORE: **Call for directions**

PHONE: **816-229-3670**

FAX: **816-224-3171**

MINIMUM ORDER: **No**

DALLAS CHILLI BY WAY OF CHICAGO

In 1914, a Portuguese kid nicknamed "Port" was tending bar in far-away Dallas, Texas, in the Adolphus Hotel, where they also had a chili parlor. All Texans loved the stuff. He soon became attached as well, and when his family moved back to Chicago, he took along the chili recipe.

He began canning the stuff in 1922, long before Hormel or other food giants ever even thought about putting up prepared foods in cans. He eventually sold out to his brother Ray, who redesigned the label in 1952, and it has been ever thus: Ray's Delicious Chilli with Beans.

You can blame the two L's in the Chilli on a sign painter named Sheehan who hadn't been to Texas. Now, they say it's how you can tell the chilli's from Illinois. They both have two L's.

Take it from somebody who grew up eating chili at the Green Hedge cafe in Hereford, Texas, this is the real stuff. It's rich, it's red, it's brightly flavored. Buy the 15 oz. can with beans, or the 7 oz. can they call Coney Sauce, which is exactly the same thing we call chili without beans in Texas. The flavor is intense and it's perfectly balanced. It may be our own true American National Dish.

And don't think you can buy just any old can of chili and get the same results. Mimi Sheraton led a panel of fussy *New York Times* taste-

RAY'S BRAND CHILLI
1920 S. 13th St.
P.O. Box 1000
Springfield, IL
62705-1000

CHECKS OR MONEY ORDERS ONLY

CALL FOR CATALOG

PHONE: **217-523-2777**

FAX: **217-523-0514**

MINIMUM ORDER: **No**

Pasta, Rice, Beans, and Box Dinners

125

Ray's Ray-A-Roni

Heat soups with beans until boiling. Meanwhile, brown the ground chuck and drain. Also cook the pasta following package directions. Drain.

Blend all the ingredients, soup and beans, fried hamburger meat, and drained noodles.

Top with grated cheddar cheese, then heat in a 350°F. oven for 20 minutes and serve to 8 Chicago Bears' fans. Pass the beer and don't forget the tortilla chips. A big bag of tortilla chips.

Yeah, team, go.

1 can cheddar cheese soup
1 can tomato soup
2 cans Ray's chilli with beans
1 lb. ground chuck
1 7-oz. box Skroodles (pasta)
cheddar cheese

testers through a forest of tin cans. Only Ray's came up a winner. All the big commercial brands tasted thin, tinny, metallic, sour, or worse. Order a case of Ray's chilli. It's dinner in a hurry and it's as reasonably priced as the grocery store stuff, but a whole lot more flavorful. If you're in Chicago, stop by their plant. As Jim Deere, their sales manager says, it's a funky old place, but they'd love to give you a tour.

Linda Eckhardt's 1995 Guide to America's Best Foods

BRUNSWICK STEW, TAMALES, TORTILLAS, AND KNISHES.

FEARNOW BROS., INC.

P.O. Box 8, 8659 Shady
  Grove Rd.
Mechanicsville, VA
  23111

CREDIT CARDS: Yes

CALL FOR CATALOG

PHONE: 804-746-5375

FAX: 804-730-4095

MINIMUM ORDER: Yes

BRUNSWICK STEW

No doubt when Mrs. Fearnow began making her famous Brunswick stew in the 1920s, she probably added the traditional squirrel and maybe a possum, if Junior'd shot one to the pot. But, everybody liked her stew so well when made with just her farmyard chickens, that she began to can it.

Now I know you think nothing fit to eat can come in cans. But that isn't so. Mrs. Fearnow's Brunswick stew, just cranked open and heated, is delicious. It's been a long time since Lillie Fearnow first entered her stew in the State Fair of Virginia. But the integrity of the stew remains.

Brunswick stew originated in Virginia. Back in 1828, when Democrats got together to rally for Andrew Jackson, the cook, Uncle Jimmy Matthews, made the stew from the harvest of his hunt. The original stew was made up of squirrel, stale bread, onions, and tomatoes. The flavor was so honest and so heartwarming that Virginians claim the Brunswick stew is what buoyed up Mr. Jackson to make his run for President. Try Mrs. Fearnow's Hope Farm stew and you may agree.

Mrs. Fearnow also puts up a mighty fine can of black-eyed peas and stewed tomatoes. I particularly recommend this to Yankees who may never have partaken of the sacred black-eyed pea before. One bite and you'll be on the side of the angels.

*Linda
Eckhardt's
1995
Guide to
America's
Best Foods*

TEXAS TAMALES

PEDRO'S TAMALES, INC.
P.O. Box 3571
Lubbock, TX 79452

For all you folks out in California who've never had a decent tamale, help is on the way. The dreaded hockey puck tamale of the Golden state is not the only kind. In Texas, a finer, thinner tamale is made, one as delicate as a fine Cuban cigar. And, Pedro's Tamales makes them *better* than homemade and sends them out.

These first-quality tamales are made with sirloin wrapped in a stone-ground, white cornmeal masa grown in nearby Muleshoe, Texas. Then the tamales are folded into the traditional real corn shucks. The chiles and spices are perfectly balanced to bring you an authentic Texas tamale. This is the real McCoy people. Believe it.

The pork tamale is another traditional favorite. Also excellent are the bean tamales, everyday favorites with Texas Mexicans. All you need do is steam or microwave either of these tamales once you get the package. We recommend the beef and cheese tidbits made with chopped green chiles then deep-fried in a crispy crunchy batter.

They even have tee-shirts, sweatshirts, salsa, and tote bags.

CREDIT CARDS: Yes

CALL FOR CATALOG

RETAIL STORE: Call for directions

PHONE: 800-522-9531
806-745-9531

FAX: 806-745-5833

MINIMUM ORDER: No

TOFU TAMALES, ET AL

COL. SANCHEZ FOODS
P.O. Box 5848
Santa Monica, CA 90409

Would this book be complete without tofu tamales? Organic tofu tamales from California? It would not. You can order fresh frozen tofu red chile tamales, green chile cheese tamales, blue corn chicken tamales, turkey burritos, and breakfast burritos. All come overnight air and will give you California on the plate.

Col. Sanchez was started in 1981 to supply natural and gourmet foods with a Southern California accent. They call their products the traditional foods of the future and strive to produce highly-spiced foods that are nutritionally dense as well.

We got a tamale-making kit that looks like lots of fun. The kit comes complete with corn husks, chile and spices, 2 lbs. organically grown yellow or blue masa, and complete instructions for mak-

CHECKS OR MONEY ORDERS ONLY

CALL FOR CATALOG

PHONE: 310-313-6769

FAX: 310-313-6772

MINIMUM ORDER: No

Pasta, Rice, Beans, and Box Dinners

ing tamales, tortillas, and tamale pies. All I'm adding is the recipe from my own first cookbook, *The Only Texas Cookbook,* for Mary Ellen Cisneros' Christmas tamales, and our next Christmas celebration will be assured.

Col. Sanchez is a good green company and supports many environmental causes. Their intent is to leave the planet better than they found it. Eat enough tamales and you'll never want to leave the earth at all.

TORTILLERIA

EL GALLINDO

1601 East Sixth St.
Austin, TX 78702

CREDIT CARDS: Yes

CALL FOR CATALOG

RETAIL STORE: Yes

PHONE: 800-447-8905

FAX: 512-478-5839

MINIMUM ORDER: $15

Thomas Gallindo and his wife, Ernestine, began their business in 1940. They came from a family who'd sold tortillas to Pancho Villa's troops at the turn of the century. So it did not daunt them to begin with 90 cents and Mrs. Gallindo's experience making tortillas. They started in Austin's east side barrio. Later, their business, named El Fenix, transferred to the next generation who modernized the plant and called it El Gallindo. Now, even three generations and dozens of products later, the Gallindo family still calls Austin's Sixth Street home.

If you live in one of those godforsaken places without tortillas, your prayers are answered. Order 'em any way you want them. Corn—yellow or white. Flour—whole wheat or white. Fried—chalupa shell or crispy rounds. In chips of many persuasions: quarters, restaurant-style, lime and chili-flavored, Mexican fiesta, guacamole flavor, blue corn, unsalted, and last but not least—the New Age baked-not-fried chips that are high in calcium but fat-free.

Also available are authentic Austin-style salsas—deep red, fiery hot, and a little salty. All you need to complete the menu is a big margarita and some mariachi music. That is authentic Tex-Mex dining.

CALIFORNIA KNISHES

MRS. MALTZ'S KNISHES

2686-B Middlefield Rd.
Redwood City, CA
94063

CREDIT CARDS: Yes

CALL FOR CATALOG

PHONE: 800-87-KNISH
415-368-1682

FAX: 415-368-1778

MINIMUM ORDER: 1 Dozen

From pushcarts to Fed Ex, the beloved knish is still a winner among people with Eastern European roots. These knishes can be shipped anywhere and will make your bubbe proud.

Mona Maltz started the business in 1986 after she and a friend from New York kvetched over a cup of coffee that there was a lack of good Jewish food west of the Mississippi. Not for long.

Soon Mona Maltz was supplying weddings, get-well knishes, love-and-knishes packs, and best-knishes-for-your-birthday packs. She uses the most modern packaging and ships them frozen. The knishes themselves are handmade, stuffed pockets of dough. The local rabbi certifies five different varieties: potato, veggie, kasha, broccoli-cheese, and spinach-mushroom. The company even uses *cholov Yisroel* cheese, made from cows owned and milked by strictly observant Jews.

The knishes are baked, not fried, and are, in fact, quite healthy and nutritious as well as being delicious. In a modern kitchen, what could be more welcome than a dozen precooked fresh knishes. This is even easier than the Just-Add-Water entrees.

*Pasta, Rice, Beans,
and Box Dinners*

THE PROTEIN PURVEYORS

Patés and sausages, hams and bacon. Corn-fed Midwestern beefsteaks. Poultry, including Thanksgiving turkeys, game, and chickens. Fish and shellfish, fresh, canned, and smoked. Using old family recipes and newfangled shipping techniques, these people will send to you fresh patés, free-range poultry, buffalo, whole lamb, milk-fed veal, live lobsters, fresh littleneck clams, and live crawfish. All guaranteed. All fresh.

Give them great meals of beef and iron and steel, they will eat like wolves and fight like devils.

—SHAKESPEARE, *Henry V*

PATÉS AND SAUSAGES, HAMS AND BACON. CORN-FED MIDWESTERN BEEFSTEAKS. POULTRY, INCLUDING THANKSGIVING TURKEYS, GAME, AND CHICKENS.

This dish of meat is too good for any anglers, or very honest men.

IZAAK WALTON (1593–1683)

AMERICAN FOIE GRAS

D'ARTAGNAN

399 St. Paul Ave.
Jersey City, NJ 07306

CHECKS OR MONEY
ORDERS ONLY

CALL FOR CATALOG

RETAIL STORE: **Yes**

PHONE: 800-537-7283
212-219-1230

FAX: 212-941-9726

MINIMUM ORDER: **No**

A s Suzanne Hamlin of the *New York Daily News* says about foie gras, "Maybe you'll be lucky and hate it, thereby being able to set aside the foie gras money for potential college educations." Now that Ariane Daguin, the daughter of an internationally-acclaimed French chef and the former apprentice at Three Little Pigs, has started not only cooking and selling this velvety smooth, unforgettable duck liver, but also giving all sorts of advice on its use, we're all doomed.

Used to be you could only get the real article from France, but now that Daguin's in business and has an American supply, you can get authentic foie gras in five versions shipped overnight. Also available is *magret*, the best duck breast, and it comes smoked and plain.

Also available are first quality sausages, duck with foie gras, venison with juniper berries, wild boar with sage, rabbit with ginger, buffalo with cumin, and duck sausage confit. Game birds available include: poussin, chicken, quail, squab, pigeon, wild turkeys, guineas, geese, and partridges. Game meats available include rabbit, wild boar, buffalo, venison, and hare.

In the heat-and-eat category, god bless her, Ariane is making sublime cassoulet, a venison daube, and a petit sale with lentils. None of her products have been frozen. They come to you overnight air, and are fresh. The quality is unassailable. Call for a catalog.

BIG APPLE PATÉS

LES TROIS PETITS COCHONS

(THREE LITTLE PIGS)

453 Greenwich St.
New York, NY 10013

CREDIT CARDS: **Yes**

CALL FOR CATALOG

PHONE: 800-327-8246
201-792-0748

FAX: 201-792-6113

MINIMUM ORDER: **No**

A lain Sinturel and Jean Pierre Pradie, both coming from families of French chefs and charcutiers, first met in London, then later by chance in New York. Pooling their resources, they were able to acquire an 11 × 13-foot two-story carriage house where, with second-hand equipment, a loan, and Gallic guts, they were able to get their charcuterie going in 1975. It wasn't long before James Beard, Mimi Sheraton, and Craig Claiborne found them. Their place was assured.

Today, they offer patés in handy 11½-oz. petit loaves that will last two weeks—provided you can stay out of them that long. Our favorite is the *Mousse au Poivre Noir*, a dark, spicy, feathery light turkey liver mousse smoothed with brandy and cream. They're famous for their patés—all recommended. *Paté de Campagne*, is a country paté made from pork, onions, garlic, and herbs. Their *Forestier* won the NASFT

Grand Show Award and rightly so. It's made skillfully of chicken liver, pork, white wine, and cepes marinated in Madeira. Yum.

They also make admirable terrines: a three-layer veggie, a salmon, a luscious spinach, and a shrimp with saffron that's sprinkled with salmon roe. You can buy great cornichons here, garlic sausage, and a selection of excellent game patés.

Bruce Aidells Apple-Sausage Risotto

makes 4 servings

Heat skillet over medium heat with 1 tablespoon oil and sauté sausage with 1 tablespoon water, covered, until cooked through and browned on all sides. Remove sausage from the skillet and set aside.

Then add remaining oil, onion, pepper, and mushrooms. Slowly sauté until the onion is translucent—about 5 minutes. Cut sausage into bite-sized rings, then add to the skillet along with tomatoes and juice, wine, salt, and pepper. Simmer uncovered about 5 minutes over low flame, just until well blended. Add rice and broth. Cover and simmer about 30 minutes, or until all liquid is absorbed. Serve hot or at room temperature. Garnish with apple rings, either spiced—from a jar, or with fresh apples you've sautéed in a little butter.

1 lb. (about 5 small links or 2 large ones) low-fat chicken sausage with apples

⅛ cup olive oil

1 medium onion, peeled and finely chopped

1 red bell pepper, seeded and finely chopped

1 cup brown mushrooms

½ teaspoon freshly milled black pepper

1 16-oz. can Italian-style tomatoes and juice

¼ cup dry white wine

YUPPIE SAUSAGES

AIDELLS SAUSAGE COMPANY

1575 Minnesota St.
San Francisco, CA
94107

CREDIT CARDS: Yes

CALL FOR CATALOG

PHONE: 800-541-2233

FAX: 415-421-5153

MINIMUM ORDER: No

When Bruce Aidells was in graduate school, he started a cheap on-campus restaurant that featured ethnic cuisine. A biologist, he went to London for post-grad work and got desperate, facing endless links of British bangers. So, in one long night of frenzied experimentation, Bruce Aidells invented his first sausages.

Necessity mothered invention once more, and within five years, Aidells was out of the lab and into the kitchen for good. Considered the big daddy of yuppie sausages, Aidells now makes eleven varieties of low-fat, low-salt, high-flavored sausages that represent today's food trends.

Most popular and especially recommended are the smoked chicken apple sausages. Sweet, smoky, and aromatic, these sausages give new meaning to the notion that low-fat foods can be high in flavor. We also adore the fresh Thai chicken and turkey with cilantro, lemon grass, and garlic. Aidells doesn't neglect pork sausages, knowing they're the traditional favorites, and makes a hearty Hunter's sausage that begs for sauerkraut and applesauce. Pass the beer.

We find a that freezer stocked with Aidells sausages means you can have a better meal at home than you can buy in many restaurants. Don't be surprised when you dial up this 800 number and they answer Williams Sonoma. They're handling mail order for Bruce.

The Protein Purveyors

GERHARD'S NAPA VALLEY SAUSAGE

901 Enterprise Way
Napa, CA 94558

~~~~~~~~~~~~~~~~~~~~~~

CREDIT CARDS: Yes

CALL FOR CATALOG

RETAIL STORE: Yes

PHONE: 707-252-4116

FAX: 707-252-0879

MINIMUM ORDER: 5 lbs.

CALIFORNIA CHARCUTERIE

Praised by Margaret Fox of Cafe Beaujolais and Marian Burros of the *New York Times*, this neighborhood charcuterie has been turning out best quality sausages without harmful preservatives for several years. Especially recommended are the East Indian-style chicken apple sausages and the Thai chicken and ginger ones.

Gerhard Twele began making sausages for sale from a 180-square-foot kitchen in 1985. He uses low-fat, low-cholesterol poultry and stresses flavor and purity in his lean products. Served in such far flung places as the Greenbriar in West Virginia and Meadowwood in Napa Valley, you can cook these no-damage gourmet sausages at home.

Ask for the latest brochure to see what new flavors Gerhard's come up with. At last notice, he was making Lyonaise with Madeira and Pistachios, Smoked Duck with Roasted Almonds, Syrian Lamb, and Fresh Chorizo with Brandy.

If you're driving around the wine country, stop by his original tiny storefront and pick up some sausage for a picnic or to take home. We keep Gerhard's sausages on hand in the freezer for quick, flavorful dinners.

BRENHAM SAUSAGE CO.

Hwy 36 North
P.O. Box 615
Brenham, TX 77834

~~~~~~~~~~~~~~~~~~~~~~

CHECKS OR MONEY ORDERS ONLY

CALL FOR CATALOG

RETAIL STORE: Call for directions

PHONE: 800-460-5030
   409-836-3152

FAX: 409-836-1908

MINIMUM ORDER: No

AIR-DRIED SAUSAGE

Did you ever step inside an old-fashioned butcher shop? The aroma of pecan smoke, the hearty scent of beef, and the peppered additions make for a mouthwatering nostalgic moment.

Ran Newman makes sausage here. Old-fashioned, air-dried sausage, made the way German immigrants to this part of Texas made them when refrigeration was nothing more than a good snowstorm every three years or so. The sausage is crinkled up, brightly-flavored, and a good staple for a campout, hunting trip, or couch potato watching a ball game.

Ran calls this sausage Texas Star. He also makes a full line of country-smoked sausages, German-Texas style: Green chile-smoked sausage, La Sauteeya (a sausage in a tortilla), South Texas Firecracker (a hot sausage in a tortilla), and Grandma Skrabanek's Sausage Roll, a sausage kolache. He also makes and sells jerky, a turkey drumstick on a roll, and regular pork and beef sausage links and rings.

Do stop in the little old store. And while you're in Brenham, don't forget to pop by the old Blue Bell Creamery. Now there's an aroma for you. Cream, cream, cream. It's where they make ice cream—famous ice cream and worth the trip. Drive down to Washington-on-the-Brazos state park and have a take-out feast, Texas-style. Texas sausage and an ice cream cone for dessert. Don't forget to pick up some Lone Star at the 7-11 to go with it.

SAN FRANCISCO ITALIAN SALAMI

You want your dry salami, you want your two-way loaf. You want old-fashioned Italian Salsiccia, you want your Sweet Sicilian Sausage. It's all here. Every permutation on authentic Italian-style sausages you could ever imagine. And all made by the Molinari family in San Francisco since 1896.

Four generations of sausage makers must be doing something right. Order from them and you'll see. The choices are legendary: pancetta, bresaola, mortadella, coppa veneziana, headcheese, galantina—it goes on and on. If you want it and it's from Italy, call them.

MOLINARI & SONS
1401 Yosemite Ave.
San Francisco, CA
94124

CHECKS OR MONEY
ORDERS ONLY

CALL FOR CATALOG

PHONE: 415-822-5555

FAX: 415-822-5834

MINIMUM ORDER: No

THIS IS NO BALONEY

If you thought that pale, smooth stuff they sell in the deli case—almost quivering with pigs' snouts and lips and ears and white bread pudding—was baloney, I have good news. Real baloney—or, as adults are supposed to say, bologna—is made from 100 percent beef, 90 percent lean, and is about the color and texture of a real good San Francisco salami. Around Lebanon, Pennsylvania, famous for this German-style sausage, the best source for real Lebanon bologna is Daniel Weaver.

Weaver first tried his luck in Mexico after emigrating from Germany, but his smokehouse was burned down by Pancho Villa so he retreated to his German relatives in Pennsylvania and began again. Now, nearly a hundred years later, his sweet-sour, smoky bologna is still made his stubborn German way, and it is divine.

THE DANIEL WEAVER CO.
P.O. Box 525
Lebanon, PA 17042

CREDIT CARDS: Yes

CALL FOR CATALOG

RETAIL STORE: Call for
directions

PHONE: 800-932-8377
717-274-6100

FAX: 717-274-6103

MINIMUM ORDER: No

The Weavers also make a heavenly sweet bologna called Baum's that's a sweet cure of the same meats and yields a tangier bologna. They also sell very fine Canadian bacon, smoked bacon, ham, and dried beef.

This is exceptional cured beef and pork. Once you taste Weaver's, you'll order again.

AUTHENTIC MEXICAN CHORIZO

CHORIZO DE SAN MANUEL, INC.

Rt. 3, Box Ex-9
Edinburg, TX 78539

CREDIT CARDS: Yes

CALL FOR CATALOG

RETAIL STORE: Call for directions

PHONE: 210-383-8751

FAX: 210-383-0334

MINIMUM ORDER: No

The de los Santos family has been making the Guerra brand of Mexican-style pork sausage known as chorizo since World War II, when the father, known as Shorty, began blending pork with his own mix of spices. The way you serve the sausage is to remove it from the natural casings, fry it up, and you get a bright red product that you then scramble with eggs and fold into a corn or flour tortilla for a Mexican breakfast or lunch sandwich.

The sausage is not fatty, it's all natural, and it's *muy autentico*. The de los Santos butchers don't add any cereal or fillers, or any artificial color, flavor, or preservatives. They use only the "Boston Butt" cut of pork and what you get is a highly-seasoned, desirable Mexican sausage.

HONEST TO GOD PASTRAMI

PASTRAMI KING
124-24 Queens Blvd.
Kew Gardens, NY 11415

CREDIT CARDS: Yes

RETAIL STORE: Call for directions

PHONE: 718-263-1717

FAX: 718-263-1841

MINIMUM ORDER: No

I never tasted pastrami before. I didn't know pastrami, but once I'd tasted the handmade pastrami from Pastrami King, I finally knew what all the old-timers were sighing about.

Making pastrami is almost a lost art. Old-time New Yorkers mourn its passing. In traditional delis, it was made on the premises, a gentle, moist, garlicky, peppered smoked beef that was hand-sliced for sandwiches. Alas, today, most places buy chemically perverted stuff that's just not the same.

Get on the subway and hie yourself to Queens. The Pastrami King out in Kew Gardens still handmakes pastrami and corned beef. The meat is pickled three weeks. It's dry cured, smoked patiently, then simmered to perfection. The result is meat that's firm, gentle, and grainy as pot roast. If you can't get to Queens, he'll mail it. And it's certified kosher.

Mimi Sheraton told *New York* magazine, "One look at the bright rose-red color, and the fine-grained texture, and the simmering slim edge of ivory fat, and any aficionado will know he is in the presence of the real McCoy. A single taste corroborates that glorious first impression."

Visit the store and you'll get a huge sandwich on rye with a half sour dill and garlic pickle, a side of handmade potato salad, made on the place, and—complimentary when you sit down—some of the best cole slaw you ever tasted. Cabbage hand-shaved and made fresh every day. It's extraordinary.

EUROPEAN-STYLE SMOKED MEATS

J im Nueske is this kind of guy. When he went to San Francisco on business, he looked in the phone book for other Nueskes and called up the only one he found. Turned out it was his cousin, who remembered swimming in the river back in Wisconsin when he was a kid.

The Nueske brothers, Jim and Robert, operate their father's smoking business using the time-honored European method of 24 hours of slow smoking that brings out the best in the fine pork they begin with. Applewood is the origin of the fine, sweet, mysterious flavor you'll find in Nueske hams, bacon, and sausages. Along with California's mahogany-smoked hams and one Vermont cob-smoked ham. These hams were found to be the best in the country in a survey done by *Cuisine* magazine. Moist, lean, sweet, and a deep red color, these pork products are first rate. Never any added fillers, binders, or extenders. The Nueske ham has no water added.

Their sausages are just lean, tender meat and natural spices. I recommend their Applewood Smoked bacon. In 1992, it won a Gold Medal in a Chefs in America Foundation contest. They called it *Best* in taste, appearance, and overall impression. We just call it breakfast whenever we have Jim Nueske's bacon on the table.

NUESKE HILLCREST FARM MEATS

Rural Rt. 2
Wittenberg, WI 54499

CREDIT CARDS: Yes

CALL FOR CATALOG

RETAIL STORE: Call for directions

PHONE: 800-392-2266
715-253-2226

FAX: 715-253-2021

MINIMUM ORDER: No

The Protein Purveyors

141

USINGER'S FAMOUS
SAUSAGE

1030 N. Old World
Third St.
Milwaukee, WI 53203

~~~~~~~~~~~~~~~

CREDIT CARDS: Yes

RETAIL STORE: Yes

PHONE: 800-558-9997

MINIMUM ORDER:

GERMAN-STYLE SAUSAGES

With more than 80 sausages on their list, all made using German and Eastern European traditional recipes, most without chemical additives and packed in natural casings, the Usingers have a place in Milwaukeean's hearts—Milwaukee being the kind of town where five kinds of sausages are sold at the ball park. Usinger's has been making sausage since the 1880s: blood sausages, liver sausages, sausages to be cooked, summer sausages, and lunchmeats, everything from Milwaukee's favorite bratwurst to a renowned *landjaeger*, heavy with garlic.

We found the *Braunschweiger* to be as pale and delicate as paté. Lean, it has the slight aroma of suet. The little *Hildescheimer*, on the other hand, was softer, rosier in color, with a mild, gentle flavor. Their goose liver studded with pistachios is heaven. Even the weiners are good.

MAHOGANY-
SMOKED MEATS

P.O. Box 1387
Bishop, CA 93514

~~~~~~~~~~~~~~~

CREDIT CARDS: Yes

CALL FOR CATALOG

RETAIL STORE: Call for
directions

PHONE: 619-873-5311

FAX: 619-873-8761

MINIMUM ORDER: No

MAHOGANY-SMOKED MEATS

Roi Ballard drives high into the Southern California desert mountains for aged mahogany with which to smoke his meats. This dense, exotic wood creates a smoky aroma so intense it permeates the box in which he sends you the ham. The ham itself is pale, moist, flavorful, and quite distinct in its mahogany smoke flavor. According to *Cuisine's* taste-test, Roi Ballard's ham was the only wet-cure ham to buy west of the Mississippi. It is absolutely wonderful.

We loved Roi Ballard's hams and bacon. And the jerky is smoky, sweet, and would keep you going clear across the dead sea or where ever it is you might have to go. Ballard also smokes poultry. If you'll just give him a call, he'll send you a virtual snowstorm of information about his products. His first occupation was marketing, and he knows how to get you to buy a pig in a poke. The flavor will bring you back.

*Linda
Eckhardt's
1995
Guide to
America's
Best Foods*

142

COUNTRY ATTIC HAMS

BURGERS' SMOKEHOUSE

Rt. 3, Box 3248
Hwy 87 South
California, MO 65018

The Burgers began curing hams for sale during the Depression to augment their farm's earnings. They hung them in the attic, where the combination of cold winter and hot summer heightened the natural aging process and produced the best-quality country-style hams. Now their company cures hundreds of thousands of hams per year, but they still pick out the best 2,000 and attic-hang them. For this connoisseur and devotee of country-cured ham, this is nonpareil. Call early and ask them to reserve one for you. You'll get the most pronounced, aged, country-cured flavor of any country ham on the market. In our package this fall, we also took a deep breath and drank in the aroma of country-cured bacon and whole hog sausage—the rope kind, full of flavor, and begging for a pot of beans. Now we can never go back to grocery store bacon—full of chemicals, or grocery store sausage—full of god only knows what. We like everything the Burgers smoke: bacon, sausage, ham, poultry, and beef.

CREDIT CARDS: **Yes**

CALL FOR CATALOG

RETAIL STORE: **Yes**

PHONE: 314-796-3134

FAX: 314-796-3137

MINIMUM ORDER: **No**

VIRGINIA HAMS AND BACON

S. WALLACE EDWARDS & SONS, INC.

P.O. Box 25
Surry, VA 23883

When we received a red leather box with gold engraving, my Southern husband Joe thought it was presentation pistols. It had that look and feel to it. But no, it was another Southern specialty, pure Virginia ham, sliced paper-thin, a deep brick-red, and lean as a Vogue model. This is the special gift box you can buy from Wallace Edwards who dry-cures hams after the fashion of the East Coast Indians who taught the first Virginia settlers how to do it. He calls his specialty the Wigwam and it is smoked and cured for a whole year, creating a highly flavorful ham that has gained a national reputation. They've won First Place or Grand Champion at the Virginia State Fair for their Virginia hams and bacons for 10 years straight.

One of the best Edwards' products we've tasted lately is the barbecued pork and sauce. It's what I'm serving for the Christmas buffet this year. One five-pound bucket yields enough for 40 sandwiches. It looks kind of alarming when you open it. The meat is fine ground and the pungent vinegar sauce is stirred in. But not to worry. Make Southern-style milk buns about the size of a goose egg. Use an ice cream scoop to measure out the barbecue. Lay in some coleslaw. Put the buns in a chafing dish to keep warm. It will knock 'em dead.

CREDIT CARDS: **Yes**

CALL FOR CATALOG

RETAIL STORE: **Call for directions**

PHONE: 800-222-4267
804-294-3121

FAX: 804-294-5378

MINIMUM ORDER: **No**

The Protein Purveyors

Edwards also makes succulent hickory-smoked sausage, a tangy rich product that can be steamed, fried, microwaved or grilled. It keeps up to a month—what a joke. It will get eaten up in a hurry.

Additionally, Edwards receives high marks for his Atlantic seafood products.

His catalog is filled with other Virginia specialties. Piggy Muffins and Mix from Byrd Mill—six little piggies in a cast aluminum mold will delight the kids. Authentic Maryland Crab cakes come by air, as do traditional Stuffed Crabs Imperial and a smoked seafood sampler that includes apple oak-smoked rainbow trout, catfish, salmon, and bay scallops.

But back to the mainstay: bacon, sausage, and hams in many forms are here. And they're all as good as it gets.

VERMONT COB-SMOKED HAMS AND BACON

Until recently, the Lefebvre family has been making fine cured and smoked meats using old family recipes and traditions just for custom orders. Now, the public has demanded they sell through the mail. Whew! Traditional cob-smoked hams and bacons are unlike any other product—a purely New England idea—and the Lefebvres do a great job. Lucky you can order them.

The ham we tried was sweet, delicate, aromatic, and had a fine texture with very little fat. It was too good for a ham sandwich and demanded a place of honor on the plate, with maybe just some dark bread and good mustard to accompany. They cure their hams with maple syrup before cob-smoking them. Their summer sausage is vinegary sweet and highly recommended. They also smoked cheddar, which goes nicely with the ham.

This is still a very small family operation and the Lefebvres welcome you at their store. They love to talk hams with people. You can get a great ham sandwich there, made from their own smoked meats, or a variety of sausage sandwiches as well. They offer a gorgeous Vermont gift basket that would be a great remembrance of a visit to the state: a 7-ounce summer sausage, an 8-ounce cheddar, a half-pint of maple syrup, 8 ounces of honey, 1½ ounces of maple candy, Vermont common crackers, 8 ounces of strawberry jam, 8 ounces of tangy maple mustard, and the official Vermont Maple Cookbook. All you need to add to the order is one spiral-sliced ham. It's Vermont.

ROLAND & SON SMOKEHOUSE MEATS

P.O. Box 278
South Barre, VT 05670

CREDIT CARDS: Yes

CALL FOR CATALOG

RETAIL STORE: **Call for directions**

PHONE: 800-457-6066
802-476-6066

FAX: 802-479-0475

MINIMUM ORDER: No

Linda Eckhardt's 1995 Guide to America's Best Foods

CORN-FED MIDWESTERN BEEF

OMAHA STEAKS INTERNATIONAL
4400 South 96th St.
P.O. Box 3300
Omaha, NE 68103

CREDIT CARDS: Yes

CALL FOR CATALOG

RETAIL STORE: Call for directions

PHONE: 800-288-9055

FAX: 800-428-1593

MINIMUM ORDER: No

Omaha makes steak look easy. All you do is pick up the phone and before you know it you've ordered more steak than you'd ever imagined. Six-ounce filet mignons, boneless strips, chateaubriands, even gourmet burgers. Who could blame you? The steaks come frozen and will await your desire in the freezer, ready to grill on the barby or in a pan in the kitchen.

Some people turn up their nose at beef that's been frozen. So, terrific: if they live close enough to a butcher who cuts prime meat, good for them. For the rest of us, Omaha Steaks are about as good as it gets.

The meat is guaranteed, it's tender, and it's succulent. The steaks come with storage and cooking suggestions. Once they get one order from you they'll keep calling you. If you're like me, you'll say yes more than you say nay.

There's just nothing like a good steak. And these are good steaks.

SLOW-COOKED TEXAS PIT BARBECUE

GUADALUPE PIT SMOKED MEAT CO.
1299 Gruene Rd.
New Braunfels, TX 78130

CREDIT CARDS: Yes

CALL FOR CATALOG

PHONE: 800-880-0416

FAX: 210-625-5520

MINIMUM ORDER: No

Texas wouldn't be Texas without barbecue and in the barbecue belt that girdles the state, there's no better representative barbecue than what Janie Macredie and her daughter, Erin Hartman, smoke and serve at their hill country restaurant on the banks of the lazy Guadalupe river.

The area's become a mecca for desperate Houstonians who drive frantically from the city every weekend in search of antiques and a little reality. They can sit on Janie's deck, eat barbecue, lick their fingers and feel whole again, before getting back on the freeway to head home for the city come Sunday afternoon.

Al Seymour, their partner in smoke, says that basically if you cook a brisket long enough and slow enough, "It gives up. It says, OK. I'll be tender." Seymour says they only use green hickory that makes a lot of dense, aromatic smoke. They smoke the meat at least 15 hours. What you get is a succulent, tender piece of brisket, pork tenderloin, sausage, turkey, chicken, or ribs.

They've got this ancient Texas craft down to a science. You can cut the meat with a fork. All you need do to make a true Texas barbecue dinner once you get it home is spread your table with butcher

The Protein Purveyors

paper, slice up a big yellow onion, get out a bunch of pickled jalapenos, buy a loaf of white bread, pop a beer, and get ready to lick your fingers while you eat. If you want to get fancy, make a bowl of potato salad and a side order of beans. They send you a mason jar of sauce. And that, my friends, is Texas.

STEVE'S BARBECUE

I lived on Steve's barbecue sandwiches on my first job in Houston, in downtown Foley's. All you had to do was walk out the back door and across the street, then elbow your way up through the kazillions of other downtown workers to the take-out counter. The choices were simple: on a half-sized hamburger bun you could order a sliced brisket, sliced ham, sausage, or chopped brisket sandwich—with or without sauce.

The sandwich seemed little, but it was so rich, so steamy, so aromatic with the barbecue rub they'd used in the hickory smoker out back, that one little sandwich was all you needed. Oh, lots of folks stopped off at the stand-up bar in the middle of the place to slather on sweet pickle relish, slices of Spanish onion, and maybe mustard or mayo. Then a handful of paper napkins, pop back out on the street, and eat in the blinking gulf coast Texas sunshine.

It was heaven. It still is. Now, Steve Caloudas and his wife, Susan, along with original owners George Caloudas and his wife, Beverly, have moved to the hill country. But they're still selling barbecue. Order a whole slow-cooked brisket for genuine Texas-style barbecue. Get a real Texas-smoked turkey for Thanksgiving, or Texas-style smoked sausage, or heavenly smoked-hams. The prices are quite modest considering the quality. This is Texas, delivered to your door.

NUECES CANYON RANCH

9501 US Hwy 290 West Brenham, TX 77833

CREDIT CARDS: **Yes**

CALL FOR CATALOG

PHONE: **800-925-5058 409-289-5600**

FAX: **409-289-2411**

MINIMUM ORDER: **No**

WHERE THE BUFFALO ROAM

WHITEFEATHER BISON COMPANY

3360 Greenwich St.
Wadsworth, OH 44281

Can Jane Fonda and Ted Turner be wrong? If they say that buffalo should replace beef in the wild west can we argue? They buy their bison meat from the Perkins family in Ohio who traded their cattle off for buffalo and began growing these wily ancient beasts.

Visit the country store that they and all their children built with their own hands, much the way their ancestors might have, and you can buy buffalo meat and an assortment of fine Ohio products and local crafts.

They love for people to visit the farm and see the buffalo grazing in the fields. It's awesome to stand up close to a buffalo. They're just so enormous you can hardly believe it.

The meat is flavorful, dark, and lean. It has less cholesterol and fat than beef. The Perkins ship it out frozen and you can keep on hand a supply of buffalo burgers, Bison steaks, or buffalo pot roast. It will certainly liven up the dinner table conversation and it will offer the fewest calories and fat grams per serving you can find in the meat department.

3 oz. serving	calories	fat	cholesterol
bison	93	1.8 g.	43 mg.
turkey	125	3.0 g.	59 mg.
beef	183	8.7 g.	55 mg.
chicken	140	3.0 g.	73 mg.

CREDIT CARDS: Yes

CALL FOR CATALOG

RETAIL STORE: Yes

PHONE: 800-328-2476
 216-336-3487

FAX: 216-335-3208

MINIMUM ORDER: No

THE PERKINS FAMILY
Whitefeather Farm

The Protein Purveyors

JAMISON FARM
171 Jamison Lane
Latrobe, PA 15650

CREDIT CARDS: Yes

CALL FOR CATALOG

PHONE: 800-237-5262
    412-834-7424

FAX: 412-837-2287

MINIMUM ORDER: Yes

SPRING LAMB

John and Sukey Jamison are urban people who had a dream. They wanted to provide a peaceful, slower-paced environment for their three young children. So, nearly 20 years ago, they traded in the Volvo for a pickup truck, gave up their apartment lease, and bought 108 acres on the outskirts of Crabtree, Westmoreland County, Pennsylvania. For a while they worked on the 100-year old farmhouse and fences, while John kept his job as a high-powered coal salesman. But they soon stocked the place with sheep and now make their entire living raising lambs and sheep. They do everything with great care, from choosing breeding stock, to feeding and finishing the animals. What you get from the Jamisons is prime, pampered lamb.

You can buy a regular young spring lamb, about 40–50 pounds hanging weight, and cut to order: two legs, two shoulders, two racks, two loins, four shanks, and ground lamb. You can also order any particular cuts you like. In addition, Sukey sells her succulent ready-made lamb stew and a divine lamb pasta sauce put up in glass jars.

The Jamisons do a lot of charity work and jet around barbecuing lamb for all sorts of special occasions. If you're looking to put on a really fancy picnic, give them a call. If you'd like to show the kids a real working farm with lambs and sheep, call and make an appointment and the Jamisons will show you around.

SUMMERFIELD FARM
10044 James Monroe
    Highway
Culpeper, VA 22701

CREDIT CARDS: Yes

CALL FOR CATALOG

RETAIL STORE: Yes

PHONE: 703-547-9600

FAX: 703-547-9628

MINIMUM ORDER: Yes

LUXURY VEAL

When I met Jamie Nicoll he was selling veal out of the back of his car. Now, less than ten years later, he and wife Rachel are nationally respected purveyors of the finest veal products money can buy. They raise their calves in hay-filled stalls and feed them only on mother's milk. This yields a rosy pink product that you've likely never seen, unless you visited some of New York's most upscale restaurants.

But now, you can order thick veal chops for home cooking. Rachel also makes and bottles *glace de veau*, the very essence of fine sauces and as good as any you can get in a fine French restaurant. Haul out your Julia Child, volumes 1 or 2. Use Jamie and Rachel's veal chops and *glace*, and your guests will faint from pleasure.

The Nicolls have an adorable farm store out in the country that you can visit too. There you'll find not only their fine veal products but other meat products to take home or send out for gifts: Frenched leg of lamb, venison Osso Bucco, venison stew meat, venison saddle, veal shoulder roasts, and a wide variety of free-range veal and farm-raised venison and lamb products. Recently, they've added pheasants, rabbits, smoked trout, and free-range chickens and quail.

Craig Claiborne said it for all of us: "I've worked with the best and I find your products excellent." Amen to that.

SMOKED TURKEY

Deep in the heart of the Texas hill country, close to the LBJ ranch, is an old-fashioned smokehouse like the kind found on the German farmsteads that first civilized this wild and untamed part of Texas.

The New Braunfels Smokehouse practices old-fashioned German-style smoking and turns out some of the best smoked turkey and ham that I know of. We adore their peppered beef jerky, and think their smoked brisket is like a trip back home.

Ask for Comal County bacon and you'll know what the German farmer-pioneers fed their families. A lean, rindless slab, slow-cured and hickory-smoked. It smells so good before you even start to cook it that you just can't believe it. Ask for their Smokehouse fajitas. It's fusion cooking. What can I say? Mexican-style fajitas slow-smoked in German-Texan fashion. The result is pure Texas and purely delicious.

NEW BRAUNFELS
SMOKEHOUSE

P.O. Box 311159
New Braunfels, TX
78131-1159

CREDIT CARDS: Yes

CALL FOR CATALOG

RETAIL STORE: Call for directions

**PHONE: 800-537-6932
210-625-7316**

FAX: 210-625-7660

MINIMUM ORDER: No

The Protein Purveyors

BEAR CREEK SMOKEHOUSE

Rt. 5, Box 154
Marshall, TX 75670

CREDIT CARDS: **Yes**

CALL FOR CATALOG

RETAIL STORE: **Call for directions**

PHONE: **800-950-2327**

FAX: **214-935-2871**

MINIMUM ORDER: **No**

FINE QUALITY SMOKED TEXAS TURKEYS

Nick and Nellie Shoults have been talking turkey since the early fifties when they began smoking and sending turkeys out by phone order. They were so taken with telephone orders back then, they let the phone company use them to advertise the value of the telephone for order-taking and building a business. *The Mighty Marshall,* a publication put out by the local chamber of commerce, bragged that the Shoults had been featured in eleven national magazines, Mr. Shoults eagerly talking on the phone while Missus looked through her card file.

The Shoults were already a success story. They'd begun in the early forties, in the piney woods of deep east Texas. They raised turkeys and hogs, grain-feeding them until they were just right, then farm-butchering and smoking the meats with local hickory they'd cut off their place. Now, Hick and Nellie have turned the business over to the kids. Bobby and Brenda, with son Robbie, work there, along with sister Becky Shoults Bibb. They all work to get the turkeys plucked and the sausage made.

Not that the kids have anything to complain about. When Mama started, she had no electricity and dipped the birds in scalding water in a black pot out in the yard. Then they got that telephone way out in the country and could quit relying on the county agent to relay messages.

Some things have changed since then, but the quality of their smoked meats remains as high as ever. Order smoked turkey, heavenly bacon, great hams, sausage, Peking duck, and peppered pork tenderloin so succulent it's irresistible. They also sell authentic Poorman's Caviar, which is really black-eyed pea relish in a mason jar, and their own version of East Texas barbecue sauce, sweet, smoky, and red with rich tomato.

The smoking may not be done in the little cinder block building they started out in, but the method's remained the same slow, labor-intensive way. You can tell. Their products are superior.

Linda Eckhardt's 1995 Guide to America's Best Foods

150

SMOKED TEXAS TURKEYS

SUNDAY SMOKEHAUS, INC.
122 East Main Street
Fredericksburg, TX
78624

When my daughter Katherine married in New York and we knew we had to feed 150 Easterners a wedding feast they'd never forget, we called Sunday Smokehaus first and ordered up real Texas Smoked Turkeys. No one was disappointed.

A tradition for Texas celebrations, these turkeys are pale pink, succulent, and dense with oak wood smoke. Made in a real Sunday House in the heart of the German population in Texas, these products say "Welcome" to those of us who grew up in Texas.

Sunday Houses were built in the town of Fredericksburg by farmers who spent one day of rest in town on Sunday—going to church, feasting, and visiting with friends. Today, the whole town is practically a museum and worth a visit by anyone who's in the neighborhood. And in Texas, we call Dallas-Houston-San Antonio and Austin the neighborhood, even if it is the better part of a day to get out to Fredericksburg and back. It's worth it.

Especially in the spring when the bluebonnets and the Indian paintbrush are in full bloom. Stop in the Sunday Smokehaus for lunch while you're there. They've got German-style deli sandwiches on hearty country bread, with sides of German potato salad, sauerkraut, Texas baked beans and whole crunchy pickles.

Order or take home German-style smoked meats: chicken, turkey or turkey breast, pork loin, sausages, jerky, and beef tenderloin. It made our wedding a hit.

CREDIT CARDS: Yes

CALL FOR CATALOG

RETAIL STORE: Yes

PHONE: 800-270-8292
210-997-8292

FAX: 210-997-0990

MINIMUM ORDER: No

The Protein Purveyors

CAVANAUGH
LAKEVIEW FARMS

821 Lowery Rd.,
Box 580
Chelsea, MI 48118-0580

CREDIT CARDS: Yes

CALL FOR CATALOG

PHONE: 800-243-4438

FAX: 313-475-1133

MINIMUM ORDER: No

FINE POULTRY PRODUCTS

Cynthia Feller carefully feeds her birds grain and produces a fine chicken. She also offers capon, duckling, turkey, goose, pheasant, and quail. No chemicals or hormones are accidently introduced to these birds. She raises them, butchers them, and flash freezes them right on the farm. Order these and you're getting a fresher bird than the so-called "fresh" birds from a grocery store, which may sit under plastic wrap up to a week before you buy them.

Cynthia's perfected a honey glaze she sprays onto birds and ham before smoking them. The smokehouse is right on the farm and uses choice local hardwoods and scientifically controlled time and temperature to yield a succulent, smoky-sweet product. Call for a catalog and see what the farm's produced this year.

BREEZY HILL MEAT
COMPANY

Hwy 59 North
P.O. Box 507
Bowie, TX 76230

CREDIT CARDS: Yes

CALL FOR CATALOG

RETAIL STORE: Call for
    directions

PHONE: 817-872-5635

MINIMUM ORDER: Yes

OSTRICH MEAT

Want something different for your next dinner party? Serve ostrich steaks. They're a lot like beef except they don't have all the fat and cholesterol. And think of it this way. If you've invited somebody over that you don't really know all that well and you want to make conversation, here's your topic. If you get tired of talking about ostrich meat and how it doesn't actually taste much like chicken at all, you can talk about ostrich feathers, ostrich boots, and ostrich belts—you could actually wear yours if you've got them. Before long, you'll get the idea that Randy Reaves did. You can use everything but the squeal on these big birds.

They're the wave of the future. Just ask Randy Reaves if you don't believe me.

Linda
Eckhardt's
1995
Guide to
America's
Best Foods

152

FISH AND SHELLFISH, FRESH, CANNED, AND SMOKED.

*Ah! Who has seen the mailed lobster rise, clap her broad wings,
and soaring claim the skies?*

—JOHN HOOKHAM FRERE (1769–1846)

THE ANTIQUE MALL AND CROWN RESTAURANT

P.O. Box 540
Indianola, MS 38751

CREDIT CARDS: **Yes**

CALL FOR CATALOG

RETAIL STORE: **Call for directions**

PHONE: 800-833-7731

FAX: 601-887-5547

MINIMUM ORDER: **No**

CATFISH CUISINE

When I first heard Food Editor Laurin Stamm rave about catfish paté, I thought she must be kidding. Laurin says she wouldn't go anywhere without Crown smoked catfish paté for a hostess gift. Let me tell you. This is no joke. The pale pink, silky smooth paté made at the Crown Restaurant deserves the accolades it's gotten. And the Roughtons have been praised for this catfish paté everywhere from *Food and Wine* to the *Catfish Journal*. In fact, in 1990, the Fancy Food Show named it the best hors d'oeuvre of the year. And rightly so.

Not only is the catfish fine, but they've made their reputation with a dessert they call Mississippi Delta Fudge Pie. Basically a smooth brownie, it only requires a dollop of vanilla ice cream to make it heaven. The good news is that you can get both by mail order.

The Crown is a country plantation style restaurant in the Mississippi Delta that only serves lunch. It's famous for miles around for divine Southern food. Evelyn and Tony Roughton have been cooking and serving these gracious Southern lunches since 1976. Actually, the Crown Restaurant began as a adjunct to their original business known as the Antique Mall.

Because of never ending requests, they branched out into the specialty food business and began making and selling food products for people to take home. Now, Tony says the specialty food business is larger than either the antique or the on-site restaurant business. But if you're travelling the delta area, take that short drive out to Indianola. The drive is lovely, the lunch is divine.

For cookbook collectors, their new book, *Classic Catfish* is a must. It has 150 pages of gourmet catfish recipes they've developed using the farm-raised catfish that abound in the delta.

Catfish Allison

Every day at lunch the Crown offers two entrees. One is always catfish. This recipe has become a favorite. The recipe was developed by Claudia Ainsworth who, with her husband Bill, are friends and neighbors of the Roughtons. Try it with other white, firm-fleshed fish, such as codfish or halibut.

Mix together in a bowl the cheese, butter, mayonnaise, onion, Worcestershire, and Tabasco. This can be made as much as 24 hours ahead.

Poach the catfish fillets in lightly simmering water for 4–5 minutes. Gently lift the fillets from the water and set aside to drain.

For individual servings, place each fillet in an au gratin dish and cover with about 2 tablespoons of cheese mixture. Run it under the broiler 2–3 minutes, or until the cheese mixture browns. Serve hot with a side dish of rice pilaf and peas.

1 cup freshly grated Parmesan cheese

½ cup soft butter

6 tablespoons mayonnaise

6 green onions and tops, chopped fine

½ teaspoon Worcestershire sauce

generous dash of Tabasco

6 catfish fillets

ATLANTIC SEAFOOD DIRECT

21 Merrill Drive
Rockland, ME 04841

~~~~~~~~~~~~~~

CREDIT CARDS: **Yes**

CALL FOR CATALOG

PHONE: **800-227-1116**

FAX: **914-621-2394**

MINIMUM ORDER: **No**

NEW ENGLAND LOBSTER AND CLAMBAKE

Talk about your luxury gift. How about a complete lobster dinner flown to you overnight from Maine and so fresh the lobsters are still kicking? Not only will you get a lobster apiece, but you'll also receive a serving for each person of a lovely, subtle lobster bisque, a bunch of fresh or smoked mussels and clams, perhaps some smoked salmon, and to top it all off, truffles all around—made by the former White House pastry chef and chocolatier, Albert Kumin.

You can decide before you order just how big you want your lobsters. Perhaps little chicken lobsters about a pound apiece, or 1½ pounders, or maybe you'd like to go all the way up to Woody Allen-sized two-pounders. You remember the kind Woody chased around the kitchen in *Annie Hall*?

I'll tell you one thing. You won't have to worry if you feel a little Woody Allen-ish about dispatching the lobsters. Complete cooking and storing directions come with the dinner. The Atlantic people will tell you how to steam, boil, or broil the lobsters. They provide Lobster Bibs, napkins, and placemats. And once you taste Atlantic Seafood Direct lobsters, you'll see how much better they are than any you can buy from the tank in your local supermarket. They're fresh, sweet, and succulent—just as if you'd plucked them from the sea yourself.

Atlantic offers splendid smoked fish as well. They offer Ducktrap River Fish Farm smoked fish: farm-raised trout that are smoked with no chemical preservatives. They also cold-smoke scallops and mussels so that they're mouthwatering. Their salmon paté and trout paté are so delicious, you could make a meal of them and forget about the rest of dinner. We adored them.

If you have a big blue pot, you can make your own clambake by layering live lobsters on top of clams and mussels, then adding new potatoes, corn on the cob, yellow onions, and a piece of linguica sausage to the steam pot. Pour in a beer and bring it all to a boil. It's a Clambake Celebration and you made it yourself.

Shirley Barr's Golden Crabmeat Quiche

Make this in a pastry shell or in individual tarts.

serves 6–8 for lunch

Preheat the oven to 300°F. Whisk together eggs, sour cream, and Worcestershire sauce and set aside. Sauté onion in butter until golden, then stir in the cheese, crabmeat, and eggs. Pour into the partially baked pastry shell. Lightly salt and pepper. Bake 55–60 minutes or until the custard is set and a knife inserted into the center comes out clean. Serve hot in wedges garnished with a sprig of Italian parsley.

3 large eggs, slightly beaten

1 cup light sour cream

½ teaspoon Worcestershire Sauce

1 medium onion, sliced paper-thin

3 tablespoons unsalted butter

1 cup (¼ lb.) shredded Swiss cheese

½ lb. fresh lump crabmeat

1 9-inch half-baked pastry shell

salt and freshly milled black pepper to taste

Italian parsley leaves for garnish

GUARANTEED FRESH SEAFOOD

Here's the market made famous by Julia Child who not only shops here with regularity but says so. An enormously busy mail-order firm, they've been sending out the provender of the cold North Atlantic for years. Prime soft shell crabs in the spring and summer, scrod, Cape Cod scallops, clams, blue mussels, monkfish, swordfish, and blue fish—their list is long, their catalog impressive. Call and just ask for what you want. Not only do they carry local seafood, but they will also try to locate fish from all over the world for you. They have a motto about their freshness: "If it ain't fresh, it ain't legal."

LEGAL SEAFOODS MARKET

5 Cambridge Center
Main at 6th
Cambridge, MA 02139

CREDIT CARDS: Yes

CALL FOR CATALOG

RETAIL STORE: Nine stores in greater Boston area

PHONE: 800-343-5804 (Nationwide) 617-864-3400 (MA)

FAX: 617-254-5809

MINIMUM ORDER: No

BAYOU-TO-GO SEAFOOD, INC.

P.O. Box 20104
New Orleans, LA 70141

CREDIT CARDS: Yes

CALL FOR CATALOG

RETAIL STORE: In the airport

PHONE: 800-541-6610
504-468-8040

MINIMUM ORDER: Yes

TAKING HOME FRESH CRAWFISH AND OTHER CAJUN SPECIALTIES

A lot of the airport stuff you see is nothing more than a cliche, but Bayou-To-Go seems to have captured the essence of Cajun and Creole cooking and made it available to travellers who are heading out of Louisiana and already missing the food. And now, you don't have to be lounging around the New Orleans airport to get Bayou's foods.

Linda Hobbs calls her business "a portable idea." She began with a cold cabinet in the airport offering live blue crabs and crawfish to go, as well as alligator steaks, sausage, and turtle meat. Linda's the daughter of a South Louisiana fisherman and knows her stuff. She's now added freshly-made gumbo and a long list of other Cajun prepared foods, as well as all the Louisiana hot sauces, mixes, creole mixes, and River Road spices your Cajun heart could crave.

Think about it. You can call up Linda's 800 number and she'll deliver Louisiana to you by express mail.

BLUE CRAB BAY COMPANY

108 Market St.
P.O. Box 180
Onancock, VA 23417

CREDIT CARDS: Yes

CALL FOR CATALOG

PHONE: 800-221-2722
804-787-3602

FAX: 804-787-3430

MINIMUM ORDER: $10

CHESAPEAKE BAY SPECIALTIES

P amela Barefoot began this mail order business in 1985. From the beginning, her Chesapeake Bay specialties won prizes. Recognized by Julia Child and the American Institute of Wine and Food for her outstanding regional preparations, Barefoot continues to create and sell custom-canned Atlantic clams, white and red clam sauces, herb blends, cocktail sauces, horseradish mustard and honey. Her seafood marinade is particularly delicious.

We're crazy about Maryland crab cakes and using Barefoot's herbed cracker crumbs and the recipe on the back of the box, we turned out some cakes that were as good as any we'd had in New York restaurants. One of the best new ideas Pamela's come up with is a way to ship live little neck clams, frozen soft shell crabs, and pas-

Linda Eckhardt's 1995 Guide to America's Best Foods

158

teurized fresh crab meat. These products are available year-round. As Pamela said about her own dinner last night with her husband—fresh little neck clams, so tiny, sweet, and succulent—all you have to do is dip them in her own clam dip and, "They'll make you moan, they're so good."

THE INTERNATIONAL CAVIAR SUPERMARKET

CAVIARTERIA
29 E. 60th St.
New York, NY 10022

CREDIT CARDS: Yes

CALL FOR CATALOG

RETAIL STORE: Yes

PHONE: 800-221-1020
212-759-7410

MINIMUM ORDER: No

Louis Sobol sells everything from domestic and imported caviars to caviar cruises. Here's where you can get fresh, broken-grain Caspian caviar—mild, perishable, and a bargain because the berries aren't perfect, Swedish gravlax (dill-marinated salmon), smoked eel, smoked salmon, and imported caviars, such as Russian Imperial and Beluga Prime. They also offer American caviars, fresh foie gras, and Italian truffles in season, both black and white.

Stop in the upper east side store next time you're in New York. You'll see all manner of caviar paraphenalia as well as enough of the briney fish eggs to boggle the mind if not the pocketbook.

LEGENDARY SMOKED FISH

RUSS & DAUGHTERS
179 E. Houston St.
New York, NY 10002

CREDIT CARDS: Yes

CALL FOR CATALOG

RETAIL STORE: Call for directions

PHONE: 212-465-4880

FAX: 212-475-0345

MINIMUM ORDER: No

I swear Russ and Daughters could make a living if they could just figure out how to bottle the aroma that overtakes you when you enter their 90-year-old-plus business on New York's lower east side. It's a heavenly smoked and pickled fish smell that will set your taste buds tingling before you can elbow your way up to the counter.

Russ and Daughters first became known to me—and to many others—by Calvin Trillin, who wrote of taking his own daughters there for Sunday brunch. A good bagel and an order of Russ's sturgeon is heaven on earth. Now I take my daughter there whenever I'm in town.

The real manager these days is Mark Russ Federman, the third generation Russ to run this business, and he's keeping tradition intact. You can still get divine gravlax, and salmon from Ireland, Scotland, Norway, Denmark, the Gaspe Peninsula, and the good old U.S. of A.

The lake sturgeon is incredible. Firm, smoky, and a golden color, it is a purely New York product.

The Protein Purveyors

159

Order for a party and get best quality fresh caviar, salmon, or sturgeon. Try pickled herring in several versions—with sour cream, pickled onions, and some in mustard with dill. You can get exotic fish products here as well. Old fashioned belly lox, whitefish club, gefilte fish, and schmaltz herring fillet. If it's pickled and smoked and comes from the sea, Russ and Daughters probably has it.

If you're in the city, do not miss the opportunity to visit this piece of Old New York.

APPLEWOOD-SMOKED TROUT

Stop in this converted gas station and take a whiff. The aroma of woodsmoke and herbs will assail your senses. The store is charming, filled with baskets, herbs heaped in bushels, locally grown produce, rainbows of peppers, pastas, oils, and locally prepared sauces.

But the best thing about this is the trout smoked by Richard Pla and Kyle Strohmann. They got into the fish smoking business in a roundabout way. They'd escaped from the city and bought a farm which they hoped to turn to profit. But a drought the first summer showed them what a risky venture that could be. Then, at a yard sale, they bought a smoker. Reading up on the subject, gathering local applewood and buying local farm-raised trout, they soon had developed a method that's won them every prize in the book.

As if the trout wasn't good enough on its own, they even bone it for you. You get a whole trout in a paper sack that smells sweet before you even cut into the fish. This is far and away the best smoked trout we've ever tasted. Our focus group dropped their forks, it tasted so good.

If you're in the Washington D.C. area, whip on down to their country store. They have fresh breads available. Get yourself a bottle of good Virginia wine, a loaf of bread, and one smoked trout. It will make a picnic you won't soon forget.

THE FARM AT MT. WALDEN

Main Street, Box 189
The Plains, VA 22171

CREDIT CARDS: Yes

CALL FOR CATALOG

RETAIL STORE: Call for directions

PHONE: 703-253-9800

FAX: 703-253-9807

MINIMUM ORDER: No

SMOKED CATFISH

PICKWICK CATFISH FARM

4155 Hwy 57
Counce, TN 38326

Betty and Quentin Knussmann raise catfish in a pond. When the fish get to be about a pound, the Knussmanns catch them and smoke them in a homemade smoker. Because they're thoroughly smoked, they don't really even need refrigeration. They're sent out through the regular mail; no shipments in the summer.

When we got ours—two fished wrapped in a plastic bag, pepper-hot, moist, and smoky, with creamy chunks of mild, fine catfish—we intended to be circumspect about them and try one of Betty's recipes. But we were so taken with the taste we nearly ate the fish all in one sitting. I swear, I had to hide the second fish. The prices are more than reasonable, and this old Southern standby is a treat.

CREDIT CARDS: **Yes**

CALL FOR CATALOG

RETAIL STORE: **Call for directions**

PHONE: **901-689-3805**

MINIMUM ORDER: **2 fish**

NORTHWEST INDIAN-STYLE SMOKED SALMON

SILETZ TRIBAL SMOKEHOUSE

P.O. Box 1004
Depoe Bay, OR 97341

The Native American Indians of the Pacific Northwest made salmon their primary meat source. To keep the catch, they smoked it. Indian hot-smoked salmon is different from lox or any of that pale, quivery stuff you buy at the deli. Indian smoked salmon is rich-flavored, sweet, dry, smoky, and moist all at once. The ancient process begins by filleting salmon sides, then layering the meat in salt and spice until the juices run. Then the salmon is heated in a smoke house to 200°F. and held at that temperature until the juices are sealed in and the meat has achieved it's deep coral color.

The Siletz Tribal Smokehouse, on Oregon's Pacific coast, makes and sells first quality hot-smoked salmon and albacore tuna in tins and foil pouches. The Siletz Confederated Tribes regained their status as a sovereign tribal group in 1977 and developed their fish smoking business out of a former state fish hatchery.

Today, you can visit the Siletz Smokehouse and store as you drive the breathtaking Oregon coast. The store is located right on highway 101 at Depoe Bay. Not only do they sell smoked salmon, but a full array of fresh seafood, including the famous Dungeness crab,

CREDIT CARDS: **Yes**

CALL FOR CATALOG

RETAIL STORE: **Call for directions**

PHONE: **800-828-4269
503-765-2286**

FAX: **503-765-2743**

MINIMUM ORDER: **No**

The Protein Purveyors

161

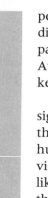

petrale sole, ling cod, and halibut. Here you can see for yourself the difference between brilliant red Coho salmon and the sweeter tasting, pale pink chinook. You can also taste divine smoked Albacore tuna. At the gift shop, they offer many Native American crafts: Zuni blankets, beadwork, and crafts made by local tribal members.

Drive east off highway 101 onto highway 20 and you'll soon see signs to Siletz, located deep in the coastal mountains and the home of the tribe's annual powwow. Held the second weekend in August, hundreds of dancers and other visitors come from the world over to visit the Tribal Center and participate in the ancient ritual. If you'd like a look at what Oregon was like before the Europeans got here, this is your chance.

SMOKED OYSTERS

Nick and Joanne Jambor, along with Bob Anderson, grow, fresh-smoke, and ship these Pacific oysters all over the nation from their 40-acre oyster farm. They raise the shellfish in Willapa Bay, now believed to be one of the cleanest in the country. They buy the larvae from another hatchery, then when it's reached the swimming stage and almost ready to "set," they put the larvae into their tanks, with shells, and within a day or so the larvae will set on the shell.

Next, they transport the shells—strung on long ropes—out to the tideflats. There the strings are suspended while the oysters grow in their borrowed shells to delectable maturity.

Joanne and Nick sell some of their oysters raw, but they save the best for smoking. These are steamed, shucked, and put first into a salt brine, then into brown sugar and spices. They're alder-smoked about five hours. The Jambors also smoke other Pacific seafood. Call them and ask what's in the smoker today.

EKONE OYSTER CO.

Star Route, Box 465
South Bend, WA 98586

CHECKS OR MONEY ORDERS ONLY

CALL FOR CATALOG

Ekone Oyster Co. ships only to Oregon and Washington

PHONE: 206-875-5494

MINIMUM ORDER: Yes

SMOKED SALMON, OYSTERS, AND MUSSELS

SPECIALTY SEAFOODS

605 30th St., Box 591
Anacortes, WA 98221

CREDIT CARDS: **Yes**

CALL FOR CATALOG

RETAIL STORE: **Call for directions**

PHONE: **800-645-3474
206-293-4661**

FAX: **206-293-4097**

MINIMUM ORDER: **No**

Specialty Seafoods started this whole business of vacuum-packed smoked salmon back in the seventies and is still doing a land office business with it. And no wonder. They keep the quality control up. Choosing the best quality salmon—both sockeyes and Kings—they hot-smoke them, the Northwestern way, then vacuum seal them in a foil pouch. Next, they're wrapped in a giftable brown box with great looking calligraphy. We hardly know whether to say these are best for gifts—they present so well—or for ourselves, since they provide on-the-spot cocktail party food that's dramatic to look at and successful to serve.

Using the Northwest hot-smoking technique, Specialty gets an aromatic, sweet, moist, and smoky product that tastes great by itself or when used in a recipe. They'll send you several to choose from.

In addition to Northwest hot-smoked salmon, they also smoke Washington state oysters and Penn Cove mussels. We're particularly fond of the mussels. Bright black and tan with orange fringes, they look terrific on a buffet table and taste even better.

You've never tasted canned salmon until you've tried custom-canned salmon. And theirs is as good as it gets. Keep some on hand. Their canned smoked salmon paté makes a great hostess gift—for your hostess or for you. Recently, they began offering Nova-style salmon as well as the Northwest style. Whatever you want in the way of smoked salmon, they'll provide it.

*The Protein
Purveyors*

JOSEPHSON'S
SMOKEHOUSE

P.O. Box 412
Astoria, OR 97103

CREDIT CARDS: Yes

CALL FOR CATALOG

RETAIL STORE: Call for
directions

PHONE: 800-772-3474
503-325-2190

MINIMUM ORDER: No

FRESH PICKLED AND SMOKED PACIFIC FISHES

Michael and Linda Josephson are third-generation owners of a dockside fish company that offers not only smoked fish but fresh Pacific fish as well. They made their national reputation, however, with their Grandfather Anton's recipe for traditional smoked salmon, which is firm, with a deep brown-orange skin and a pale shell-pink meat inside. This is a rich, complex, irresistible flavor that comes either vacuum-packed—from 1- to 10-pound pieces—in plastic or in a can. They also cold-smoke lox, and this produces a soft, rosy, but saltier product, something like a seafaring ham. Salmon jerky, sometimes known as squaw candy, is hard stuff to chew but has a kind of smoky-sweet flavor and is popular with kids.

The Josephsons will ship fresh West Coast specialties: whole coho or chinook salmon, salmon steaks, halibut, sturgeon, lingcod, Pacific snapper, albacore tuna, petrale, English sole, and mouth-watering razor clams in season.

These people are reliable. Call them.

HOMARUS INC.

76 Kisco Avenue
Mt. Kisco, NY
10549-9979

CREDIT CARDS: Yes

CALL FOR CATALOG

PHONE: 800-666-8992

FAX: 914-666-8734

MINIMUM ORDER: No

CLASSIC EUROPEAN-STYLE SMOKED FISH

OK. You know about pastrami, but do you know they can treat salmon the same way, brining and cold-smoking it, with the surface packed with peppercorns, and what you get is simply heaven? Homarus calls it *Poivre Lachs* and it's a rosy moist delicacy that would lift any buffet table into the stratosphere.

Karen Ransom and her partner Peter Heineman began smoking fish in 1976. Karen boldly walked into some of New York's top kitchens and dared the chefs to try her smoked fish products. Fresh out of college, the pair began smoking and selling trout and salmon first to restaurants, then to expanded markets. They now smoke a variety of seafood along with trout and salmon, including such esoterica as eels, sablefish, scallops, shrimp, sturgeon, tuna, and whitefish. They will also custom-smoke fish to your specifications.

Order a side of salmon smoked in various manners: a gravlax using dill, peppercorns, brown sugar and salt; or salmon cured with cilantro, rosemary and mint, aquavit, tequila, chrysanthemum petals and tangerine zest, lemon dill or—you name it and they'll try it.

*Linda
Eckhardt's
1995
Guide to
America's
Best Foods*

164

Northwest Caesar's Salad

makes 2 main dish servings

Preheat the oven to 400°F. Cut bread into ½-inch cubes. Toss in olive oil then arrange one layer deep on a baking sheet. Toast in the oven 5 minutes, or until golden brown.

Meanwhile, smash garlic cloves and combine with salmon. Mash with a fork or in a mortar and pestle. Add a little olive oil to make a buttery puree then spread this onto the toasted croutons and set aside.

Remove outer leaves of romaine and discard. Cut remaining leaves into bite sized pieces and place in a large salad bowl.

In a small saucepan filled with boiling water, precook the egg for two minutes. Then, scoop the egg white and yolk into a small bowl. Add olive oil and whisk to make an emulsion. Whisk in lime juice and Worcestershire sauce, then toss with the salad greens. Toss Parmesan into the salad and season to taste with a little salt and a lot of pepper. Add flavored croutons. Divide between two dinner plates and serve at once.

6 slices French bread

¼ cup olive oil

4 cloves garlic

2 tablespoons Northwest-style smoked salmon

1 head Romaine lettuce, outer 6 leaves discarded

1 large egg

juice of a lime

1 teaspoon Worcestershire sauce

¼ cup freshly grated Parmesan Cheese

salt and freshly grated black pepper to taste

NORTHWEST FRESH AND SMOKED SALMON

So you thought you had to go fishing to catch a salmon on a line. No. You can pick up the telephone and these folks will send you a line-caught salmon, never frozen, either chinook or a locally farm-raised fish. Order a 6- or 10-pound fish. It comes to you the next day. Then all you have to do to be ready for a dinner party is poach it.

They will also send you fresh caught, fully-cooked Dungeness crab, pacific oysters in the shell or shucked, steamer clams live in the shell, and salmon steaks or fillets. Order the crab and all you have to do is tear into it and start sucking that sweet crab meat out of the shell. It's the West Coast at its best. Do try to remember to buy a loaf of sourdough bread and melt some butter, maybe accompanied by a green salad and a light chardonnay—how we like to eat in the West.

And this isn't even what Fred Hegg is famous for. What's created

HEGG & HEGG SMOKED SALMON

801 Marine Drive
Port Angeles, WA
98362

CREDIT CARDS: Yes

CALL FOR CATALOG

RETAIL STORE: 3 locations in Port Angeles

PHONE: 800-435-3474
206-457-3344

FAX: 206-457-1205

MINIMUM ORDER: No

devoted customers is Fred's ability to smoke Northwest seafood. He smokes salmon, tuna, sturgeon, shad, oysters, crab, and clams. His smoking method derives from the Northwest Indian formula that uses alder and creates a dry, flavorful product. He's been mail-ordering smoked and canned fish for over forty years to customers who just keep coming back. His reputation is sterling.

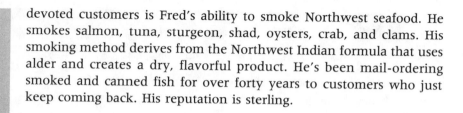
CREDIT CARDS: Yes

CALL FOR CATALOG

RETAIL STORE: Yes

PHONE: 800-622-7775
  212-490-6650

FAX: 212-949-5210

MINIMUM ORDER: No

*Linda
Eckhardt's
1995
Guide to
America's
Best Foods*

HEART OF NEW YORK SMOKED FISHES

A visit to New York is not complete without a trip to Grand Central Station, the main terminal used by locals to move in, around, and out of the city. While the gargantuan lobby is genuinely grand, the real surprise is below. If you follow the arrows to the restaurant deep underground you're going to see an even greater spectacle. The Oyster Bar Restaurant is large and hushed, the ceilings paved in glistening white tiles. First opened in 1913, the restaurant feels like a temple.

The waiters are quintessential New York, the seafood is divine. I also like it because the tables aren't so crowded that you can hear the details of the fight or the tête-à-tête going on at the next table. Sit at the bar, watch the oyster bar men expertly opening oysters with their special knives, and soak in New York's story. Just listen.

They open more than a million raw oysters a year here, some fifteen different varieties. We particularly loved the pan-roasted oysters we ordered when we were there.

What you can't see is the kitchen. Every meal in the cavernous dining room is cooked from scratch. Every biscuit is baked in-house. Every gallon of clam chowder starts here with fresh clams and cream. They built a full smokehouse right there, underground, so that they can control the quality of their smoked salmon and other fishes. They never freeze their smoked fish—it breaks down the cells and destroys the taste—and if you order a glistening side of salmon for your next party, they will simply custom-smoke it to suit you and ship it out.

When we got our smoked salmon side, glistening pink, moist, and mouthwatering, we arranged to have a party. We laid that salmon out, sliced it paper thin, served it with nothing but lemon wedges and capers, a little freshly ground pepper and some chopped onion. Believe me, that was a party. What was left over we scrambled with eggs the next day for breakfast.

The Oyster Bar sends out other smoked fishes besides salmon:

smoked brook trout, smoked sturgeon, luxury Balik salmon. They even have their very own cheesecake. Everything is Four Star Quality.

CUSTOM-CANNED SALMON

This is not the salmon my mother cranked out of a can to make salmon croquettes when I was a kid. No. This is custom-canned salmon that makes even the fresh salmon stand back at a respectful distance.

An old tradition on the Pacific coast, salmon caught by sports fishermen is sometimes taken to a custom-canner for putting up. Dick and Casey also can commercially caught salmon and what you get are big chunks of salmon—not overprocessed and not oversalted—but just meltingly rich and delicious.

You can order the salmon plain or with a variety of seasonings: Cajun, Italian, No-Salt, Zesty, and Smoked. They're all better than anything you ever bought in a store. We laid in a case. After opening two cans, we never want to be without it.

If you're in Brookings, stop by the cannery and smokehouse at the Port of Brookings Public Launch and Marina. If you can't get there, call up and get a variety of smoked and canned first quality Pacific fish products: smoked salmon fillet, smoked albacore fillet, cans of smoked salmon, and albacore. Also available are divine Cozetts cranberries in port wine and brandied cranberries. Remember that this coast grows more cranberries than New England. And they're big, flavorful, and juicy. The bounty of Oregon. It's here. Come and get it.

DICK AND CASEY'S

P.O. Box 2392
Harbor, OR 97415

CREDIT CARDS: **Yes**

CALL FOR CATALOG

RETAIL STORE: **Call for directions**

PHONE: **800-662-9494**

MINIMUM ORDER: **No**

The Protein Purveyors

LAZIO FAMILY PRODUCTS

327 Second St.
Eureka, CA 95501

CREDIT CARDS: **Yes**

CALL FOR CATALOG

RETAIL STORE: **Yes**

PHONE: **800-737-6688**
    707-442-6688

FAX: **707-442-5867**

MINIMUM ORDER: **No**

GOURMET TUNA

Lawrence G. Lazio and family are custom-canners on California's far Northcoast. What they put up in a can and call tuna fish you will hardly recognize. The meat is white albacore and is packed in either spring water or extra virgin olive oil—your call. It has nothing but great taste and only 100 calories per serving.

The Lazios use an ancient Mediterranean method and use only superior albacore. The first time I opened one of these cans, I could hardly recognize the stuff. I didn't get a jolt of that fishy odor you get from grocery store tuna. It didn't look too much like cat food. It looked more like tuna I'd just poached.

The Lazios catch their tuna with a hook. No nets, no dolphins, and no other fish are ever touched. They catch the fish, flash-freeze it, then pack the fish in their Northcoast California packing plant. Their tuna is what you'll soon be calling "the good stuff." Be sure and ask for the recipe sheet the Lazios have developed—four pages of genuine Mediterranean specialties using albacore. Yum.

Lawrence sells this tuna out of his seafood restaurant. It's a good stop if you're ravenous after a day of sight-seeing the area Victorians and the tall trees.

Coho salmon spawn for an average of five days.
—U.S. Army Corps of Engineers

Female coho salmon deposit an average of 2,500 eggs when spawning.
—U.S. Army Corps of Engineers

Pink salmon have a two-year life cycle, which is so invariable that fish running in odd-numbered calendar years are isolated from even-numbered years, so no gene flow occurs between them.
—U.S. Army Corps of Engineers

In 1986, 3,909 tons of blue mussel meat was harvested off the Maine and Massachusetts coasts, with an estimated value of $4 million.
—U.S. Army Corps of Engineers

Seafood should be chilled between 32° and 40°F.
—Department of Health and Human Services

HOT STUFF

S alsa, chili, and steak sauces. Dry spices. Ethnic herbs and spices. Chili peppers every which way. Chutneys and fruit sauces. Pickled fruits and vegetables. Relishes. Fruit and berry vinegars, mustards, mayos, olives, oils, and salad dressings. Some of the most innovative concoctions occur within this category, including many salt-free, fat-free, and sugar-free salad dressings and jams. Raspberry walnut. Lemon chardonnay. Champagne mustard. Yum.

The food that to him now is as luscious as locusts shall be to him shortly as bitter as coloquintida.

—SHAKESPEARE, *Othello*

SALSA, CHILI, AND STEAK SAUCES. ETHNIC HERBS AND SPICES. CHILI PEPPERS EVERY WHICH WAY.

"I probably shouldn't learn to cook Creole food anyway. It's too complicated." "Sheeit. Ain't nothing but onions, green peppers and garlic. Put that in everything and you get Creole food."

—MAYA ANGELOU (1928–)

Red Peril Chicken

makes 4 servings in 20 minutes

In a large skillet over medium high heat, melt the butter and saute chicken breasts until golden on both sides, about 5 minutes. Add stock, wine, lemon juice, and zest and half the salsa to the skillet, cover and poach until the breasts are done, about 15 minutes. Lift from the poaching liquid to hot plates. Garnish with the remaining salsa, adding a dollop atop each breast.

1 tablespoon unsalted butter

2 whole chicken breasts, boned, skinned, and halved

1 cup chicken stock

1 cup white wine

juice and zest of a lemon

1 cup Red Peril salsa

MIGHTY FINE SALSA

This salsa is good. The original California Chipotle Chile Salsa is a hot and smoky dip that will give the name salsa new meaning. Other heavenly flavors are also available. Tomato Corn Salsa is a mild and chunky salsa with corn kernels, green chiles, onions, garlic, and jalapenos. Tomatillo Garlic is a green salsa redolent of garlic, red bells, green chiles, red wine vinegar, and jalapenos. The tomato pineapple is slightly sweetish, Caribbean-influenced salsa is made with pineapple onion, lime juice, mint, jalapenos, spices and a hint of butter. Yum.

All these salsas are low in salt, sugar, and fats. A nutritional readout is included on the label. We love this stuff. It's way beyond ordinary bottled salsas.

SALSA SABROSA
2343 Roosevelt Ave.
Berkeley, CA 94703

CHECKS OR MONEY ORDERS ONLY

CALL FOR CATALOG

PHONE: 510-486-0510

FAX: 510-486-1757

MINIMUM ORDER: 1 Case

INSTANT SALSA FIXIN'S

If you're growing tomatoes out in the backyard or if you have access to some from a good farmer's market, you can make an instantly delicious salsa by mixing up these dry seasonings with dead-ripe tomatoes and a shot of lemon juice.

The dry mix also makes a good marinade for chicken breasts when slurried with real lime juice, tequila, and a shot of olive oil. They also recommend a Texas Red Peril ranch dip made from ranch dressing and their dry salsa. Eat it at your own peril. It's howling hot and good.

TEXAS RED PERIL HOT SALSA FIX'NS
P.O. Box 732
Fort Worth, TX 76101

CHECKS OR MONEY ORDERS ONLY

CALL FOR CATALOG

PHONE: 817-731-6949

MINIMUM ORDER: No

K-PAUL'S

**824 Distributors Row
P.O. Box 13342
Harahan, LA
70183-0342**

CREDIT CARDS: **Yes**

CALL FOR CATALOG

RETAIL STORE: **In the restaurant**

PHONE: **800-457-2857
504-731-3590**

FAX: **504-731-3576**

MINIMUM ORDER: **$15**

KING PAUL COOKS

Paul Prudhomme brought South Louisiana to the world. He taught me that mixing three kinds of peppers—red, white, and black—made flavors jump on the tongue. He taught all of us to consider food that was charred to be highly desirable, not something you'd skulk away with to the back garbage can.

He and his wife, Kay, began a restaurant in New Orleans known as K-Paul's that still has them lined up around the block. His beloved wife died, but Paul keeps the business going and his empire's growing.

Now, he's into mail order. You can get magic seasoning blends so you can make your own blackened redfish or chicken meals, and seasonings for meat, poultry and seafood that are carefully-blended mixtures of Cajun spices and herbs. He also sells gumbo file and cayenne pepper. You can order any of Paul's books and they'll come autographed.

Maybe best of all, you can order K-Paul's Mail-A-Meal. Want Jambalaya for 6 or 16? Order it. Want shrimp creole for your next dinner party? Let K-Paul's cook and send it. How about etouffee? Order crawfish, shrimp, or chicken and within 45 minutes, your dinner party is done. These dinners come via overnight air and should be served the day you get them. So make out your guest list, set the table, and pick up the phone. That's an easy dinner party. And talk about good.

ANDY'S GOOD 'N HOT

**P.O. Box 284
D'Lo, MS 39062**

CREDIT CARDS: **Yes**

CALL FOR CATALOG

PHONE: **800-468-4399
601-847-GOOD**

MINIMUM ORDER: **No**

HOT SOUTHERN SALSAS

Would you believe D'Lo Mississippi could spawn a line of salsas to rival those made in Texas? Trust me on this. It has. Andy Burkhart makes it. But, in truth, Andy is a roughneck straight from the oil patch in Texas. He moved to Mississippi with an oil company but couldn't find decent salsas in the stores. "I started making it to spoil myself," he says.

Before long, demand for his hot, spicy, fresh-tasting salsa became so great that he quit his job and started cooking full-time. So full-time that he's been known to cook and stir for eighteen hours at a stretch.

Although even the mildest can be called spicy, Burkhart's sauces come in medium hot, extra hot, and XXX hot habanero which is only for macho munchers. They also make a green salsa and a classic Texas-style barbecue sauce. All Andy's sauces have a homemade fresh taste and contain no preservatives. Andy and his wife, Billie, intend to keep it that way.

SATISFYING SALSAS

Georgia Pisciotta not only makes salsas so good you'll nearly drop your chip, they're good for you besides. Low-salt, no-fat, they're just good tasting. We're especially crazed over the chipotle salsa. Freckled with fire-roasted jalapenos, the flavor is rich, complex, hot, and sweet. We love it.

Visit the plant and you can buy Georgia's potato chips hot from the kettle. *Fancy Foods* awarded Saguaro (suh-whar-o) a prize for the best in "Outstanding Healthy Products" for her spicy black bean dip. Black as sin, hot as the devil, it has neither salt nor fat. It's all good taste. She also makes a good and spicy, no-fat pinto bean dip, and offers an authentic southwestern salsa made from tomatoes, chilis, onions, cilantro, and garlic.

Last, but not least, they sell blue corn chips to dip into all those great salsas and dips. Also available are pinto bean chips, yellow corn chips, and white corn chips. Each one is better than the last.

SAGUARO FOOD PRODUCTS

860 East 46th St.
Tucson, AZ 85713

CREDIT CARDS: **Yes**

CALL FOR CATALOG

RETAIL STORE: **Call for directions**

PHONE: 800-732-CHIP (Nationwide)
602-884-8049 (Arizona)

FAX: 602-884-9704

MINIMUM ORDER: **Yes**

SAN TONE SALSAS AND DRY RUBS FOR BARBECUE

Dry rubs are useful to people who wish to season meats for grilling or roasting without the use of oils. Arthur Stroeck, an old Texan with the gravelly voice of a man who sounds like he's lived every day of his life, offers a line of dry rubs that can be used not only to marinate and season meats, but to spike salads as well.

His lemon pepper contains salt, garlic, onion, chili pepper, lemon zest, sugar, and monosodium glutamate (MSG). The mesquite grill seasoning contains salt, onion, garlic, and MSG. The Mexican-style salad seasoning contains salt, parmesan, garlic, paprika, lemon and orange zest, and MSG. All of these dry rubs are flavorful—despite the fact their laced with MSG. I do wish he'd take that ingredient out.

Arthur also makes a line of traditional Texas salsas that he calls, "San Tone Salsas." They come in various flavors like border mamas used to make: kidney bean, hot or mild picante, garlic, yellow squash, black-eyed pea, and hot mesquite. The salsas have a deep, rich flavor and will seem very familiar to anyone who has ever done time in Texas. Arthur's salsas are free of chemical preservatives or salt. Their good flavors come from all natural spices.

ARTHUR'S

P.O. Box 165
1020 Macon St.
Fort Worth, TX
76101-0165

CHECKS OR MONEY ORDERS ONLY

CALL FOR CATALOG

PHONE: 817-332-9495

FAX: 817-336-2222

MINIMUM ORDER: **No**

Hot Stuff

EL PASO CHILE COMPANY

909 Texas Ave.
El Paso, TX 79901

~~~~~~~~~~~~~~~~~~~

CREDIT CARDS: Yes

CALL FOR CATALOG

RETAIL STORE: Yes

PHONE: 800-274-7468
915-544-3434

FAX: 915-544-7552

MINIMUM ORDER: No

STALKING THE WILD ENCHILADA

P ark Kerr not only knows how to cook like an angel from hell, he also offers playful, sound advice for all those who'd like to try Tex-Mex and Mex-Mex cooking for the first time.

In the downtown store he and his sister Monica own in El Paso, Park dispenses equal parts good cheer, good advice, and good products. He's written a book—*muy autentico*—called *The Texas Border Cookbook* and it's a must for great border recipes. Ask him and he'll autograph it anyway you wish.

Walk into the old brick storefront in historic downtown El Paso. It's like walking into somebody's 500-square-foot pantry. Interesting table top stuff and good junk: a hunt through the haystack for a golden needle. You'll find it. Like the parakeets by the blue front cash register. The store is a treasure. Small and precious. Go.

But back to the food. We love Chipotle Cha Cha Cha so much we don't know whether to dip our chips in it or our whole bodies. After a couple of Snakebite salsa Bloody Marys, made from Park's mix, anything might happen.

He knows his barbecue too—as any real honest-to-god Texan must. His barbecue meat marinade will turn a brisket to ambrosia and make a believer out of any of the folks who never had the real article. He also makes a good table sauce from beer, and an even better one from tequila.

Try Coyote nuts—local peanuts roasted and tossed with red chile powder and garlic. Caramba, that's good. And for the true trial by fire, order El Paso chili mix. You'll get several recipes—you can hear Park's soothing voice if you listen—and you'll get real Texas chili.

POWDERED HELLFIRE/BOTTLED DYNAMITE

TEXAS GUNPOWDER, INC.

15330 LBJ Fwy,
Suite 41
Mesquite, TX
75185-2573

CHECKS OR MONEY
ORDERS ONLY

CALL FOR CATALOG

RETAIL STORE: **Call for
directions**

PHONE: 214-279-5766

MINIMUM ORDER: **No**

Janice Pinnell's daddy, W.L., ground jalapenos for his own convenience. Everybody called W.L. "Pappy", and they screamed bloody murder when he started out grinding and drying those peppers in mama's kitchen. The smell of jalapenos drove everbody, even the dog, out of the house.

So Pappy moved his operation to the garage. But the thing of it was, when Pappy put his pale, gray-green powder up in bottles, everbody had to admit that it was deadly delicious: a taste as special as fresh jalapenos only neater to use and all natural, with no salt, no preservatives, and no artificial coloring. His wife, Jan, who was on a low-salt diet, found her life had zest again, or at least her meals did.

Eventually, after Pappy had sprinkled his powdered jalapeno on everbody's eggs—and everything else—everybody said, Pappy, you might as well sell that stuff. So he did. Somebody noted if you used too much it could blow your head off, and so Pappy started calling it Gunpowder. And so it is.

Janice made this a business and has found it takes up all her time just filling mail orders. They sold a boatload of it to the boys in the Persian Gulf, and the rock group Genesis took two cases back to England with them last summer. Suppose that's why they jump around the stage like that?

Gunpowder's good on popcorn. It's great in gazpacho. It's the devil in deviled eggs.

Mrs. Dog's Chicken Wings

Mix Mrs. Dog's Jamaican Jerk, cooking oil, and chicken wings. Marinate, covered, in the refrigerator for up to 24 hours. Lift from marinade to a rack over a baking pan and sprinkle with cheese. Bake 1 hour at 350°F. Mrs. Dog says it's better prepared the day before and reheated just before serving.

5 lbs. chicken wings

5 tablespoons Mrs. Dog's Jamaican Jerk

5 tablespoons cooking oil

1½ cups grated parmesan or asiago cheese

MRS. DOG'S PRODUCTS, INC.

P.O. Box 6034
Grand Rapids, MI
  49516

CREDIT CARDS: Yes

CALL FOR "DOGALOG"

PHONE: 616-940-1778

FAX: 616-774-0193

MINIMUM ORDER: No

Linda Eckhardt's 1995 Guide to America's Best Foods

MICHIGAN HOT DOGS

Julie Applegate's making Scotch bonnet pepper sauce and jerk marinade that she calls Mrs. Dog. In taste-tests, ours and the National Fiery Foods Show in Albuquerque this year, her jerk marinade has topped all comers in the hot foods category.

We rubbed this marinade on a pheasant Joe shot, and let it stand in the refrigerator overnight before grilling the bird. The flavor was tender, hot, moist, and sweet. The pheasant was better than most, which can be quite stringy and lean. Thanks, Mrs. Dog. You just tamed one wild bird with the wily Scotch bonnet.

Mrs. Dog's marinade also gives chicken salad a lift. Ms. Applegate says she finds the peppers quite therapeutic and says they cured her chronic fatigue syndrome. She named the stuff after her own Golden Retriever who appears with her at food shows, decked out in three strands of pearls. That's no misplaced modifier there. The dog's decked out. Not Mrs. Dog. She wears cooking clothes and manages to look like an artist in the kitchen.

Mrs. Dog also makes a great Sweet and Hot mustard that's terrific on sandwiches. It's a world-class made-in-Michigan treat.

Hot, Hotter, Hottest

Don Alfonso says around 9,000 years ago the natives of southeast Mexico were already spicing their foods with chiles. They knew the vast difference in hotness among chiles. But not until a scientist named Scoville measured the heat in different varieties did we get any explanation for the differences.

chili varieties	Scoville Units
Habanero (hottest)	100,000 to 300,000
Piquin, Thai	50,000 to 100,000
Tecpin, Cayenne	30,000 to 50,000
De Arbol	15,000 to 30,000
Serrano	5,000 to 15,000
Chipotle, Morita	2,500 to 5,000
Cascabel, Guajillo, Puya	1,500 to 2,500
Ancho, Mulato, Pasilla	1,000 to 1,500
NM 6-4	500 to 1,000
Cherry (mildest)	100 to 500

THE APOCALYPSE IS NEAR, AS NEAR AS YOUR TELEPHONE

You won't be a virgin long after you try this Habanero Hot Paste. It's so potent that just a little dab will do you. Take the recipes they send and cut the hot stuff in half before you begin cooking. Otherwise, you may be walking around with the top of your head blown off.

They make this deadly Habanero Hot Paste, a Caribbean meat sauce and Apocalyptic Hot Sauce. They're not kidding. But the taste is marvellous once you get past the heat. They also make fine ginger, curry, and herbal sauces to use as condiments for your next Caribbean dinner.

What is it about hot places and hot foods? Must be the counter-irritant theory of cuisine. If you eat something this hot, you break out in a sweat and forget that you're sitting in the steam bath that is the climate.

VIRGIN ISLANDS HERB AND PEPPER COMPANY

P.O. Box 9519,
St. Thomas
U.S. Virgin Islands
  00801

CREDIT CARDS: **Yes**

CALL FOR CATALOG

PHONE: **809-776-2145**

MINIMUM ORDER: **No**

Hot Stuff

177

DON ALFONSO

P.O. Box 201988
Austin, TX 78720-1988

CREDIT CARDS: Yes

CALL FOR CATALOG

RETAIL STORE: **Call for directions**

PHONE: 800-456-6100

FAX: 800-765-7373

MINIMUM ORDER: No

AUTHENTIC TEX-MEX CONDIMENTS OLÉ

Austin, Texas has produced many a fine purveyor of Tex-Mex cuisine. Standing in the front row is Jose Marmolejo, president of Don Alfonso. He uses only natural ingredients and traditional processes. He uses family recipes to produce authentic Mexican-style salsas, adobos, and mole.

Open a jar of the chocolate brown-colored salsa de chipotle and you'll know what all the excitement's about when the word chipotle is mentioned. Chipotles—which Don Alfonso also sells dried—are simply ripe jalapenos that have been smoked and dried. But when added to a traditional tomato salsa, the whole concoction simply sings.

First in line in the heat-and-eat category is the mole poblano. A blend of chiles, peanuts, chocolate, sesame seeds, herbs, and spices, all you add is cooked chicken, leftover turkey, and rice for a traditional Mexican feast.

Besides his own fiery products, Don Alfonso also sells dozens of chiles and chile powders, frozen gourmet tamales with everything from green chile and smoked gouda, to chicken with mango habanero barbecue sauce, to a tamale with black tiger shrimp, pineapple, and chipotle sauce.

He sells Mexican cooking utensils including molcajete, tortilla presses, and comals. By the time this book comes out, he'll be ready to give tours. Stand by.

*Linda
Eckhardt's
1995
Guide to
America's
Best Foods*

178

HOTCHA TEXAS TASTES

TASTE TEASERS

P.O. Box 516382
Dallas, TX 75251

I t had to happen. Some Texan was bound to put jalapenos in chocolates. Sure enough, Susanne Hilou's made a green slime filling of jalapeno jell and then formed it into a miniature bittersweet chocolate brick with a jalapeno logo on the top. She packs these in a small red box with a gold inner foil blanket. This is food for foolishness, fit for those on whom whimsy is not lost.

More delicious are Susanne's hot and sweet jalapenos. Think of sweet, clear pickles and substitute jalapenos—that's what she's done. They're delightful. Also available are jalapeno spread, a Texas jam for a cream cheese brick. She makes corn relish, marinated black beans, garlic dill jalapenos, and a Southwestern dip mix.

CHECKS OR MONEY
ORDERS ONLY

CALL FOR CATALOG

PHONE: 214-458-2873

FAX: 214-490-3608

MINIMUM ORDER: No

Susanne encourages you to make a custom gift using two, three, or four products, and she'll pack them in a good-looking wooden crate and tie it all up with jalapeno ribbon. Hotcha.

HOT STUFF TO EAT

TONY PACKO'S CAFE

1902 Front St.
Toledo, OH 43465

T ony started his cafe in the thirties, making a sandwich he called a Hungarian Hot Dog by splitting a sausage, putting it into a bun, and slathering it with a hearty beef sauce. He charged a nickel. His wife made a great chili and soon "Two Dogs and a Chili" became the favorite lunch for Toledo's working public. The cafe still stands. You can go there for a hot dog, although I'm afraid they may charge you more than a nickel, and the third generation Tony may wait on you.

The Packos like a little playfulness in their foods and they bottle and sell a variety of Hungarian-inspired products: sweet hot pickles and peppers, Brittany tomatoes, Hungarian salsa, pickle relish, chunky peppers, really chunky dills, a great hot dog sauce, a mustard relish, and a spoonable ketchup. The flavors are honest and punched up, about as American as "The Star Spangled Banner." They'll custom-pack a gift for you. As Tony says, "U Pick it, we Pack it."

CREDIT CARDS: Yes

CALL FOR CATALOG

RETAIL STORE: Call for
directions

PHONE: 800-366-4218
419-691-1953

FAX: 419-691-4865

MINIMUM ORDER: No

Hot Stuff

HILL COUNTRY FOODS

2933 Ladybird Lane
Dallas, TX 75220

~~~~~~~~~~~~~~~~~~~~~~~

CREDIT CARDS: Yes

CALL FOR CATALOG

RETAIL STORE: Call for
directions

PHONE: 214-350-3370

FAX: 214-352-5886

MINIMUM ORDER: No

ISLA VIEQUES CONDIMENT CO.

P.O. Box 1496
Vieques, PR 00765

~~~~~~~~~~~~~~~~~~~~~~~

CREDIT CARDS: Yes

CALL FOR CATALOG

RETAIL STORE: Call for
directions

PHONE: 800-741-0848
809-741-0848

FAX: 809-741-2700

MINIMUM ORDER: No

*Linda
Eckhardt's
1995
Guide to
America's
Best Foods*

ACROSS THE BORDER

If you want your old-fashioned Texas chili, the kind that kept the prisoners from riotin' in the county jail, you get you some Jailhouse chili, blend and cook it up according to the box directions, and you'll be willing to stay in your own little prison called home.

Also available are Shotgun Shells, Texas' own hot-pickled okra, and Buckshot, otherwise known as jalapeno stuffed olives. They've made the chili seasoning in several varieties for the chilihead crowd: Frank's #201, #202, and #301. They've got your Desperado's Hot Chow Chow and Boogie Woogie B-B-Q sauce.

We like the Desert Surprise—I'll say—a cactus salsa and dip. Tastes great with fresh veggie dippers. We call this Texas fun food. Gives you something to talk about if the company is boring.

PARADISE FOUND AND BOTTLED

Diana and Jim Starke moved to Puerto Rico from New England and loved it so much they had to figure out a way to make a living. Seeing the number of peppers and mangos grown in that hot tropical climate, and loving the local foods, they began a cottage business from their mountain top home: "When we saw people shovelling mangos out of their yards and remembered stateside price tags of $1.99 apiece, we knew we were onto something." At first they had to do odd jobs to keep body and soul together, but pretty quickly their product line—put up in half-pint whiskey bottles—took off and now they're steaming.

You'll be steaming too once you taste their condiment line. They make several grades of hot sauce from hot to hellfire, and a variety of piquant steak sauces, chutneys, and marmalades—all based on Vieques native provender: peppers, mangos, bananas, papayas, honey, herbs, and citrus. They make good use of longleaf coriander and habaneros, those hotter than hell Scotch bonnet peppers.

We're addicted to their Mountain Herb Hot Pepper Sauce, a sweet spicy picante that's a great marinade for chicken breasts. We also love Pique Puertoriqueno, a vinegar-based whole pepper and herb sauce put up in a little whiskey bottle. It's great splashed onto rice and beans. No sissies need try to eat their Caribe Fire, a smooth satanic blend of mustard, papaya, garlic, and habaneros. It's hotter than the proverbial hell, but complex and seductive, with grassy overtones.

TEXAS CONDIMENTS

JARDINE'S TEXAS
FOODS

P.O. Box 160
Buda, TX 78610

CREDIT CARDS: Yes

CALL FOR CATALOG

RETAIL STORE: Call for
   directions

PHONE: 512-295-4600

FAX: 512-295-3020

MINIMUM ORDER: No

Dan Jardine (say Jar-deen) is a Texas good old boy who knows his picante. He began making and selling Texas-style condiments in 1979 and has expanded his near-to-Austin empire until now he has the most gorgeous site I've seen in ages. It's perfect for a picnic and buying trip you can take as a day trip just out of Austin. I went there for a chuckwagon breakfast with a bunch of people who'd gathered in Austin for the Texas Hill Country Wine and Food Festival. It was dazzling on an April morning.

Visit Dan's ranch in the spring time and see a blanket of bluebonnets and Indian paintbrush. The limestone ranch house sits in such a field and is home to his business and a great place to visit. Order from them or buy on the spot such Jardine specialties as Texas Caviar, a jalapeno-stuffed olive. He also sells a lip-smacking good 5-Star barbecue sauce, a picante sauce he calls Texacante, and a variety of chili mixes. His Shotgun Willie Texas Chili won a taste-off when compared to a dozen or so national brands of chili.

We particularly like his Texas Red Snapper and Texarita drink mixes. Put up in glass, fifth-of-whiskey bottles, these brightly-flavored drink mixes will turn a bottle of vodka into a hero.

If you're looking for authentic Texas flavors that reflect the Six flags heritage, look no further than Dan Jardine. He's bottled that strange brew of cowboy-Mexican-German-Southern tradition that is Texas Cuisine. It's the real thing.

Hot Stuff

MIGUEL'S STOWE AWAY

RR3 Box 2086
Waterbury, VT 05676

CREDIT CARDS: Yes

CALL FOR CATALOG

RETAIL STORE: Call for directions

PHONE: 802-244-7886

FAX: 802-244-7804

MINIMUM ORDER: No

MEXICO NORTH

How on earth did Mexican foods find their way to Vermont? What can we say? Michael Henzel fell in love with Mexico and took it home with him to snowy Vermont. He operates an inn and restaurant in the country between Stowe and Mt. Mansfield. He's learned that skiers love to down that salsa after a day on the snowy slopes.

Stop in this 1793 farmhouse in the Green mountains and you can eat everything from chile verde to tostados. Yes, for you cowards, they still cook chicken and steaks. But for those who want to take Mexican-Vermont home, send for Miguel's red chile sauce. It's a deep red, spicy, and not too hot sauce, best remembered when doused onto a brick of cream cheese then finished with a dab of Miguel's green chile salsa. Serve warm with Miguel's white or blue corn tortilla chips.

Miguel's also makes smoked jalapeno fajita sauce that's a splendid marinade for beef or chicken fajitas. Also available are several salsas. Their best tomato-based salsa was called by the *New York Times* a "preferred product, chunky and fresh-tasting, a good balance of spice and acid." How do they do that so far away from the border?

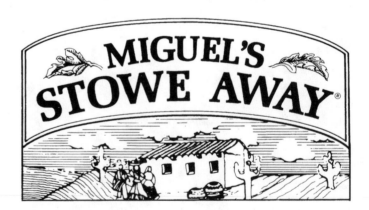

*Linda
Eckhardt's
1995
Guide to
America's
Best Foods*

182

AMAZING RED CHILE PRODUCTS

SANTA CRUZ CHILI & SPICE CO.

Box 177
Tumacacori, AZ 85640

The Santa Cruz valley is only a few miles north of Mexico into Arizona. Jesuits established a mission here in the 17th century. Visit today—it's about 50 miles south of Tucson—and you'll find a sleepy town that's a home for ranching, mining, and farming. Visit Gene Holland's Chili Center and you'll find an impressive array of chilis and chili products, along with a fine Western museum. There, you'll see McClellan tree saddles like the ones used by the American Army in the nineteenth century and invented by one of Holland's grandfathers. You can learn, first hand, just exactly what the ranchers contributed to American life. Even if you have to drive out of your way to get there, you should do it. This is the West. Period.

In 1942, Gene Holland perfected a method for grinding chiles into a paste that makes border cooking a breeze. The surprising thing about the chili paste is that it's not particularly hot. Bright orange in color, it's rich in the flavor of chiles grown in Arizona, with a sweet, astringent aroma and the texture of tomato paste. A spoonful will perk up many a recipe.

Gene and Judy England's daughter, Jean England Neubauer, now runs the business and dispenses recipes, salsas, chili pastes, and a fabulous chili powder with equal aplomb. After nearly fifty years in the business, the family has developed sources for rare and exotic chilies, herbs, and spices. Call Jean if you're looking for something rare and wonderful.

You can order chile paste by mail, as well as chili barbecue sauce, green salsa, hot picante sauce, and a wealth of spices and herbs. Their list of what's available changes. Call and ask what they've got in stock. As for me, I'm happy to find a sometime-source for *epazote,* the Mexican version of lamb's-quarter used in so many Mexican-style soups and stews.

CHECKS OR MONEY ORDERS ONLY

CALL FOR CATALOG

RETAIL STORE: **Call for directions**

PHONE: 602-398-2591

MINIMUM ORDER: **No**

Hot Stuff

PAT'S PIMIENTOS

P.O. Box 5
King City, CA 93930

CHECKS OR MONEY
ORDERS ONLY

CALL FOR CATALOG

PHONE: 408-385-5756

FAX: 408-385-4839

MINIMUM ORDER: 2 cases

PIMIENTO JAM

Pat Gill and her husband, Allen, farm in the sunny central valley of California. They grow and sell red, yellow, chocolate, and orange pimientos. You can buy them fresh from late September until the first frost.

But Pat's also figured out a way to bottle that California sunshine with a series of good pepper products. We're crazy for her pimiento jam, a bright red, piquant jam made with sugar, vinegar, salt, and butter. How could you go wrong? She also makes a pimiento relish that's dazzling red, and made with onion, sugar, vinegar, spices, and salt. No artificial preservatives or additives.

If you visit the farmer's market in Oakland during the harvest, you're likely to see Pat Gill there with her peppers. She's the Earth Mother of the market and known by everybody.

STONEWALL CHILI
PEPPER CO.

P.O. Box 241
Hwy 290 East
Stonewall, TX 78671

CREDIT CARDS: Yes

CALL FOR CATALOG

PHONE: 800-232-2995
210-644-2667

FAX: 210-644-2377

MINIMUM ORDER: Yes

CHILIS, CHILIS, CHILIS

Jeff Campbell figured out that the hot Texas hill country was ideal for growing his favorite chili peppers and became the first commercial producer of deadly hot habaneros before the trend-setters had even dreamed them up. Last year, riding the crest of the hot chili wave, Jeff put 100,000 pepper plants in the ground. Hotcha!

You can order Salsa del Diablo made from habaneros, tomatoes, onion, garlic, and cilantro in a not-to-kill-you, but just-to-warn-you hot sauce. There's half a dozen more hot sauces and one local product—a blending of good Stonewall peaches, sweet as a kiss, with red ripe jalapenos into a hot peachy preserve. It's good for the next time you cook a goat out in the backyard and are looking for the perfect accompaniment.

Here's your source for Texas Chili Pepper Christmas Lights, jalapeno lollipops, and hot habanero or jalapeno jellies. Best of all, Jeff will box up and send you FRESH chiles in season: Anaheim, poblano, cascabel, cayenne, caribe, hot cherries, piquin, jalapeno, habanero, serranos, tabasco, or Texas chili petins.

Linda
Eckhardt's
1995
Guide to
America's
Best Foods

184

TEXAS CHILI

OLD PETTY FARMS

P.O. Box 136112
Lake Worth, TX 76136

Gordon Pettey puts up chili fixins the way God intended for chili fixins to be put up. In a long, clear plastic sleeve, you get a whole head of garlic, 6 black chili pasilla peppers—dried, a little ziplock bag of killer red chili cayenne pepper flakes, a big bag of chili powder, a little doodad of masa, and another of cumin and oregano. In addition, Gordon puts in the pack his own personal recipe for Classic Texas Chili. And it makes six pounds. All you add is beef stew meat or venison to complete.

Besides making your basic bowl of red—without beans, please—Gordon suggests you might use his classic chili to do the following:

• Crumble cornbread in a bowl. Add some cooked pintos and top with chili. Dust with a little grated longhorn cheese.

• Ladle chili over scrambled eggs. Sprinkle with longhorn and serve with tortillas.

• Open up a pack of Fritos and ladle the chili on top.

• Make Aztec tamales by adding 2 teaspoons unsweetened cocoa to 2 cups chili. Serve over tamales. (See listing for Pedro's Tamales.)

Gordon Pettey also sells a gallon tin lunch bucket filled with cracked Texas pecans. Here's where you can find rare Ribbon Cane syrup in a glass pitcher. And he makes a Texas Sun Chili Kit, as well as selling toasted pecans and fruit in honey. He makes small batch jellies from wild texas fruits and herbed vinegars with flowers inside.

Maybe the oldest of the old-fashioned things this old restaurateur makes are country hams. They're as perfect as nature permits. Hand-processed the old Southern way, the hams are heavily smoked, aged for months, and do not have one drop of water added.

CHECKS OR MONEY ORDERS ONLY

CALL FOR CATALOG

PHONE: 214-601-4256

FAX: 817-738-5040

MINIMUM ORDER: No

Hot Stuff

CHUGWATER CHILI CO.

P.O. Box 92
210 First St.
Chugwater, WY 82210

~~~~~~~~~~~~~~~~~~~~~~~

CHECKS OR MONEY
ORDERS ONLY

CALL FOR CATALOG

PHONE: 307-422-3345

MINIMUM ORDER: No

WYOMING CHILI

In case you're wondering what Chugwater is, it's the name of a little prairie town way out on the Oregon trail that had a little pitiful creek running through it. Now it's ranching country and the home to the estimable Chugwater Chili Co.

Basically what we have here is a dried chili powder mix that looks like the stuff in the grocery store but doesn't taste like it. Mix this with your venison and your beans and what you get is chili with a fresh, pumped-up flavor that's just like what the boys had on the trail when they were driving the cattle way out west.

The chili mix comes in a cute little apothecary jar and will pep up even a pot of plain old beans so that you'll be whistling, "Get along little Dogie" before you're through eating it.

LA COUR DE FERME

1019 Delcambre Road
Breaux Bridge, LA
70517

~~~~~~~~~~~~~~~~~~~~~~~

CREDIT CARDS: Yes

CALL FOR CATALOG

RETAIL STORE: Call for
directions

PHONE: 800-467-3616
318-332-3613

FAX: 318-332-1467

MINIMUM ORDER: 2 jars

CAJUN POWER

Breaux Bridge, Louisiana is the heart of the coonass country and the Gauthier family is 100 percent. They make good Cajun foods using mama's Cajun recipes. Get Static's Barbecue Sauce. It's been slow-cooked for hours from onions, garlic, cayenne, and spices to give it a lovely caramel color and a taste that will improve barbecued beef, pork, or chicken. We also use it at the table and think it's a damn sight better than catsup.

Peewee's Cajun Cayenne Juice is spicy, savory, and hot as Cajun hell. Marinate seafood in it. Add zip to potatoes and vegetables. A shot of Peewee's makes a bowl of red beans and rice do the do-si-do.

T-Loui's Cajun Chow Chow is nothing but coarsely ground cayenne seasoned with onions, garlic, and Cajun spices. Put it in your gumbo. OOOOOeeeee. Pont Breaux Cajun Powder can be used in place of salt and pepper to give your meals a little Cajun zip. Andre's Rouge, a spiced cajun hot sauce, will take the top of your head off, but you won't mind.

*Linda
Eckhardt's
1995
Guide to
America's
Best Foods*

186

NOW YOU'RE COOKIN' CHINESE

If you ever wondered how to make fried ice cream, Pat Tung will teach you. She gives cooking lessons in suburban Rocky River, just outside of Cleveland, and she's taught thousands of Ohioans to cook and love Chinese foods.

Her specialty is a super batter mix that will guarantee light, nongreasy tempura. She also bottles and sells an authentic Szechuan-tasting sauce she calls Spicy Garlic sauce. Her Oriental marinade is heaven. She also makes a Brown sauce, a Sweet and Sour sauce, and sends out a cookbook so that you can have the benefit of her teacher's approach at home.

Pat Tung provides excellent products and instructions for those who want to learn Chinese cooking at home.

PAT TUNG'S INTERNATIONAL GOURMET DELIGHTS, INC.

P.O. Box 16868
Rocky River, OH 44116

CHECKS OR MONEY ORDERS ONLY

CALL FOR CATALOG

PHONE: 216-356-1987

MINIMUM ORDER: No

A CHICKEN IN EVERY POT—AN ETHIOPIAN CHICKEN, IF YOU PLEASE

Cathy Molla served in the Peace Corp in the Sixties and was assigned to Ethiopia. She loved the sights, smells, and sounds of the market. She came to adore the food and the ceremony around meals. At lunch, which might go on for three hours, the family sat around a table and a large, handwoven basket filled with steaming foods was placed in the middle. You tore off a piece of flat bread and scooped up the stew, using the bread as an edible spoon.

At the bottom of the basket an *injera* or flat bread, held a variety of *wots* or stews, spiced with a peppery mixture known as *berbere*. Now, Cathy has made it possible for you to cook and enjoy authentic Ethiopian dinners at home.

Buy Cathy's *Berbere* Hot or Extra Hot dry spices. Ask for a copy of her homemade cookbook, and you'll be on your way to Ethiopian cuisine. Learn to make *Ibe,* a homemade cheese similar to ricotta. Learn to make both vegetarian and chicken stews pepped up with *berbere*. Learn to make authentic *injera,* the flat bread. It's fun. It's easy. It's dinner with no knives and forks. We especially enjoyed our dinner of *Doro Wot,* a chicken stew. And we were glad we didn't have to pluck the chicken. Although, in Cathy's book, the instructions for making Ethiopian chicken stew begin when you're looking the bird in the eye. You can take it from there.

MIKAEL THEODROS ETHIOPIAN PRODUCTS

P.O. Box 12761
Tucson, AZ 85715

CHECKS OR MONEY ORDERS ONLY

CALL FOR CATALOG

PHONE: 602-885-7255 (No phone orders)

MINIMUM ORDER: No

Hot Stuff

**CINNABAR
SPECIALTY FOODS**

1134 West Haining St.
Prescott, AZ 86301

xxxxxxxxxxxxxx

CREDIT CARDS: **Yes**

CALL FOR CATALOG

PHONE: **800-824-4563
602-778-3587**

FAX: **602-778-4289**

MINIMUM ORDER: **No**

INDIAN CONDIMENTS

Neera Tandon, a native of India, moved to Arizona where she met food retailer Ted Schleicher. About eight years ago, the two teamed up to begin bottling Neera's Indian-style chutneys to sell in Ted's store. They called the products "Cinnabar," after Neera's catering business, and before long the clamor was so great they had to devote all their energies to the business of making and selling the Cinnabar line.

The Cinnabar kitchens use only the finest and freshest ingredients without any preservatives or fillers. The result is quite simply magic. Pear Cardamom Chutney is authentic, rich, sweet, and mysterious tasting. The Thai Seafood Marinade, that's made from tamarind, fish sauce, brown sugar, and red pepper is excellent. We used up our bottle of Spicy Tandoori Indian Grilling Paste in a week, smearing it on everything in sight.

Their list is dazzling. Chutneys including tomato, tomato-mint, mango, and peach in addition to the Pear Cardamom. Tomarmalade comes from colonial Virginia and is a heady mixture of tomatoes, oranges, zest, cinnamon, and clove. Also try Kashmiri marinade, Barbados Honey Pepper sauce, Asian Tamarind sauce, and Shahi Pilau—a mixture of basmati, cashews, raisins, almonds and spices that creates an "add-water only" side dish for any Indian-style dinner.

Cinnabar's products are four star. Praise is not enough. Order them.

*Linda
Eckhardt's
1995
Guide to
America's
Best Foods*

188

INDONESIAN SPICES

MRS. DeWILDT'S SPICES

Fox Gap Rd., R.D. 3
Bangor, PA. 18013

Spices, in antiquity, were used as currency. The Boot's family found them indispensable during World War II when the family became separated. Born and raised in the Dutch East Indies, Ann DeWildt Boots had just graduated high school in Australia when the rest of her family were imprisoned by the Japanese back home in the East Indies.

After the war, Ann and her husband John came to New York. Her mother, still in the East Indies, was prohibited by law from transferring money, but she could send spices. And so she did. The Boots began selling them and so began a business that has prospered for more than forty years. The mail order business is now operated by daughter Cathleen, who carries on a family tradition of teaching people the colonial foods of the Dutch East Indies.

Order Indonesian spices here: a fiery sambal, a chile paste, sweet soy sauce, krupuk, and various prepared foods are all available. Reflecting their Dutch heritage, the Boots also offer Dutch specialties including cheeses, chocolate, and cookbooks.

Ask for the Boots' instructions for making a traditional Indonesian *Rijsttafel,* or rice table. It makes for a splendid party.

CREDIT CARDS: Yes

CALL FOR CATALOG

PHONE: 215-588-0600

MINIMUM ORDER: $14

Hot Stuff

LE CORDON BLEU, INC.

404 Irvington, St.
Pleasantville, NY 10570

~~~~~~~~~~~~~~~~~

CREDIT CARDS: Yes

CALL FOR CATALOG

RETAIL STORE: Call for directions

PHONE: 800-457-2433
914-741-0606

FAX: 914-741-0869

MINIMUM ORDER: $25

FINEST FRENCH CONDIMENTS IMPORTED FOR CORDON BLEU

Famous for their French cooking schools, Le Cordon Bleu also supplies U.S. customers with imported fine foods, including exquisite preserves of rose petals and black figs, peach and raspberry preserves, tea jams, fine quality chocolates, and various French cookies including palets and galettes, which may be the best butter cookies on the planet.

If salad is your thing, order French olive oil, Bordeaux or Champagne vinegar, and Dijon or tarragon mustard. Also available are hazelnut oil, pear and sherry wine vinegars, classic whole grain mustards, raspberry mustard, and a variety of hard goods including cookbooks, videos, a chef's toque and apron, a tea towel, and a wine map.

If you want information about Cordon Bleu's cooking schools in France, England, Canada, or Japan, call the 800 number. They've got all the data.

In New York, stop in Trump Tower for a look at the Cordon Bleu Boutique. Everything they offer has been personally approved by the Cordon Bleu chefs at the school in France. With choices that range from mustards to jams to toques, it's all here. If you're travelling to Paris, stop in 8 rue Leon Delhomme, 75015 Paris. You can sign up for a one day demonstration class, sign the kids up for a Children's Class on a Wednesday afternoon, or attend a group workshop. Call the 800 number to make arrangements. And let's face it. If you go to France and don't take a classic cooking lesson, you may as well have stayed home.

PIGGIE PARK BARBECUE

Maurice Bessinger calls his business Piggie Park but that shouldn't fool you. He makes barbeque sauce that's number one with guess who? The American Heart Association. A rich mustard South Carolina-style barbecue sauce, it makes pork (the other white meat) into a divine barbecue.

When I was growing up, Pig Stand restaurants were as common as McDonald's are now. You could get a sandwich on a hamburger bun made of thin slices of barbecued pork, pale pink and tan meat with crisp mahogany edges, piled high on the bun then finished with a dab of sauce and some sweet relish. Buy Maurice Bessinger's sauce and a pork shoulder. Barbecue it out in the backyard and, my friends, you can still get a pig-style sandwich. No matter where you live.

This taste at Piggie Park is as old as Dixie and just about as mysterious. If you're in the south, anywhere in the south, make a detour to West Columbia and wheel into Piggie Park. It's got everything including the carhops. If you want to give your kids a sense of what it was like to grow up in the fifties, stop by Piggie Park. You can eat those pig sandwiches until you pop.

MAURICE'S GOURMET BARBEQUE

1600 Charleston Hwy
P.O. Box 6847
West Colombia, SC
29171

CREDIT CARDS: **Yes**

CALL FOR CATALOG

RETAIL STORE: **Call for directions**

PHONE: **800-628-7423**

FAX: **803-791-8707**

MINIMUM ORDER: **No**

TEXAS BARBECUE FIXINS'

Craig Conlee was working in his dad's barbecue joint in downtown Bryan. Seemed like the Texas A&M parents who came through just always wanted to know where they could buy some of that good barbecue sauce to take home.

And so a new mail order business began. Craig isn't the first of his family to feed people though. His grandmother Florence, known as Meme, was a famous cook in the county and even took care of the strays who wound up in the county jail. Her husband was the sheriff. He swore people would get "throwed in jail" just so's they could get a good meal.

Today, you can not only order terrific, authentic "sops," or cooking sauces, for Texas-style barbecue, you can also buy a bloody mary mix called "Lonesome Red" that's so good people have been known to splash it onto eggs for breakfast. Chili seasoning, black-eyed pea dip, salsas, and relishes make up the rest of these authentic Texas products. Our new favorite from Brazos Beef is the "Greengoes". Per-

BRAZOS BEEF EMPORIUM

700 South Bryan St.
Bryan, TX 77803-3928

CREDIT CARDS: **Yes**

CALL FOR CATALOG

RETAIL STORE: **Yes**

PHONE: **800-872-8737**
 409-775-1611

FAX: **409-775-1917**

MINIMUM ORDER: **Yes**

Hot Stuff

191

fectly sized small tomatillos, peeled, pickled, and put up like olives, they're meant for gringo martin-*eyes*. Some Texas ranch salsa in one bowl, some award-winning Texas ranch caviar in another. Some blue corn chips. It's cocktail time in Texas.

SOUTHWESTERN BARBECUE

God, I love America. Where else would you find an Italian chef, living in a Southern town, making Southwestern foods—and doing a good job of it. Nick Luciano does just that. He makes and bottles barbecue sauce—a deep, smoky, red thick sauce, a green chile pepper salad dressing that begins with a mayonnaise base, and a couple of interesting salsas. His hot salsa is tomato based, complex and not too hot. His avocado salsa has a fresh avocado flavor, but I warn you, you will have to get past how it looks. You know how avocados look when they've sat out too long? That's what this salsa looks like. He also makes and bottles fine, roasted pepper barbecue sauce, a tequila lime fajita marinade, and a nacho cheese mix.

Perhaps his best product is canned chile spice. He's blended chiles with other typical Mexican-style herbs and spices, and put them up in paste form in little cans. You only have to add meat, beans, and maybe some onions to get a fine pot of chili. By rendering the dry spices into paste form, you'll get the most intense, complex flavor and you'll get it quick. You can have the same flavor normally delivered in an all-day cooking session in just a fraction of the time.

GREAT BARBECUE SAUCE FROM OHIO

It is quite impossible to make decent barbecue sauce outside the state of Texas. Or at least that's what we always thought, until we tasted Mom's Barbecue Sauce from the state of Ohio. How can this be? Perhaps Mom came from the South.

Who knows? All we can say is that Wes Parsons had made his barbecue sauce at home for years, to lots of applause. When he entered it in a local Cleveland taste test, it came in third place out of twenty-three entrants. This sauce is hand-packed by Wes himself, and comes to you in a Kerr jar with flat and lid.

It's quite good. Wes' secret tastes like orange zest to me, but the basic sauce is tomato and vinegar-based, with chunks of tomato, flecks of black pepper, and an aroma so smoky it's mouthwatering. It begs for a chicken. We like it.

CHEF NICK'S LUCIANO FOODS

3709 Lamar #5
Memphis, TN 38118

CREDIT CARDS: Yes

CALL FOR CATALOG

PHONE: 800-653-6425

FAX: 901-367-1781

MINIMUM ORDER: $25

MOM'S BARBECUE SAUCE (BY PARC KITCHENS)

591 Treeside Drive
Stow, OH 44224

CHECKS OR MONEY ORDERS ONLY

CALL FOR CATALOG

PHONE: 216-929-7290

MINIMUM ORDER: No

BEST BARBECUE SAUCE

WICKER'S BARBECUE SAUCE
P.O. Box 126
Hornersville, MO 63855

A fellow named Peck Wicker, from this 200-resident hamlet in the bootheel of Missouri, invented this barbecue sauce for daubing on the pork he sold from his natural pit. Like others, he began bottling and selling it because of customer demand. I was leery of the stuff when it came in, because it looks like water with cayenne pepper floating in it. But this vinegar-based sauce with Peck Wicker's own combination of spices has proved to be a valuable addition to the larder. A chicken, marinated in this sauce for the day, then simply roasted in the oven, comes out golden, crisp, and about as satisfying as if I'd cranked up the barbecue.

Besides the good tangy taste that Wicker's sauce gives to chicken, shrimp, pork, or beef, the good news is that the whole 28-ounce bottle only has 70 calories and no fat at all. Weight Watchers calls this a free one. In fact, it's sold as a diet condiment. It's all natural, has only pure ingredients, and no chemicals or other preservatives. Besides the original, Wickers also offers Mesquite-flavored sauce, and a low-sodium version that has 75 percent less salt than the original.

Order a mixed six-pack and see what you like best. You can even get a tee-shirt or apron that says, "I'm on the sauce."

CREDIT CARDS: Yes

CALL FOR CATALOG

PHONE: 800-847-0032

FAX: 314-737-2113

MINIMUM ORDER:
 3 Bottles

JAMAICAN JERK

CARIBBEAN CREATIONS
P.O. Box 1073
Bethel, CT 06801

Talk about hot. Caribbean Jamaican Jerk marinade is hot. But not too hot. And when paired with Peanut Ginger sauce for the finished dish, it makes for brightly flavored barbecue in the style of the tropical islands.

Celia Miltz, lately of Connecticut, started this business after a love affair with the lush Caribbean. She says of this style cooking, "Jerk is a method of flavoring and preserving meat developed many generations ago by the native Arawak Indians." Miltz makes her own version of the marinade by combining locally purchased onions, soy, and vinegar with Jamaican Scotch bonnet (*habanero*) peppers. She cooks the stuff in a 150-gallon kettle and stirs it with a boat oar. Then she bottles it and takes it home, where she sells it out of her garage.

Celia Miltz says, "Mealtimes are important to families. And with my products, I feel that I can participate in them and touch people's lives in a pleasurable way." She's had snazzy labels designed and has expanded from the original jerk marinade to a couple of interesting products, a pineapple salsa we particularly recommend, and a pineapple mango vinaigrette that will make your salads do the limbo.

CREDIT CARDS: Yes

CALL FOR CATALOG

PHONE: 203-730-2710

FAX: 203-730-2712

MINIMUM ORDER: $10

193

**PETER LUGER
RESTAURANT**

185 Broadway
Brooklyn, NY 11211

CHECKS OR MONEY
ORDERS ONLY

CALL FOR CATALOG

RETAIL STORE: **Yes**

PHONE: **718-387-0500**

FAX: **718-387-3523**

MINIMUM ORDER: **No**

STEAK SAUCE SUPREME

A tradition in Brooklyn for over 100 years, this is a small, old-fashioned steak house that's worth a visit, just to see how old New Yorkers ate out. The room is half-timbered, narrow and dark, with beer steins and brass plates on the walls, an ancient wide-planked floor, and leaded glass windows on the front. Order a steak and it comes just as you asked. These people know their steaks.

And you want to talk about steak sauce? This is the best. Their own steak sauce is not only great on steak, but also served on slabs of red ripe tomatoes. You can't do without this. They only began bottling and selling the sauce after customers begged. We love this sauce on hamburgers. We love it on chicken. The taste is somewhere between cocktail sauce—it's spicy with horseradish, and traditional steak sauce—being a rich brown color. The sauce is fat-free. It tastes so good you won't mind.

*Linda
Eckhardt's
1995
Guide to
America's
Best Foods*

194

SOUTHWESTERN SAUCE

MAHAN'S SOUTHWEST GOURMET SAUCES, INC.

P.O. Box 26901
El Paso, TX 79926

Here's an American story for you. Joyce and Robert Mahan are bottling and selling a Southwestern Sauce that had its beginnings in the Pennsylvania Dutch country of Robert's mother. Mom cooked ribs dabbed with a tomato sauce, beginning in Pennsylvania, then continuing as she moved all over the world with her army officer husband, Blair. Robert grew up an army brat and says of his mom's cooking, "You had to doctor up the foods so they were halfway decent."

Seemed like everywhere they moved, the sauce took a turn, until, by the time she passed the recipe on to her son Robert and his sister Joyce, it was an entirely new creation. Robert served it first in a restaurant he operated in Madison, Wisconsin, in a dish he called "Mom's Ribs." Yankees raved.

After he moved home to El Paso to take care of his elderly parents, people began to say, "Robert, that sauce is so good you should bottle it and sell it." So he did. But not without the partnership of his mother and his sister. The three of them run the business.

Now, after the sauce has won numerous prizes including first place in a *Chile Pepper* magazine contest for Fiery Foods, Robert knows he's got a winner. Order some and Robert will tell you how to make the best damn ribs you ever ate. And watch for new products he plans to add to the line next year: an extra-hot sauce, a Green Fire sauce, and a Southwest salad dressing.

CHECKS OR MONEY ORDERS ONLY

CALL FOR CATALOG

PHONE: 800-743-6242
915-584-8598

FAX: 915-585-0037

MINIMUM ORDER: No

CHUTNEYS AND FRUIT SAUCES. PICKLED FRUITS AND VEGETABLES. RELISHES.

The pellet with the poison's in the vessel with pestle. The chalice from the palace has the brew that is true.

—MILDRED NATWICK to Danny Kaye in *The Court Jester*, 1956

MY OLD KENTUCKY HOME

LA PECHE
1147 Bradstown Road
Louisville, KY 40204

CREDIT CARDS: **Yes**

CALL FOR LIST OF
PRODUCTS

RETAIL STORE: **Yes**

PHONE: 502-451-0377

FAX: 502-458-7546

MINIMUM ORDER: **No**

One of Louisville's most successful restaurateurs, Kathy Cary's made bluegrass cuisine into an art that takes the best of Kentucky traditions then gives it a French twist. Her original take-out place, La Peche, and the newer Lilly's are so popular, and have received such critical acclaim, that Kathy's been asked to cook at the Beard House in New York.

She earned raves for her cheese grits served on pools of chutney, for her Shaker lemon pie, and for—of course—the de rigueur iced tea studded with fresh orange slices. If you can't get to Louisville to try some of Kathy's cooking, order up a bottle of her Kentucky Tavern sauce. A dark brown opaque sauce made from tomatoes, vinegar, corn syrup, onions, garlic, raisins, spices, orange zest, anchovies, tamarind, mangoes, walnuts, red peppers, brown sugar, Kentucky bourbon whiskey, and other minor ingredients, this stuff is magnificent. It's a natural condiment for beef and mixed with mayo makes a great hors d'oeuvre dip for crudites.

GORGEOUS GOOD FOODS

APPLE CIDER VINEGAR
BASIL·LEMON BALM·GARLIC·TARRAGON
25 OUNCES
GRAFTON GOODJAM • GRAFTON VERMONT 05146

GRAFTON GOODJAM COMPANY
Grafton, VT 05146

CHECKS OR MONEY
ORDERS ONLY

CALL FOR CATALOG

PHONE: 802-843-2276

FAX: 802-843-2589

MINIMUM ORDER: **No**

Hands-down winner in the packaging category, Grafton puts its products up so handsomely you wouldn't much care what they tasted like. Red peppers and herbs and garlic cloves drift in crystal clear vinegars that come in square Spanish glass bottles with corks and beeswax. The honey is packed in an adorable clay pot and tied with raffia. Hot, gingered, apricot chutney is mouthwatering in a French hex canning glass, and the melt-in-your-mouth puff pastry cookies known as Palmiers are packed in a tin. Each little buttery cookie is just two bites, but before you know it, you may have eaten several dozen of them, they're so good.

Mary Schoener, who dreamed up this company, loves to cook. The chutney is made in small batches from organic apricots, apples, carrots, onions, apple cider vinear, maple syrup, ginger, garlic, chilies, and no preservatives. It's a glorious apricot color and the fruit is all firm and not cooked to death. The flavor is tart, not too sweet, and just begs for a leg of lamb.

Mary's products sell by word of mouth. No wonder. You should buy one to eat and one to stare at. If you're in Manhattan, pick up Mary's good jams at Ecce Panis, Dean & Deluca, Bergdorf's or Bloomie's. And I'll tell you one thing. Give this for a house gift and you're sure to be invited back.

SOUTHERN JAMS AND PICKLES

BAINBRIDGE FESTIVE FOODS

P.O. Box 587 HWY 47
White Bluff, TN 37187

~~~~~~~~~~~~~~~~

CHECKS OR MONEY
ORDERS ONLY

CALL FOR CATALOG

PHONE: 800-545-9205
615-797-4546

MINIMUM ORDER: Yes

Tom Bainbridge, and Win and Sally Halliday are keeping alive an old Southern tradition with their pickles, jellies, and preserves. Crisp sweet pickles, hot and spicy sweets—lord, you'll swear you're back home at Mama's for Sunday dinner.

The pickles are thick, crunchy, and sweet. You can also get 'em hot with tabasco—a must for barbecues. I first ate Bainbridge products six years ago. The black walnut jelly was so good I still remember it. Just a jot on ice cream and it's dessert. Also recommended are apple pie jelly, cherry pie jelly, and lemon honey jelly. They make a long list. Call for a brochure. Don't forget to ask about the preserves: strawberry-rhubarb, or the figs and berries. Old-fashioned good.

IN A PICKLE

BILL'S DILLS

14575 Denton
Truckee, CA 96161

~~~~~~~~~~~~~~~~

CHECKS OR MONEY
ORDERS ONLY

CALL FOR CATALOG

PHONE: 800-995-PIKL
916-587-9341

MINIMUM ORDER: 1 Case

*Linda
Eckhardt's
1995
Guide to
America's
Best Foods*

Bill Griffis likes to fuss with food and when he worked as a chef, he was usually in the soup with the boss for spending too much time on the presentation. He solved that problem by changing jobs—to a part-time pickle maker and a part-time ski instructor.

Bill's Dills are made the old-fashioned way. Nobody since World War II has attempted this pricey, labor-intensive system. Griffis uses a "fresh pack", which means pickles are sealed in their own jar with spices to ferment. What you get is an old-fashioned soft pickle, like they used to offer in country store pickle barrels. Don't be alarmed by the soapy looking juice the pickles are floating in. The only reason you've never seen that before is because you're too young to remember pickle barrels. Neither, thank gawd, can I.

SEVEN SWEETS AND SEVEN SOURS

Seven sweets and seven *sahrs* (sours), that's what the old Pennsylvania Dutch farmers wanted on their dinner tables to make a meal complete. Apple butter, pickle relish, spiced peaches, and sweet pepper relish. Chowchow and corn relish. Sweet and sour dressing and tomato preserves. Peach butter and lemon butter. Chile steak sauce and sauerkraut. The folks at Wos Wit make it all, and all first class too, using top quality, fresh ingredients and old-fashioned methods.

The genuine farm recipes they make take up a full page of an order sheet: a half dozen fruit butters, a group of horseradishes, five kinds of old-fashioned bacon salad dressings, and dozens of relishes from Dutch Sweet to Beet and Horseradish. All so good we were eating them out of the jar.

Wos Wit is Pennsylvania Dutch for "What do you want" and that pretty well describes Paul Zukovich's attitude. If it's old-fashioned and farm-like, Paul puts it up. The chowchow is heaven. It's made from 10 vegetables: celery, cauliflower, green beans, corn, peppers, lima beans, yellow beans, tomatoes, onions, and carrots—all chopped and blended with a sweet and sour dressing. Farm families could make supper with a serving of chowchow and a heaping mound of fried potatoes. Come to think of it, so could we.

GROUSE HUNT FARMS INC.

RD 4, Box 408-A
Tamaqua, PA 18252

CHECKS OR MONEY ORDERS ONLY

CALL FOR CATALOG

RETAIL STORE: **Call for directions**

PHONE: 717-467-2850

FAX: 717-467-2850

MINIMUM ORDER: No

CONDIMENTS BEYOND BELIEF

Sherri Maurer is one of those miracle cooks. She can take the humblest ingredients and turn them into condiments that hum. It all began because Sherri can't stand waste. She used to make catsup from her leftover tomatoes. One year, she didn't have quite enough tomatoes but she did have some apples, so she put the two together, seasoned it, did some adjusting and changing, and pretty soon she had something so good her friends said it was *Beyond Catsup*. The name stuck. Like many of her fellow Vermonters, she decided to go into business. With help from the Vermont Department of Agriculture, she decided she'd need two tons of tomatoes the first

JASMINE AND BREAD

RR #2, Box 256
South Royalton, VT 05068

CREDIT CARDS: Yes

CALL FOR CATALOG

PHONE: 802-763-7115

MINIMUM ORDER: Yes

Hot Stuff

year. The farmers she called were flabbergasted. Yankee thrift made them more than a little wary. But that was then. This is now. Sherri Maurer made four tons worth the first year, and now she makes many times more than that and has a dazzling product line.

Sherri's Sweet Lightning practically makes me cry it's so good. A clear amber jelly flecked with horseradish, it's one of the best condiments I know to glaze a chicken. Or heck, I just eat it with a spoon out of the jar. It's that good.

She also makes a blow-the-lid-off mustard with horseradish she calls Beyond Mustard, and a salsa that's "Beyond Belief" as well. Plum Perfect is a good lamb and veal condiment, and her Beyond Marinara uses that old Mexican trick of mixing tomatoes and oranges to create a smooth, sophisticated sauce for pasta. Her condiments are, one and all, beyond compare.

NEW ENGLAND CONDIMENTS

In the Cranberry Corner of Cape Cod, Barbara Henry's begun making perky condiments using New England recipes and the provender of Massachusetts. Her Schnappy Peach Preserve is zipped up with ginger. Her Sweet Cranberry Relish calls for its own turkey. The Perky Pear Relish is bright and subtle with Indian overtones.

All Barbara's products are salt and preservative free. They come boldly bonneted and packed in wooden crates. An assortment might include two lemon pepper mustards, a tangy cranberry chutney or relish, some peach or pear preserves or relish.

She'll pack them in assortments of three, four, or six condiments each. Just ask. And she'll stick in a card if you so require.

HENRY C. ADAMS CORP.

P.O. Box 707
Mattapoisett, MA
02739

CREDIT CARDS: Yes

CALL FOR CATALOG

RETAIL STORE: Call for directions

PHONE: 800-248-8639
508-758-2726

FAX: 508-758-2726

MINIMUM ORDER: No

Linda Eckhardt's 1995 Guide to America's Best Foods

BOMBAY SAUCE, CHUTNEYS, AND CONSERVES

LA CASA ROSA

107 Third St.
P.O. Box 380
San Juan Bautista, CA
95045

CREDIT CARDS: Yes

CALL FOR CATALOGUE

RETAIL STORE: Call for
directions

PHONE: 408-623-4563

MINIMUM ORDER: No

A central California institution, La Casa Rosa is a restaurant in a classic California mission-style house that was originally built in 1858. Since 1935, La Casa Rosa has offered condiments for sale there and by mail order. These condiments are made in the restaurant kitchen from the surrounding California provender. Their justly famous Bombay Sauce is bright yellow, sweet and sour, a perfect complement to curry. They also offer 20 to 30 chutneys, spiced watermelon rind, preserves, salad dressings, and jellies—including a spectacular pomegranate. This is genuine old style California food. Highly recommended.

FINE DINING IN-HOUSE—OR AT YOUR HOUSE—COURTESY DORIS SIMPSON

MUIRHEAD

43 Highway 202
Ringoes, NJ 08551

CREDIT CARDS: Yes

CALL FOR CATALOG

RETAIL STORE: Yes

PHONE: 800-782-7803
908-782-7803

FAX: 908-782-7803

MINIMUM ORDER: No

D oris and Edward Simpson bought an 18th-century house in Hunterdon County, New Jersey, about 20 years ago, and turned a portion of it into a restaurant. Doris is an expert with sauces and condiments. In response to demand by her customers, she now sells the following fine products: compound butters made with her own fresh, garden-grown herbs, dill and horseradish salad dressings, horseradish mustard, a "creative" cooking sauce, pesto, sherry pepper, cranberry conserve, sweet and sour honey glaze, four-seeded mustard, apricot-jalapeno jelly, apple catsup, and a sweet and sour dressing.

The "creative" cooking sauce is particularly entrancing. A deep red, sweet onion and herb-seasoned sauce—a spoonful on top of oysters on the half shell is unforgettable. Doris sends cooking suggestions with all the condiments. Each is boldly seasoned and unforgettable.

If you're in the South Jersey area, don't miss an opportunity to eat with Doris and Edward. You'll have to elbow your way into the parking lot past all the Mercedes and Lincolns, but once inside, the sense of peace and tranquility will wash over you as you experience a fine dining experience. This was the first restaurant we took our granddaughter to when she was only three weeks old. Although Natalie didn't have much to say about the food, she slept peacefully and the Simpsons treated her like an angel. Which, of course, she is.

Hot Stuff

THE POSTILION

217 Madison St.
Waukesha, WI 53188

~~~~~~~~~~~~~~~

CREDIT CARDS: Yes

CALL FOR CATALOG

RETAIL STORE: Call for directions

PHONE: 800–760–0777

MINIMUM ORDER: No

MADAME KUONY'S COMPOTES

Forty years ago, Madame Kuony and her husband established a restaurant here in a Victorian homestead. Their customers adored the small-batch compotes, sauces, mincemeats, marinades, vinaigrettes, and hazelnut pralines they were served in the restaurant. After tiring of seeing customers on their knees, begging, the good madame began bottling the products to take home. Today, every bottle that leaves her kitchen is still made, labeled, and tied by hand. This is cooking at it's finest. I found Madame at a food show, where even the most jaded buyers from gourmet shops were eagerly crowded around her, tasting everything in sight and hanging on her every word.

Besides plum puddings, Yule Logs, basting sauces, marinades, and vinaigrettes that she carefully makes and sends, her great mounds of fruit compote in crystal compotiers are a feast for the eyes and nose as well as the taste buds. Order in pairs or a quartet. Madame suggests apricot-prune blended with tart fresh limes and rum for use in a flamed omelet. Apple-kirsch is made with whole almonds, spices, and limes. Also try cherry-pineapple laced with cognac over best quality ice cream. Pear-ginger, the most exotic, is flavored with angelica, Cointreau, and raisins and can be folded into crepes or served in thin slivers of baked ham.

FRUIT AND BERRY VINEGARS, MUSTARDS, MAYOS, OLIVES, OILS, AND SALAD DRESSINGS.

Oh champagne—I love it! It tastes like your foot's asleep.

—JOAN DAVIS in *George White's Scandals*, 1945

CHRISTOPHER LAYNE FOODS

8399 Mayfield Road
Chesterland, OH 44026

~~~~~~~~~~~~~~~

CHECKS OR MONEY
ORDERS ONLY

CALL FOR CATALOG

PHONE: 216-729-9233

FAX: 216-729-9322

MINIMUM ORDER: 3 cases

LUXURY VINEGARS WITH CITRUS, HERBS, AND PEPPERS

If you're looking for a gift that's got something to eat and something to keep, look no further. Betty Anne Irwin's puts up vinegars with herbs, citrus, and peppers in imported Italian bottles and jars that offer such a good-looking product, you may not want to use them.

Talk about labor intensive. Betty Anne and her partners, Leo Rota and Sandy Plemen, hand-fill these gorgeous glass bottles. One vinegar came with strands of lemon zest strung in the bottle like a golden rope. Another had peppers. In another, nasturtiums were suspended in a lovely pink vinegar. They also make vinegars infused with berries.

You can choose from a total of nine vinegars. Also available is a jar of Lagniappe, a sweet bell pepper sauce that's sweet, smoky, and quite complex in flavor.

KIMBERLEY WINE VINEGAR WORKS

290 Pierce St.
Daly City, CA 94015

~~~~~~~~~~~~~~~

CHECKS OR MONEY
ORDERS ONLY

CALL FOR CATALOG

PHONE: 415-755-0306

FAX: 415-755-0240

MINIMUM ORDER: No

VARIETAL WINE VINEGARS

Some of America's best varietal wine vinegars are produced by Larry and Ruth Robinson, who began making vinegars in their old San Francisco Victorian. They moved a couple of times, but they still use the traditional French Orleans method of converting wine to vinegar in oak barrels. This method, filtering out bacteria rather than chemically changing or pasteurizing the wine, takes six months. The delicate esters that flavor wines are carried over to the vinegars when they're prepared in this way—without heat and without chemicals. Commercial chemical processes, in contrast, take only three days.

But the Robinsons are the patient sort. Just this year, Larry retired after teaching high school for 34 years—25 years in the same classroom at Lowell High. He's used to doing things the slow and patient way.

Their most exciting new product is a champagne vinegar. It's light, it's lovely. It's available in limited supply. Order it today.

KIMBERLEY
CALIFORNIA
Wine
Vinegar
GARLIC
CABERNET

RASPBERRY VINEGAR AND VINAIGRETTE

KENDALL-BROWN FOODS

86 Forrest Lane
San Rafael, CA 94903

CHECKS OR MONEY
ORDERS ONLY

CALL FOR CATALOG

RETAIL STORE: **Call for directions**

PHONE: 800-851-7203
415-499-1621

FAX: 415-472-5737

MINIMUM ORDER: **No**

Barbara Kendall begins with fresh raspberries and the highest quality California white wine vinegar. Her raspberry vinegar stands up in taste tests with imported vinegars and is more fruity and fresh than any of the competitors. I guard my bottle of Barbara's vinegar jealously and won't let anybody else use it. It's so intensely raspberry that just a little used to deglaze the pan will create a perfect sauce over a just-sautéed fish fillet. Barbara's vinegar is used in the best restaurant kitchens in San Francisco.

Barbara has also developed three splendid salad dressings: raspberry-walnut, dill-horseradish and a blackberry vinaigrette. The blackberry vinaigrette will turn roasted root vegetables into an aria.

HERB VINEGARS

FIREFLY FOODS CO.

P.O. Box 82096
Portland, OR 97282

CHECKS OR MONEY
ORDERS ONLY

CALL FOR CATALOG

PHONE: 503-654-6225

FAX: 503-659-2650

MINIMUM ORDER: **Yes**

Karen Williams' Portland backyard exploded in herbs one year and she, being a banker, couldn't stand to see them going to waste. So she began making herb vinegars. Soon, she had more vinegars than she could use so she began selling them locally. Unlike a lot of other homemade herb vinegars, hers were, and are, crystal clear. She cold steeps the herbs, then uses a filtration process to eliminate cloudiness. She eventually expanded beyond her backyard and began making use of Oregon's fruit bounty as well.

Besides expected flavors like basil, garlic, and dill, she also makes splendid vinegar from Oregon's marionberry. Her pear vinegar is especially recommended. We like it better for Asian stir-fries than rice vinegar. It's sweet and fruity.

After a lot of people kept asking her what to do with flavored vinegars, she finally invented a series of dried dressing mixes: cheesy-basil, cranberry-poppyseed, kitchen pepper, and a salt-free dressing. You can make a fat-free dressing easily, using a seasoned vinegar and one of these mixes.

Still using Oregon's bounty, Karen makes a fine blueberry chutney with hazelnuts, apples, and spices. Her cherry chutney, made with raisins and ginger, begs for a Thanksgiving turkey.

Hot Stuff

PRAIRIE HERB COMPANY

P.O. Box 3375
Gillette, WY 82717

CREDIT CARDS: Yes

CALL FOR CATALOG

RETAIL STORE: Call for directions

**PHONE: 800-447-2837
307-686-7531**

FAX: 307-682-4396

MINIMUM ORDER: No

ORGANIC PRAIRIE HERBS

Cec Stanford lives way out on a ranch near Gillete. She grows a big garden and puts up a bunch of stuff every short summer that Wyoming permits. She's always grown organic and she loves herbs, so it stands to reason she'd put the two together.

Out on the ranch she makes pure organic, unfiltered herb vinegars, beginning with fine quality white wine vinegars. She stuffs the bottles with herbs, and fills, corks, labels, and seals every bottle by hand. The vinegar bottles are dipped in cinnamon wax.

Of course the herb vinegars are fat-free, sugar-free, salt-free and preservative-free. They may be a little cloudy when you get them. That's because they're also unfiltered. Let them stand. They'll clear up in a day or so.

The garlic dill has a good punched-up flavor, but our favorite is the basil garlic. Must be that Wyoming soil and those short summers. Everything figures it better come up quick before the snows start blowing. The flavors are intense.

Bertman's Honey Mustard Sauce

makes 2 cups

1 cup honey
½ cup Bertman's Ballpark mustard
¼ cup water
2 tablespoons soy sauce
1 teaspoon cornstarch

Heat the mixture over medium heat until boiling, whisking frequently. Transfer to a clean jar and store in the refrigerator, covered, for up to a month.

Use this sauce with ham, shrimp, or chicken, as well as ribs, tofu or just about anything you can think of that needs to be pepped up.

BALL PARK MUSTARD

Pat Bertman Mazoh, known in Cleveland as *the mustard lady*, still makes her daddy's mustard just the way he made it for hot dogs at Cleveland Indians' games during the thirties. Bertman's Ballpark mustard is rich and brown, smooth and bitter, spicy and just the right counterpart to a steamed soft bun and an aromatic, sweet, greasy hot dog.

Although Bertman's mustard looks like Dijon, it has a distinctive eastern European flavor: more assertive, more bitter, more memorable than any subtle French mustard. Joe Bertman was from Poland and seasoned his mustard to suit himself. It's just the thing to accompany strong flavored meats. My assistant mixes equal parts Bertman's mustard with mayo and ketchup for the quintessential college-kid's baked potato topper. I like to dip raw veggies in it. My husband's made a terrific barbecue cooking sauce with it.

But the truth is that mustard is bleacher food, meant to be smeared onto hot dogs and dripped on your shirt. Bertman's is THE original ballpark mustard. Period.

JOE BERTMAN FOODS

P.O. Box 6562
Cleveland, OH
44101-1562

CHECKS OR MONEY ORDERS ONLY

CALL FOR CATALOG

RETAIL STORE: **Call for directions**

PHONE: **216-431-4460**

FAX: **216-561-6656**

MINIMUM ORDER: **No**

Hot Stuff

Boetje's Pork Chops with Honey-Mustard Sauce

makes 4 servings

Preheat outdoor charcoal or gas grill for at least 5 minutes. Grill the chops until browned on both sides with good grill marks showing. Meanwhile, mix together mustard, honey, rosemary, salt, and pepper and brush on the chops once you've turned them once. Continue cooking and turning until the glaze is browned. Watch closely and don't let it burn.

4 thin sliced pork chops

2 tablespoons Boetje's Dutch mustard

2 tablespoons honey

¼ teaspoon dried rosemary, crushed

½ teaspoon salt

¼ teaspoon freshly milled black pepper

BOETJE FOODS
2736 12th Street
Rock Island, IL 61201

CREDIT CARDS: Yes

CALL FOR CATALOG

PHONE: 309-788-4352

FAX: 309-788-4365

MINIMUM ORDER: Yes

BLOW-THE-LID-OFF MUSTARD

A 103-year-old Dutch recipe is the basis for Boetje's (boat-jeez) mustard. Originally, the owners sold it door-to-door—for a nickel—provided you had your own container. Today, Will Kropp will send it to you through the mail. It's still made from #1 brown mustard seed, imported from Canada, blended with vinegar, salt, and other "secret" spices. The mustard is aged in wood vats, then stone-ground so that all the flavors are released.

What you get is a clean tasting, smooth, brown, hot-as-hell mustard that begs for a decent bratwurst or a sack of pretzels. It's a product that says Chicago, and would be a good and cheap gift for those who love that part of the world. Buy it by the case.

Linda Eckhardt's 1995 Guide to America's Best Foods

GERMAN MUSTARD AND CREAMY HORSERADISH

If you like German-style condiments, Susan Barhyte's making some you'll like. Her stone-ground sweet mustard is perfect for sausages and cheeses and makes a hot dog sing.

She also makes a creamy horseradish, extra-hot and thick, that's good with roast beef. We love the dill mustard, creamy and delicate. Served on salmon, it turns that dish into a delicacy.

Pub mustard, made with dark beer, is a sandwich mustard, good with ham and good with pastrami. The jalapeno gold is double whammy hot and a nice addition to Tex-Mex sandwiches.

SWEET, HOT, SMOOTH-AS-SILK MUSTARD SAUCE

We had an English houseguest who practically fell into one mustard pot when we were testing the various mustards that came into the house. The one he couldn't stay out of comes from Ohio and is made by a pair of school teachers who just plain like to cook from scratch.

Michael and Kathy Walker and their three kids went skiing in Vermont one winter vacation and fell in love with a mustard dipping sauce they had there. Once they got home, Dad got to puttering around in the kitchen and before you knew it, had invented a sweet hot mustard sauce they all agreed was better than the one at the slopes.

The mustard begins with imported mustard seeds, then is blended with sweet clover honey, apple cider vinegar, and vegetable oil. There are no artificial ingredients or preservatives. Not that you'd need any. If the folks at your house are like the ones around here, this mustard will disappear in a hurry.

The mustard was a big hit in the stores. Then they decided to branch out with Kathy's mom's Thanksgiving cranberry Celebration sauce. This sauce is really quite lovely. It's a deep purple color and complex, with hidden herbs as well as the zing of cranberry. It will certainly be on our Thanksgiving table this year.

HAUS BARHYTE MUSTARDS
875 Prospect Place South
Salem, OR 97302

CHECKS OR MONEY ORDERS ONLY

CALL FOR ORDER SHEET

PHONE: 800-227-4983

FAX: 503-399-1537

MINIMUM ORDER: No

HUNTINGTON FARMS
P.O. Box 20581
Shaker Heights, OH 44120

CHECKS OR MONEY ORDERS ONLY

CALL FOR CATALOG

PHONE: 216-321-5948

MINIMUM ORDER: Yes

Hot Stuff

209

SAN FRANCISCO MUSTARD CO.

4049 Petaluma Blvd.
North
Petaluma, CA 94952

CHECKS OR MONEY
ORDERS ONLY

CALL FOR CATALOG

PHONE: 707-769-0866

FAX: 707-769-0270

MINIMUM ORDER: No

NAPA VALLEY MUSTARD

P.O. Box 125
Oakville, CA 94562

CHECKS OR MONEY
ORDERS ONLY

CALL FOR CATALOG

PHONE: 800-288-1089
707-944-8330

FAX: 707-944-9325

MINIMUM ORDER: No

*Linda
Eckhardt's
1995
Guide to
America's
Best Foods*

MUSTARDS

Robert Dickinson makes mustard in very small batches. An old-world recipe combined with fresh California ingredients makes for mustard to remember—in three flavors yet. His original traditional whole seed mustard is a favorite around here. We call it California Caviar and spread it on crostini for hors d'oeuvres. This mustard is scented with garlic, onion, paprika, and other natural spices. But not to be missed are his hot garlic and hot honey mustards. Robert uses only the best mustard seeds: *Brassica alba*, a large yellow seed, and *Brassica junicea*, a smaller, spicier variety. The mustard seeds are blended with California white wine vinegar, honey, and pure spring water. No salt, no sugar, and no artificial colors, flavors or preservatives. The original whole seeded mustard is crunchy, brown, and begs for a ham sandwich. The hot honey and garlic mustards are smooth, pungent, and dense with flavor. Ask Robert to send you a gift pack of all three flavors. For a modest price, you'll have an outstanding gift.

MUSTARD—OH, MUSTARD

The smart money says Indian food will be the next big craze in this country. And Ruthie Rydbom is ready. She's recently added to her excellent mustard line, a mustard oil that is called for in many Indian recipes. The oil is a canola oil infused with a special selection of mustards. It's clear yellow-colored and will add zip to sauteed shrimp, chicken, or pork stir fries.

This company opened in 1982 with three entrepreneurial women, Ruthie Rydbom, Ann Grace, and a partner recently replaced by Michael Moone. They began making a fine California Hot Sweet mustard that is still the cornerstone of their business. Other flavored mustards they developed include Green Chili and Garlic, a Country Catsup, a Dijon-style herbs-of-the-valley mustard, and a special Orange-Ginger mustard.

Now, ten years later, they're still known for good quality, healthy products, and help to cooks who need advice about using their products. I love to deglaze the pan after sautéeing chicken breasts with any one of their mustards. It turns a simple chicken sauté into a symphony.

Napa Valley Mustard Thai Noodle Salad

Sauté garlic and ginger with 1 tablespoon oil in a 12-inch skillet. Toss in noodles and drizzle on additional oil and soy sauce. Transfer to a large bowl and mix with peppers, cucumbers, and herbs, and dress with lemon juice and vinegar. Sprinkle with carrots and peanuts. Serve to two people.

1 clove garlic, minced

1 quarter-sized piece fresh ginger, minced

4 tablespoons spiced Napa Valley Mustard Oil, divided

12 oz. fresh thin Chinese noodles, boiled briefly, then rinsed and drained

1 tablespoon soy sauce

½ cup diced red bell pepper

½ cup diced cucumber

1 tablespoon each: basil, parsley, cilantro, and mint

1 tablespoon lemon juice

1 tablespoon rice vinegar

topping: long strips of carrot cut with lemon zester and chopped toasted peanuts

**NORMAN-BISHOP
CALIFORNIA
MUSTARDS AND
SAUCES**

1655 Newport Ave.
San Jose, CA 95125

CHECKS OR MONEY
ORDERS ONLY

CALL FOR CATALOG

PHONE: 408-292-1089

FAX: 408-295-0333

MINIMUM ORDER: 3 jars

**STRAWBERRY
CREEK COLLECTION**

100 Ericson Court
Suite 125
Arcata, CA 95521

CHECKS OR MONEY
ORDERS ONLY

CALL FOR CATALOG

PHONE: 707-822-9128

MINIMUM ORDER: No

*Linda
Eckhardt's
1995
Guide to
America's
Best Foods*

MAYO AND MUSTARD

Carrol Norman makes mustards, mayos, and sauces that are piquant and distinctive. And every single one is low calorie with no preservatives. Carrol's Dill Garlic mustard makes a wonderful sauce for salmon, and her California Raspberry will admirably deglaze a pan in which you have cooked a chicken breast.

Tonight, we mixed the well-balanced Raspberry mustard with extra virgin olive oil for a vinaigrette that made our mesclun exceptional. It also makes a great spread for sandwiches in place of mayo, if you're trying to cut back on the fat grams.

She's made a smoky sweet mustard just right for ham sandwiches, and a garlic mayo that's good to dip coldboiled shrimp in.

We fell in love with her Original Mexican sauce. A red hot spicy sauce, it's a good chip dipper, and made our Mexican breakfast when we stirred it into scrambled eggs then folded them into a hot corn tortilla. Caramba.

FANCY MAYONNAISE

Arcata, California, deep in the Redwoods on the far north coast of the Pacific, is developing quite a reputation for fine specialty food production. Stephanie Tejada is doing her part by making fancy mayonnaise. Her fresh garlic mayo, white and innocent-looking, is a joy to behold and will wake up any sandwich. Even better is Fiesta mayo that's spiked with jalapenos and red pepper flakes. We particularly adore that—a jot on top of grilled fish is fantastic.

These mayos are better than butter on sandwich breads or garlic bread. Mix them with anchovies and it's instant Caesar Salad.

Stephanie makes the mayos with a mixture of canola and olive oil, whole eggs, vinegar, lemon juice, and fresh garlic and herbs. Terrific.

SPECIALTY OLIVES AND OILS FROM CALIFORNIA

FUSANO CALIFORNIA VALLEY SPECIALTY OLIVE COMPANY

P.O. Box 11576
Piedmont, CA 94611

CREDIT CARDS: Yes

CALL FOR CATALOG

PHONE: 800-916-5483
510-530-3516

FAX: 510-531-1083

MINIMUM ORDER: Yes

Through Ellis Island to San Francisco in 1909, came Papa-Non Cristo Fusano, homesick as hell and trying to recreate his beloved Italy as quickly as possible. He planted an olive orchard and with Nana raised eleven children on the results.

From the beginning he cold-pressed extra virgin olive oil and sold "San Fernando Valley brand" olives in a variety of cures. Now, third generation-Rosemarie Fusano carries on delivering traditional Italian and other Mediterranean olive products.

Her extra virgin olive oil is a lovely light green, aromatic but not overpowering, a medium weight, and a nice fragrant choice for light vinaigrettes. A little goes a long way.

I swear, you'd pick these products out of a line up because Rosemarie's developed such good-looking labels. A kind of art nouveau self-portrait, in front of a spreading apron of olive trees, the picture well represents the products. Choose from Sicilian style olives, or kosher, or Greek, or garlic-stuffed, or jalapeno-stuffed, or cantina, or kalamatas, or onion-stuffed or—our favorite—the California Deli Mix. The mix includes pepperocini, pitted green and black olives, garlic, sliced red peppers blended with Italian spices, a pinch of salt, and white wine vinaigrette. Besides it's obvious use for antipasti, we find it makes a mean addition to a California martini. I only did this because Rosemarie said, "Let your culinary imagination run wild." Buon Appetito.

Hot Stuff

213

SIMPSON & VAIL, INC.

38 Clinton St., Box 309
Pleasantville, NY 10570

CREDIT CARDS: **Yes**

CALL FOR CATALOG

RETAIN STORE: **Call for directions**

PHONE: **800-282-8327**
914-747-1336

FAX: **914-741-6942**

MINIMUM ORDER: **No**

CRESPI OLIVE OIL

I went to a focused taste test for olive oils this spring at the Fancy Foods show in San Francisco. Needless to say, they featured only the best—about 50 of the best oils were tasted. Now the problem with some of the rarest imported oils, is that they're hard to get if you're outside a major metropolitan area. Enter Simpson & Vail, a purveyor of fine food products, both domestic and imported.

Order Crespi olive oil and pestos from S&V. It's the best. They also offer a wide variety of other well-known and not so well-known culinary treasures, including Dundee marmalades, and teas and coffees from around the world. All sorts of teapots and accessories, including cozies, are here. They offer a formidable list of bean products, including some terrific heirloom beans: rattlesnake beans, rice beans, scarlet runners, snow caps, Steuben Yellow Eyes, Tongues of Fire, and Jacob's Cattle among others.

Also available are Indian foods, chutneys, sauces, pastes; polentas, and Tahitian vanilla. The list is long and luscious. Call and ask for a catalog.

SANTA BARBARA OLIVE CO.

P.O. Box 1570
Santa Ynez, CA 93460

CREDIT CARDS: **Yes**

CALL FOR CATALOG

RETAIL STORE: **Call for directions**

PHONE: **800-624-4896**
805-688-9917

FAX: **805-686-1659**

MINIMUM ORDER: **No**

CALIFORNIA OLIVES EVERY WHICH WAY FROM SUNDAY

For two generations, the Makela family has grown olives in this central coastal valley of California. In 1983, son Craig began pressing the best into extra-virgin olive oil. To my mind, it's one of the best money can buy. Cold-pressed, a lovely green-gold color, clear as a crystal, it's fruity but not overbearing.

Besides oils, the Makelas also sell premium olives in a variety of packs, including jalapeno-stuffed olives and perfect vermouth-soaked martini olives, stuffed and spiced. The Makelas claim every bottle is handpicked, handpacked, and all natural. One of their good new products is chunky olive salsa. A mixture of green and black olives with fresh tomatoes, herbs, and spices, you can get it medium or hot. It will make your mouth water. It also makes a great spread for crostini.

The Makelas recently added salad dressings: Garlic Galore, Ravishing Raspberry, Basil Bravado, Cucumber, Caesar, and Chunky Olive. We especially like the Chunky Olive. It's a creamy blend of olives, olive paste, and extra virgin olive expertly seasoned with herbs. Yum.

Tapenade

Place olives in the food processor fitted with the steel blade. Pulse to coarsely chop. Add anchovies, capers, and garlic. With the machine running, pour the oil through the feed tube and process until you have a coarse puree (about 10 seconds). Season to taste with freshly milled black pepper and store in a clean covered jar in the refrigerator. Let it steep two to three days before using. Spread it on toast, or use it to spice up hard boiled eggs, raw veggies, or pasta.

1 cup black olives
½ cup green olives
8 anchovy fillets
2 tablespoons capers
3 garlic cloves, peeled
½ cup extra-virgin olive oil
freshly milled black pepper to taste

OLIVE SPREAD

Talk about your fusion cooking. When Jackie Pometta decided to take salsa to Italy, this is the product she came up with. It's a dense olive spread made with sweet red peppers, olive oil, wine vinegar, a mixture of olives, and definitely Italian spices. They serve it in their deli as a spread atop crostini. We used it on a homemade pizza and once on a boboli. Terrific.

They also make a garlic version that's made of the same sweet red peppers, black and green olives with olive oil, wine vinegar, Italian spices, and a great jolt of garlic.

Hot Sicilian is the same thing, but with enough red pepper flakes to give it some punch.

Use these salsas on sourdough rolls or as a dip for raw veggies. Stir them into pasta salads. It's dinner in an instant.

You can pick up Pometta's Italian salsas at their deli in the heart of the Napa Valley if you're out doing a wine tour. Located in Oakville, this deli has outdoor seating, is a full service deli in the California Italian-style, which translates into great bread, a good selection of meats and cheeses, and big smiles for all their customers.

POMETTA'S ITALIAN SALSA

P.O. Box 351
Oakville, CA 94562

CHECKS OR MONEY ORDERS ONLY

CALL FOR CATALOG

RETAIL STORE: **Call for directions**

PHONE: 707-944-8523
707-944-1550

FAX: 707-944-9534

MINIMUM ORDER: **No**

Hot Stuff

215

**NICK SCIABICA &
SONS**

P.O. Box 1246
Modesto, CA 95353

~~~~~~~~~~~~~~

CREDIT CARDS: **Yes**

CALL FOR CATALOG

RETAIL STORE: **Call for
directions**

PHONE: **800-551-9612
209-577-5067**

FAX: **209-524-5367**

MINIMUM ORDER: **No**

VARIETAL OLIVE OILS

Dan Sciabica now heads a family venture that's been in place for four generations. Growing olives and producing oil using the time-honored methods practiced by his Sicilian grandfather, Dan makes a splendid extra-virgin olive oil from pesticide-free fruit carefully picked from the tree, *not* off the ground. Dan's mother, Gemma, is in charge of quality control. Here's how that works.

In Gemma's kitchen, around the stove and spilling off the countertops, are bottles and bottles of different pressings of olive oil from dark green to light gold. When Gemma gets one to test, she opens it, rubs some on the back of her hand, sniffs it, and holds it up to the light. Then she tastes it. If the oil is cloudy, off-tasting, rough to the touch, or a dozen other subtle cues that only Gemma understands, it's rejected and won't get either the Sciabica or Marsala brand name label.

Buy a Sciabica olive oil that comes from a particular variety of tree: Mission, Mission Organic Green, or Manzanillo Variety Organic Green. The Mission is the more common variety used for oils, but the Manzanillo is rare—fruity, light, and delicious oils result. I find I can use about half as much Manzanillo oil as I do more common oils. It's that brightly-flavored.

**THE HAWAIIAN
MACADAMIA NUT
OIL COMPANY**

P.O. Box 685
Waialua, HI 96791

~~~~~~~~~~~~~~

CREDIT CARDS: **Yes**

CALL FOR CATALOG

PHONE: **800-367-6010
808-637-5620**

FAX: **808-637-6194**

MINIMUM ORDER: **2 items**

GOOD COOKING OIL

In Hawaii they use macadamia nuts for everything. It only stands to reason that somebody would decide to sell just the oil of the nut. It's nutritious, it has a high flash point, and it's great for salad dressings. Just imagine a vinaigrette with the hint of that nutty, sweet macadamia in it. That's what you get. It keeps up to a year in the cupboard and is useful in many ways.

PROVENCE IN A BOTTLE

PROVENCE
2001 Sul Ross St.
Houston, TX 77098

CREDIT CARDS: **Yes**

CALL FOR CATALOG

PHONE: **713-522-0205**

FAX: **713-526-2456**

MINIMUM ORDER: 3
Bottles

What happens when a chef and a graphic designer team up? You get salad dressings that taste fabulous and are put up in bottles beautiful enough to give away. The formulas, developed by German Chef Klaus Huebner, were then run through the Texas A&M lab to produce a product that would be shelf-stable. The resulting dressings are highly flavored, low in fats and cholesterol—nutritional data on the label—and aromatic. Graphic artist Steve Collier worked his magic with the pen and came up with labels so delightful, I'm tempted to soak them off and paste them up on my walls. Each salad dressing flavor gets a different, delicious-looking label, reminiscent of Toulouse-Lautrec's prints.

We adore the sherry dressing with it's dense brown texture and the label that looks like a Toulouse-Lautrec woman visiting the South of France. The bright yellow *Avignon*, is a creamy dressing redolent with the aroma of curry. The country mustard begins with—of course—Dijon, and is a hearty, full-bodied dressing.

All of these products just cry out for Mesclun. Toss some prepared greens with one of these dressings and for me, it's lunch. They taste better than most bottled dressings.

EXQUISITE SALAD DRESSINGS FROM FRESH FRUIT AND WINE

CUISINE PEREL
P.O. Box 1064
Tiburon, CA 94920

CHECKS OR MONEY
ORDERS ONLY

CALL FOR CATALOG

PHONE: **415-456-4406**

MINIMUM ORDER: **No**

Leonardo and Silvia Perel are two of the most innovative cooks I know. Coming to Northern California from Argentina less than ten years ago, they bring classic cooking techniques and Latin American influences to the bounty of West Coast cuisine. Their salad dressings, free of artificial preservatives and made with the fresh fruits and wines they find locally, are just simply too good. The lemon Chardonnay has won "Best of Show" in national contests where the competition is fierce. Their Champagne mustard dressing is my personal favorite. Both dressings are smooth, creamy, pungent, and perfectly balanced, and can lift salad greens to new heights.

The Perels are constantly coming up with new products. Lately they've added mustards, blended with fine California wines: chardonnay, sauterne, chenin blanc, and champagne. Their new Zinfandel orange mustard is everything you could ask for: sweet, hot, smoky, oaky. Their chutneys are original as well: grape apricot, grape peach,

Hot Stuff

and a piquant grape. Their Zinfandel tomato sauce makes pasta a banquet. Particularly interesting are the new oils. Christmas tree green basil and garlic grapeseed oil are splendid tossed with fresh pasta.

Finish off dinner with Perel's Coffee-Chocolate Fudge sauce over Haagen Dazs vanilla ice cream. Don't blame us for the satisfied glaze that comes over you.

NARSAI'S SPECIALTY FOODS

350 Berkely Park Blvd
Kensington, CA 94707

CHECKS OR MONEY ORDERS ONLY

CALL FOR CATALOG

RETAIL STORE: Call for directions

PHONE: 510-527-7900

FAX: 510-527-6633

MINIMUM ORDER: Yes

NARSAI DAVID'S CONDIMENTS

Narsai sells the dressings and mustards that make his northern California restaurant famous. You can take home Citronnade, a delicate, lemony dressing with Dijon mustard and coarse black pepper. In the restaurant, they toss it with salad greens, bunches of fresh herbs, and cheeses and fruits on a plate. Narsai also makes pure stone-ground mustards, flavored with white wine. These include tarragon, green peppercorn, or sweet old-fashioned, made with brown sugar—the German way. He also makes a fine feta cheese salad dressing made with olive oil, lemon, mint and garlic, as well as a basil dressing vinaigrette that brings alive just-blanched vegetables.

Just today, for lunch, we made a Narsai burger by adding a teaspoon of his Assyrian marinade to good ground beef before grilling it outside. Yum.

When you call, don't forget that Narsai made his reputation with dessert toppings he calls Decadence. With good reason. Order Chocolate Caramel Decadence, or Chocolate Raspberry Decadence, along with the original Chocolate Decadence. Each is smooth, rich, dark, and divine atop a bowl of vanilla Haagen Dazs.

Chutney Dip

Stir together a half cup each of mayo and yogurt with a cup of chutney. Add curry powder to taste and ¼ cup finely chopped cucumber. Cover and refrigerate a half hour or so. Serve with *crudites* and crackers.

CALIFORNIA SUNSHINE IN A BOTTLE

CALIFORNIA SOLEIL VINEYARDS

P.O. Box 3150
Yountville, CA 94599

CHECKS OR MONEY
ORDERS ONLY

CALL FOR CATALOG

PHONE: 800-225-8463
       707-944-8585

FAX: 707-224-7989

MINIMUM ORDER: No

CALIFORNIA SOLEIL VINEYARDS

NAPA VALLEY

CHARDONNAY

Vinaigrette

DRESSING FOR SALADS

12 OZ . 336G

Harriet and Ray Mayeri have done the inevitable. They've created a line of products that begin with California wines. I mean there's just so much of it—Somebody had to use it in other products. And their products are as good as the wines they start with.

Harriet has invented some splendid vinaigrettes. None contain added sugar or salt. They're low in fat and have no cholesterol, but the best news of all is that the taste is lovely. The cabernet is robust, with the taste of fresh smashed garlic, the pinot noir is a lovely sweet-sour scented vinaigrette, and the chardonnay is a light mustard-garlic that's just the ticket for delicate butter lettuce.

In addition, Harriet's made wine grape preserves that beg for a croissant, wine syrups for Belgian waffles, and chutneys in several wine flavors that are—one and all—subtle, mysterious, and impossible to stop eating. Apple chardonnay, cranberry cabernet, plum pinot noir, and pear riesling make the perfect glazes for poultry, lamb, fish, or to accompany curries.

RISING SUN FARMS

5126 South Pacific
Highway
Phoenix, OR 97535

CREDIT CARDS: Yes

CALL FOR CATALOG

RETAIL STORE: Yes

PHONE: 800-888-0795
503-535-8331

FAX: 503-535-8350

MINIMUM ORDER: No

ORGANIC HERBS AND HERB PRODUCTS

When I first met Elizabeth and Richard Fujas they were living in a Yurt, a circular tent, in the Colestine Valley with an apron of herbs and vegetables spreading out in front of their dwelling. It was a kind of post-60's paradise. They had run-off pure water from snow to grow their certified organic herbs and veggies. They sold their provender from the back of a truck at farmers' markets. But, like a fine crop, their business grew.

Today, the Fujas's have a list of organic products as long as your arm. Perhaps their most successful is a *torta* Elizabeth invented that's a blend of cream cheese and butter, interlaced with her own home-made pesto and sun-dried tomatoes. People who eat it fall to their knees. In fact, it was named Best-of-Show at a Fancy Food show a couple of years back. And rightly so.

In addition to the Pesto Dried Tomato Torta, they make a variety of fine fresh pestos, and dried tomatoes in oil and in cello packs. They also have invented some exceptional vinaigrettes and marinades. All are made with their own certified organic herbs, blended with canola and olive oils and rice vinegar. Elizabeth has exquisite taste. You'll like every one of these. From Garlic Lovers' vinaigrette, to a classic Tarragon Dijon Mustard vinaigrette, these dressings are to die for.

She also slurries local honey with interesting flavors: fresh orange and spice, mint, almonds and spice, ginger and lemon, garlic-rosemary-sage, lemon thyme, or a pure Oregon honey.

Additionally, she sells two good mustards. Razzberry, made ruby-red with local raspberries, and lemon thyme, made zesty with their own herb and lemon zest.

These products are first-rate. I cannot recommend them highly enough.

*Linda
Eckhardt's
1995
Guide to
America's
Best Foods*

220

MASTERPIECE IN A MOMENT

TO MARKET TO MARKET
4880 Ireland Lane
West Linn, OR 97068

Kathy Parson has a way with words and a way with dry spices. She mixes up a variety of dry spices and gives you a recipe so that you can indeed make a masterpiece in a moment. Her products make cooking easy and they all taste great.

Charlie's Choice is one of the best seasonings I've ever tried for tuna fish. When I mixed it with some custom-packed tuna from Lazio, the results were stupendous. We also adore Thrill of a Dill, which she's been making for years. It's a dry dill blend that you mix with sour cream and mayo for a fantastic dipper for fresh veggies.

It's About Thyme is a dry blend that makes a herb butter for poultry, a cheese spread, or a cheese ball. She's got recipes right on the package. If you can read, you can cook. Popeye's Passion, mixed with sour cream and mayo, makes that great spinach dip that people put into a round loaf of sourdough bread. It's delicious.

Other tasty products include Ginger and Spice with Curry is Nice, Shrimply Delicious, Jack and the Bean Dip, hot-as-hell Cravin' Creole, the Paragon of Tarragon, and the original Sweet'n Sauce Mix-up Mustard. Ask Kathy to make up a special gift basket. That's her real strength. And don't forget to order her little cookbook. It will make your dinners sing.

CHECKS OR MONEY ORDERS ONLY

CALL FOR CATALOG

PHONE: 503-659-9192

FAX: 503-655-3390

MINIMUM ORDER: No

Hot Stuff

THE CONFECTIONERY

All the sweet goodies: ice cream, custom-made chocolate gifts, truffles, nuts, hand-dipped chocolates, dessert sauces and ice cream toppings, old-fashioned hard candies, toffees, taffies, caramels. Newfangled candy bars. Even chocolate in a jar. Real Pennsylvania pretzels, popcorn balls. Other good stuff.

On a desert island, I would want a whopper of a bittersweet chocolate bar with almonds—with the added property of being able to grow back any piece that was bitten off.

—ISAAC ASIMOV when asked what he'd wish for should he be stranded on a desert island

ALL THE SWEET GOODIES: ICE CREAM, CUSTOM-MADE CHOCOLATE GIFTS, TRUFFELS, NUTS, HAND-DIPPED CHOCOLATES, DESSERT SAUCES AND ICE CREAM TOPPINGS, OLD-FASHIONED HARD CANDIES, TOFFEES, TAFFIES, CARAMELS. NEWFANGLED CANDY BARS. EVEN CHOCOLATE IN A JAR.

I call him the boy with the ice-cream face.

—EMILE MEYER about Tony Curtis in *Sweet Smell of Success*, 1957

ICE CREAM IN THE MAIL

OUT OF A FLOWER
703 McKinney, Ste. 202
Dallas, TX 75202

CREDIT CARDS: Yes

CALL FOR CATALOG

PHONE: 214-754-0324

MINIMUM ORDER: 6 pints

You think I'm kidding, right? Ice cream in the mail? No way! Maybe not, but you can get ice cream by overnight delivery from Federal Express. And when it comes, packed in dry ice, it's rock hard and impossible to sink a spoon into until you've put it in your home freezer a couple of hours.

And what fabulous ice cream it is. Cream, milk, eggs, and sugar made into a custard then infused with natural organic fruit and herb flavors. Michel Bernard Platz and Jose Sanabria, who began with an organic herb farm, started out by making their fantastic ice creams, granitas, and sorbets scented with their own herb combinations for local Dallas upscale restaurants.

I ran into them at the Texas Hill Country Food and Wine Festival. People were standing ten deep around their booth to get a taste. No wonder. Try a watermelon-colored ice cream made with rose geranium for starters. Or how about pumpkin with roasted pumpkin seed. Or peach and champagne with mint. Or maybe fresh ginger and red port wine. Or a blend of golden raisins and champagne. Or frozen chocolate truffles infused with raspberry liqueurs. Or try a strawberry and vodka ice.

Michel and Jose make 35 flavors in all. I like to serve walnut sized balls of three flavors in a dessert dish with a sprig of mint for a garnish. It's so good you can hardly bring yourself to swallow. But make sure you're home the morning this is delivered—it won't wait!

The Confectionery

PANDORA'S
CONFECTIONS,

c/o Promises Kept
512 Second St., 2nd Fl.
San Francisco, CA
94107

CREDIT CARDS: Yes

CALL FOR CATALOG

RETAIL STORE: Call for
directions

PHONE: 415-974-5292

FAX: 415-974-5296

MINIMUM ORDER: No

CHOCOLATE MIRACLES

Alice Medrich, of the late great Cocolat, performed a great service by acting as teacher to a lucky few budding chocolatiers. Two of the happy heirs to Alice's extensive gifts in the making of fine chocolates are Trudy Kranz and Lisa Olswing who've opened their own chocolate-making business.

Trudy and Lisa are chocolatiers par excellence. They makes incredible chocolate fantasies. Hollow chocolate containers filled with chocolate surprises and every one wrapped in colorful gold foil: champagne bottles, baseball gloves, and dinosaurs. Giant chocolate Easter Eggs filled with more little chocolate Easter eggs. Chocolate Valentine heart boxes filled with little chocolate valentines. Jack O'Lanterns filled with little chocolate pumpkins. Santas in a chocolate box, and a chocolate Sun Box that's filled with the stars and the moon. You name it. And they use—as Alice so wisely taught them—the finest European milk and dark chocolates. They're limited only by their imagination.

This year their featured mail order item is a giant hollow Dinosaur Egg wrapped in bright orange foil and nestled in a cottage nest made from one of the gorgeous Slate Creek Cottage boxes with line drawings of dinosaurs. The box is wrapped in green string and comes complete with crayolas so the kids can color the dinosaurs to suit. And, as if that weren't surprise enough, when the child bites through the egg, lo and behold, what's inside but 20 baby chocolate dinos. This is a true treasure for kids of all ages.

If you're in San Francisco, stop in Fillamento, a confectionary at the corner of Sacramento and Fillmore, and ask for their latest Pandora's confections. If you're there around Easter, you'll find dazzling bunnies and eggs. Christmas? Santas of every persuasion. The Sun Box is summer. Fillamento's a wonderful stop for chocoholics. Enjoy.

Linda
Eckhardt's
1995
Guide to
America's
Best Foods

226

IMPORTED SWISS TRUFFLES

TEUSCHER CHOCOLATES
9548 Brighton Way
Beverly Hills, CA 90210

CREDIT CARDS: **Yes**

CALL FOR CATALOG

RETAIL STORE: **Yes**

PHONE: 310-276-2973

FAX: 310-276-5691

MINIMUM ORDER: **No**

Good things come in small packages and nowhere is that more true than when you order a box of truffles from Teuscher, just off Rodeo Drive in Beverly Hills. You'll get precious morsels that have been flown in from Switzerland.

Their most famous truffle is the Champagne truffle, milk chocolate outside enrobing a center of dark rich chocolate and at the very heart of the truffle, a splash of Dom Perignon creme. The truffle is dusted with confectioners' sugar.

Eleven other buttery flavors are available. Ask for the Extra Butter truffle. Your vessels may slam shut. You won't care. Order milk chocolate, bittersweet, or white chocolate truffles with almond, orange, toffee, buttercrunch, and other special centers.

The packaging from Teuscher is half the fun. Handmade Swiss boxes of the season are always available. How about a bouquet of crepe and silk flowers filled with truffles. Or would you like a smiling frog prince, or a winged lady bug? Or a wide-eyed owl, or a mouse, or a cat, or a lion, or a songbird. A clown for your birthday, a Santa for the season. Teuscher playfully packages their treasures in a treasure box for you to keep.

They also sell staggeringly good butter cookies in vanilla, amaretto, or Basler-Leckerlis from Basel. These latter cookies are iced and scented with ginger. Serve with eggnog at Christmas. You'll have a Merry Christmas indeed.

ANN ARBOR'S BEST TRUFFLES

MINERVA STREET CHOCOLATES
1053 Olivia
Ann Arbor, MI 48104

CREDIT CARDS: **Yes**

CALL FOR CATALOG

PHONE: 313-996-4090

MINIMUM ORDER: **$30.50**

Judy Weinblatt, who has been making and selling truffles for nearly ten years, got a nice boost for her business when she gained an unexpected admirer. David Letterman invited her on the show. While she taught Letterman how to make truffles, he lobbed them into the audience. What a hoot.

Her truffles are as good as European ones. Plus, she's given them her own American touch. Tender, intense, chocolate morsels that she's hand-dipped, they are fresher, finer, creamier, and more perfumed than any you can get from most import places. She fills her truffles with flavored cream, butter and egg yolk mixtures that have no added sugar. The flavors include vanilla bean, praline, rum

The Confectionery

brandy, orange, mocha, and dark chocolate. The one I like best is rolled in crushed pistachios over an intensely bitter chocolate shell and a solid white chocolate ganache studded with more pistachios. Can you believe it? Too good.

ANDRE'S CONFISERIE SUISSE

5018 Main St.
Kansas City, MO 64112

CREDIT CARDS: Yes

CALL FOR CATALOG

RETAIL STORE: Yes

PHONE: 800-892-1234
816-561-3440

FAX: 816-561-2922

MINIMUM ORDER: No

CREDIT CARDS: Yes

EUROPE MEETS AMERICA IN KANSAS CITY FOR TRUFFLES

The next time Calvin Trillin flies home to Kansas City for dinner, I can tell him where to go for dessert after barbecue. Andre Bollier may not be a native, but he's brought Swiss confections to plain old Kansas and made it, dare we say, more Continental.

These are among the best domestic truffles and chocolates you can find, plus, Andre's will ship year round. Small, dense, enrobed in light or dark chocolate couvertour or rolled in best quality cocoa. Also dramatic are the chocolate wine bottles. Molded, then filled with chocolate enrobed roasted California almonds, this is possibly better than the wine you were thinking of buying for Aunt Velma's birthday.

Especially recommended are the chocolate mint leaves. A perfect after dinner mint, they're European-style, top quality, bittersweet chocolate, perfectly balanced by mint. A new favorite is the Engadiner Nut Torte. Alternating layers of light and dark chocolate, each wedge is fantastically rich with pecans, cream, butter, honey, and sugar, then baked in a crust and dipped in chocolate. Serve these wedges to company and you can forget about making dinner. A thimble of port, a cup of espresso. It's all you need for impromptu entertaining.

OLD-FASHIONED BOXED CHOCOLATES

CRAND'S CANDY CASTLE

Rt. 5, Box 3023
Enfield, CT 06082

Robert Crand doesn't claim to make truffles. He just says they make "the best in homestyle candies." Out of what home, I'd like to ask? When I opened up this box of assorted chocolates, the perfume of chocolate, raspberry, and nuts wafted up even before I had the inner box open. No home candymaker that I know can even come close.

Like so many other master chocolatiers, the Crands learned their craft from their father and still operate the business that he began. And keep the same hours: 9 to 9, seven days a week. Oh, that Yankee work ethic. For the natives, a visit to the candy castle, which looks like your standard New England saltbox house with candy-striped awnings over the lower windows and big letters announcing the name, is a ritual for Christmas shopping.

The Crands make candy using old recipes and old techniques. They do not use assembly line machines, artificial flavors, or preservatives. Emma Rousseau has been hand-dipping chocolates for more than 50 years and can artistically drip a distinguishing letter in chocolate on each candy—"r" for raspberry, "p" for pineapple. Ever try to do that? Forget about it. Their prices are so low, I hate to let on. But if you want to know what the original "Sweetheart" box of chocolates was supposed to be like, this is it.

CALL FOR CATALOG

RETAIL STORE: Yes

PHONE: 203-623-5515

MINIMUM ORDER: No

OLD-FASHIONED SWEETHEART CANDIES

CUMMINGS STUDIO CHOCOLATES

679 E. 900 South
Salt Lake City, UT
84105

The boxes of candies you see in drugstores and discount shopping malls look good but usually taste ghastly. Order from old-fashioned Cummings and you get honest-to-god chocolates that taste so good your eyes will glaze over.

Packed in gold foil boxes, they offer a variety of good old-fashioned chocolates that are fresh, fresh, fresh. Choose from nut-filled creme fondants, an assortment that includes nut fondants, cremes, caramels, and covered nuts in dark or milk chocolate. Order truffles that combine rare Tehuantepec chocolate with whipped cream—an international award winning truffle. Or try Slowpokes, a caramel on a bed of pecans and coated with chocolate.

Then there are fruit and nuts dipped in chocolate. And double-

CREDIT CARDS: Yes

CALL FOR CATALOG

RETAIL STORE: Yes

PHONE: 800-537-3957
801-328-4858

FAX: 801-328-4801

MINIMUM ORDER: No

dipped mint, marzipan, English toffee, nut brittles, glazed salted nuts, pecan logs, Mint Delights, molded Santas, Bunnies, golfbags, roses and other chocolates all formed and wrapped in colored foils.

The quality here is second to none.

NEW AGE DESIGNER CANDY BARS AND BUTTERCREAM ICE CREAM TOPPINGS

GRAND FINALE
200 Hillcrest Road
Berkeley, CA 94705

CREDIT CARDS: Yes

CALL FOR CATALOG

PHONE: 800-748-6271
510-655-8414

FAX: 510-655-3509

MINIMUM ORDER: No

Barbara Holzrichter makes the best buttercream confections I know of. Working from the basement of her house and using a Willy Wonka candy machine invented and built by her physicist husband, she's created some dynamite desserts.

Beginning with buttercream caramels in three flavors (*New York* magazine called them the sweet shock of astonishment—the ultimate caramel), Barbara also makes heavenly ice cream sauces that will turn you into a faithful sundae worshipper. But perhaps more to the point, Barbara has reinvented the wheel. She's making candy bars that give new meaning to the term.

Finale Bars are what a Baby Ruth ought to be but isn't. In four flavors, choose dark chocolate pecan, milk chocolate almond, dark chocolate almond, or milk chocolate pecan. Each and every one starts out with satiny caramel, then Barbara adds nuts and enrobes the whole thing in first quality chocolate. Delicious.

For those who just want a bite, she also makes the same assortment of flavors in Petit Finales, which are brightly wrapped, bite-sized bars. Bet you can't eat just one.

The trademark dessert sauces—as good as it gets—come in these flavors: buttercream caramel, triple chocolate fudge, bourbon pecan, grand marnier chocolate, and Bailey's Irish Cream.

TRUFFLES AND GREAT CANDY BARS

FRAN'S CHOCOLATES

2805 East Madison
Seattle, WA 98112-4020

After eating only one of Fran's candy bars, you'll never be content with mass-produced chocolates again. Just now, I had a "Coconut Gold", which must be what they were shooting for when they made Almond Joys. But let me tell you, Fran's candies are the real joy.

The Coconut Gold Bar is dark chocolate over a filling of white chocolate and whole roasted almonds. She also makes a Park Bar that's Belgian milk chocolate over soft caramel and peanuts. Divine. Buy them by the box.

Besides deluxe candy bars, Fran makes European creams and truffles that are small, dense, and as complicated as love. Every single candy has been hand-dipped in liquid chocolate then finished with a swirl of chocolate dripped off the index finger of the chocolate maker. Irresistible. Fran Bigelow learned her craft beginning at the California Culinary Academy then apprenticed in Europe. Her standards are the highest. She buys best quality Belgian chocolate then creates fillings using liqueurs, fruits, and nuts. The end result is as good as it gets.

For ice cream lovers, Fran bottles caramel and chocolate sauces. Try to keep from eating the sauce right out of the jar. If you're in Seattle, don't fail to stop in Fran's shop. Bill Rice of the *Chicago Tribune* says it's one of the best candy shops in the country. There, you can also purchase fresh tortes, cakes, cookies, and assorted other chocolate divinities. The intoxicating aroma of chocolate is worth the visit.

CREDIT CARDS: **Yes**

CALL FOR CATALOG

RETAIL STORE: **Call for directions**

PHONE: **800-422-3726 (out of Washington) 206-322-0233**

FAX: **206-322-0452**

MINIMUM ORDER: **No**

The Confectionery

MY SISTER'S CARAMELS

1884 Bret Harte St.
Palo Alto, CA 94303

CHECKS OR MONEY
ORDERS ONLY

CALL FOR CATALOG

PHONE: 800-735-2915

MINIMUM ORDER: $15

BEST CARAMELS ON THE PLANET EARTH OR ANY OTHER

Hilary Donahue says her caramels are the closest to homemade you've ever tasted. Well, Hilary, I don't know anybody who can make caramels like this at home. This recipe of her sister's is soft, pure, translucent, butter-colored caramel made from pure whipping cream, double A butter, and good California sugar. That's all. But, if you ever taste these, you will never forget them. Of all the taffies I tasted, these were my favorites. When I went to New York to appear on the "Today Show," I stuffed my pockets with My Sister's Caramels and handed them out all around. I did resist claiming they were my own sister's, but I did adopt Hilary as an honorary sister.

Hilary first made them for sale from her home kitchen, but this is one of those stories where the orders quickly jumped out from under her, so she now has them made professionally in a candy kitchen but still in small batches. She makes heavenly chocolate caramels. Among the flavors you can order are praline cream made with dark brown sugar and pecans, pumpkin pie, chocolate candied orange, and vanilla mallo. The flavors rotate with the season and may include raspberry cream, coffee, chocolate-praline, and peanut butter.

They do a big Chanukah business as well as being a favorite for Christmas and birthdays.

GWETZLI FOODS

P.O. Box 20298
Oakland, CA 94620

CREDIT CARDS: Yes

CALL FOR CATALOG

PHONE: 510-655-5621

FAX: 415-836-4367

MINIMUM ORDER: No

LITTLE GOODIES

Barbara Hack started making chocolate goodies in San Francisco in 1975. Then she moved to Zurich, where she perfected her art and came to know intimately the finer details about chocolate. She's been making *Gwetzli*, little goodies ever since.

And, as painters who get inspired paint a new picture, when cooks get inspired they invent a new recipe. When Barbara went to Hawaii to get married, she was taken with the Kona coffee and the luscious macadamia nuts. Before long, she'd invented a new candy that's become her signature.

Gwetzli Macadamia Toffees combine the best of the East and the West. Fine European chocolate enrobes dense buttery toffee that's chock full of macadamia nuts. She makes the toffees two ways: dark chocolate with coffee-flavored toffee and macadamia nuts, and milk chocolate with simple macadamia nut toffee. Can we say which is better? Impossible. They're both sublime. Order two tins. One of each. Then you can bite down on the little heavenly squares and make your own decision.

WEDDING TOFFEES

Berta London made her famous candies to celebrate her own wedding. Later, she made them for Christmas gifts and people said, you should sell these, and so she has.

I'm certainly glad because these homestyle English toffees are irresistible. Dark, bittersweet chocolate over hazelnut English toffee, they're rich with butter, sweet and heavenly. They come in several other luscious flavors: white chocolate with macadamia nut crunch, Original English toffee, milk chocolate with peanuts, and all packed in silver foil cake boxes that are almost too glorious to open. But not quite.

THE ENGLISH TOFFEE

During the summers when I used to visit my Aunt Jamie in Grand Junction, the talk around town was of the coming riches from uranium. But the undiscovered treasure was made by another Jamee, and that was toffee, rolled in chocolate and almonds, a toffee of such quality that one *New York Times* reporter said, "Honestly, I suggest you skip this paragraph because if you read on, and if you order, you'll be hooked." If you have ever had traditional English toffee rolled in almonds and chocolate, you'll know this is it. Perfect, buttery rich, with California almonds and fine quality chocolate. This little candy store in the fair-sized desert town has made a worldwide reputation from this single product. Available in one-, two-, three-, and five-pound boxes.

Don't order just one pound, or you may be calling the airlines for reservations to Grand Junction. It's that habit-forming.

HOMEMADE WITH LOVE

MRS. LONDON'S CONFECTIONS
P.O. Box 529
Lexington, MA 02173

CHECKS OR MONEY ORDERS ONLY

CALL FOR CATALOG

RETAIL STORE: **Call for directions**

PHONE: 617-862-7151
508-371-3074

FAX: 508-371-0396

MINIMUM ORDER: **No**

ENSTROM CANDIES
200 South Seventh St.
Box 1088
Grand Junction, CO
81502

CREDIT CARDS: **Yes**

CALL FOR CATALOG

RETAIL STORE: **Call for directions**

PHONE: 800-367-8766
303-242-1655

FAX: 303-245-7727

MINIMUM ORDER: **No**

BUCKLEY'S FANCY
FOODS

P.O. Box 14119
Baton Rouge, LA 70898

~~~~~~~~~~~~~~~~~

CREDIT CARDS: Yes

CALL FOR CATALOG

PHONE: 800-445-3957

FAX: 504-642-0146

MINIMUM ORDER: No

FANCY TOFFEES

B utter, sugar, almonds, and a little margarine, all cooked together to just the light crack stage, then poured out thin and cut into 1-inch squares. These thick, rich, buttery, golden squares of hard toffee come to you in a two-pound tin and I swear you'll want to hide it from the rest of the family so you can eat it all yourself.

Spurgeon Buckley first made it to raise money for his Newton, Mississippi church bazaar. After somebody shipped a can of it to Atlanta, Buckley got his first mail order. He soon moved his candymaking venture to a greenhouse in his backyard. For a long time he used a Rube Goldberg-type candy machine that he designed and built to fill his own needs, making candy only during the fall for Christmas mail orders. But now his daughter Beverly has taken over, moved the venture to her hometown, Baton Rouge, and sells year-round. Since I'm now addicted to the stuff, I'm grateful. You will be too once you taste it.

FENTON AND LEE

P.O. Box 3244
135 East 13th Ave.
  across from US Bank
Eugene, OR 97403

~~~~~~~~~~~~~~~~~

CHECKS OR MONEY
  ORDERS ONLY

CALL FOR CATALOG

RETAIL STORE: Call for
  directions

PHONE: 503-343-7629

FAX: 503-343-6385

MINIMUM ORDER: No

*Linda
Eckhardt's
1995
Guide to
America's
Best Foods*

CHOCOLATES NAMED FOR TWO FINE SONS

T he crunch of coffee beans, the bite of bitter chocolate. Put them together into a tablet and you'll have the dark as sin, delightful espresso Crunch candies that the Fancy Food show voted the Best Confection for 1992. The trouble with getting them is that you won't want to stop eating them. However, their real use is as a faux dessert after you've had a great big meal and don't want anything more than an exclamation point to finish.

This is only one in a line of chocolates made in a little chocolate shop in Eugene, Oregon so popular they're widely sold wholesale to some fancy Eastern establishments, who subsequently slap their own name on the product and wish they could claim them.

Janele Smith started this chocolate shop in 1982 after moving with her husband to Eugene. She could quickly see Eugene had enough nut and berry businesses to choke a horse, but chocolate they weren't overwhelmed with.

Now, Eugene's many runners try to make Fenton and Lee one of their rest stops. Fenton and Lee are, by the way, Janele's 24- and 19-

year-old sons, who have managed to get themselves clear across to the East Coast for college, on the proceeds from the shop.

Janele will make a custom chocolate to satisfy your wildest desires. The day I spoke with her she was making a 20-lb. Grand Marnier Slug for Eugene's Annual Slug Fest. The Slug Queen will get this glorious confection for a prize. For those of you who don't know what a slug is, don't ask.

Fenton and Lee's chocolates are pure—preservative and chemical free. All the flavorings are natural. Choose from boxed assortments, a fudge collection, a tin of buttercrunch stacks, hazelnut buttercrunch, or perhaps your own designer tie—made from pure solid chocolate and hand-decorated with polka dots or paisley. You can order a champagne bottle made of chocolate with a secret gift inside, or a chocolate moo cow, or a truffle-sniffer pig. All available with just one phone call—any time from October through May.

SWEET SLOOPS AND OTHER SURPRISES

Ben Strohecker says he scientifically conducted market research before plunging into the cold waters of commerce. He stopped everybody he saw and asked them what they'd want to eat if they knew they were going to die in ten minutes. "A chocolate-dipped toffee crunch," his apocryphal respondents answered.

Sweet Sloops were born. A mouthwatering, triangular-shaped toffee crunch dipped in white chocolate with the hull dipped in chopped nuts. They're the best. And don't forget Sand Dollars, molded chocolate enrobing soft, creamy, butter caramel centers studded with pecans. Marblehead mints are deep chocolate coins with sailboats embossed in their peppermint chocolate bodies. Sweet Shells are shaped like scallop shells and are made of dark sweet chocolate with a hint of orange crunch.

If Ben decides to do any more market research, I want to be the first to taste the results.

HARBOR SWEETS
Palmer Cove,
Leavitt St.
Salem, MA 01970-5546

CREDIT CARDS: **Yes**

CALL FOR CATALOG

RETAIL STORE: **Yes**

PHONE: **800-243-2115
508-745-7648**

FAX: **508-741-7811**

MINIMUM ORDER: **No**

The Confectionery

THE BRIGITTINE MONKS

23300 Walker Lane
Amity, OR 97101

CREDIT CARDS: Yes

CALL FOR CATALOG

RETAIL STORE: Yes

PHONE: 503-835-8080

FAX: 503-835-9662

MINIMUM ORDER: No

HEAVENLY FUDGE

Did you ever use the kind of fudge recipe that begins, "One jar of Hippolite cream"? That was a kind of prepared marshmallow cream known to candymakers as *mazetta*. The Amity monks have mastered the process for making homemade marshmallow cream without the chemical undertones of preservatives, and from that they make a fudge so creamy, so long-lasting, it doesn't turn to sugar shards after a week. It's so delicious that some say it's the best fudge in this world—and maybe the next. Care for ingredients, as well as the process, makes the difference. Beginning with Guittard chocolate, real cream, and that homemade mazetta made from both brown and white chocolate, this is a really good fudge.

Available in several flavors and packed in one-pound foil containers, the prayerful monks quietly go about making traditional chocolate—and chocolate cherry, with or without nuts, amaretto, and pecan pralines as well. The monks also make heavenly hand-dipped truffles in flavors ranging from mint to maple. Call for a brochure.

MARSHALL'S FUDGE

308 East Central Ave.
P.O. Box 639
Mackinaw City, MI
    49701-0639

CREDIT CARDS: Yes

CALL FOR CATALOG

RETAIL STORE: Yes

PHONE: 800-343-8343
    616-436-5082

FAX: 616-436-5107

MINIMUM ORDER: 1 pound

MACKINAC ISLAND FUDGE

A lot of tourist stops offer more local color than good quality, but Marshall's is an exception. The Marshall family has been making candies by hand for more than seventy years.

Dean, the son, now heads up the family business and continues the tradition started by his mom and dad. Now open year-round, Marshall's can send out fudge any time you want it.

Their classic fudge is made daily by hand from good, pure ingredients and it's shipped out the day they get the order. Of the twenty-six flavors, we're particularly hooked on chocolate English walnut. There's just something about that combo that's irresistible.

Many adore their pecan log and butter pecan fudge. They also make crisp cashew brittle and English toffee. Take the kids to Mackinac Island to see the candymakers. Pouring cauldrons of hot fudge onto marble slabs, they turn and fuss with it, until the fudge sets up. Watch this once and you'll order ten pounds. It's such an ancient, satisfying method. Fun to watch. Fun to eat.

BETTY BLAND'S PRALINES

ORLEANS PRALINES/ELIZARDI CANDY COMPANY

3262 Ella Lee Lane
Houston, TX 77019

Yes Virginia, there is a praline like you had that time you visited the crescent city. Thin, scrumptious, New Orleans-style pralines, these are the sugar crystal style, chocked full of pecan pieces. They're each slipped into a waxed paper wrapper with a picture of an Antebellum House and live oak tree on the front—just so you won't forget where these candies were invented. Just because their maker moved from New Orleans to Houston, doesn't mean she didn't take the recipe with her. Betty Bland is still whipping up pralines in the old Southern fashion.

A group of candies is then packed in a tin and shipped, ready to be devoured by the grateful person who receives it.

This is a small company—practically run out of a River Oaks home. But these candies are exquisite. A perfect thank you gift. Known as Betty Bland's Prawleens to the natives, they'll become a must for you if you ever eat the first one.

CREDIT CARDS: Yes

CALL FOR CATALOG

PHONE: 713-523-8003

MINIMUM ORDER: No

Wondering about the origin of pralines? Necessity being the mother of . . . these delightful candies are the result of a careless kitchen boy, an exasperated chef, and their demanding employer, a certain General Praslin. It was the seventeenth century. Renaissance cooks were just beginning to make candies, when the ill-fated kitchen boy spilled a bowl of toasted almonds on the stone-cold kitchen floor. The chef, in his temper, splashed a pot of burnt sugar onto the almonds. Because the general was ringing the bell impatiently, the desperate chef scraped the stuff up and served it. The general adored it and soon presented it to the ladies of Louis XIII's court. The ladies named the candy for the general. We can only hope the kitchen boy got a promotion.

The Confectionery

PAULINA'S ROCCA

P. O. B. 1366
Burlingame, CA 94010

~~~~~~~~~~~~~~~~~~

**CHECKS OR MONEY
ORDERS ONLY**

CALL FOR CATALOG

PHONE: 800-621-9234

FAX: 415-579-0132

MINIMUM ORDER: No

**SCHIMPFF'S
CONFECTIONERY**

347 Spring Street
Jeffersonville, IN 47130

~~~~~~~~~~~~~~~~~~

CREDIT CARDS: Yes

CALL FOR CATALOG

**RETAIL STORE: Call for
directions**

PHONE: 812-283-8367

MINIMUM ORDER: No

*Linda
Eckhardt's
1995
Guide to
America's
Best Foods*

238

ALMOND ROCCA

You've probably tasted commercial rocca, that Italian cookie made with sugar, butter, milk chocolate, almonds, and vanilla. And if you thought the mass-produced kind was good, you'll think Paula's homemade stuff is great.

Paula not only makes this divine confection by hand, she packs it in a rare and glorious box that looks like a cottage. The box itself—known as a Cottage Gift Box—is also made in California's north La Honda woods, and is available in a variety of darling designs: a Coast-side Victorian, a Log Cabin, a Potting Shed, and others. Specify which one you want when you call Paula. She'll pack your rocca to suit.

OLD-FASHIONED HARD CANDIES

Sonny Schimpff was a national treasure. One of a handful of German immigrant candy makers who knew the old crafts for making hard candies without chemicals, he died a couple of years ago. I was panicky when I heard this, because I knew Sonny was having a hard time finding somebody to apprentice. Whew. What a relief. He taught his cousin Warren and his friend, Mary Lee Wessel, a good many of the ancient formulas and methods and Schimpff's Confectionery lives. His cousin Warren Schimpff, a research chemist in California bought the store from the estate. After some remodeling and restoration, he opened up the old-fashioned soda fountain candy store once more. Four generations and going strong. We won't have to have Christmas without stockings filled with Schimpff's candies. Around here, it wouldn't be the same without Schimpff's bourbon balls in daddy's stocking.

Located in a suburb of Louisville, Kentucky, this candy shop has been in operation since 1891. Step inside the bright storefront and have an old-fashioned soda, an ice cream cone, or a sarsaparilla. Look up at the old-fashioned tin ceiling, note the wire ice cream chairs. This is the sweets biz as experienced before the beginning of the twentieth century. Trying to pick just which candies you want from the rows of gallon jars behind the marble counter is difficult. We like the clove and lemon drops. The kids want cinnamon red hots.

The Schimpffs have been making red hots and other hard candies using hand-cranked machinery since before the civil war. They're also famous for a candy called Modjeskas. Madame Modjeska was a Polish actress who struck the fancy of an elderly candymaker when she performed in Louisville in 1883. To show her his true love he invented a marshmallow dipped in caramel candy that's still popular today. Schimpff's also makes and sells fine chocolates.

> "You've got Santa Claus, the Easter Bunny and Schimpff's. You take any one of them away and you're messing with tradition."
> —*Louisville Courier Journal,* on the reopening of the store.

RIBBON CANDY

Old-fashioned ribbon candy is almost a lost craft. So is art candy—the little, round, hard candies with pictures on the inside. And candy straws, those tiny, striped, peppermint straws with the cocoa filling. And peppermint pillows, those mini-candies—tiny, but packed with flavor.

You can find these and other traditional candies at Hammond's. Or order candy apples, Rocky Mountain almond toffee, satin straws, Rocky Road eggs, truffles, sugar-free chocolates, taffies, cinnamon Santas, butter creams, and Jordan almonds. If it's candy, and it's traditional, Hammond's makes it.

The Hammond family has been making candy in Denver since 1920. Now, three generations later, the faces have changed but the recipes and the craft have been passed down so that you can taste traditional candies as made in Europe and America in the nineteenth century.

Hammond candies are beautiful. They're made with first quality ingredients and they're tailored to the season or occasion. Order wed-

HAMMOND CANDY COMPANY
2550 West 29th Ave.
Denver, CO 80211

CREDIT CARDS: **Yes**

CALL FOR CATALOG

RETAIL STORE: **Yes**

PHONE: 303-455-2320

MINIMUM ORDER: **No**

Fine candies since 1920

HAMMOND'S

The Confectionery

ding mints or Halloween candies. Get Christmas Ribbon candies for the stockings, and Jordan almonds for Easter. These candies taste as good as they look. Every last one of them.

CRANBERRY SWEETS CO.

Corner 1st and Chicago
Bandon, OR 97411

CREDIT CARDS: Yes

CALL FOR CATALOG

RETAIL STORE: Yes

PHONE: 503-347-9475

MINIMUM ORDER:

CRANBERRY CANDIES

If you're visiting the Oregon coast on your vacation this year, be sure to stop by Bandon. The downtown is charming and one of the institutions there is the Cranberry Candy Store. Stop in and buy yourself a white sack full of old-fashioned chewy candies to munch on while you stroll. Their signature cranberry-flavored candy, laced with local walnuts, is more a gel than anything else. The texture comes from the natural pectin in the cranberries, that come from the bog next door. Cut into small rectangles and rolled in sugar, these are a fabulous, fresh-tasting sweet. Using the same, old-fashioned method, the candymakers also make an outrageous wild blackberry confection and, believe it or not, a delicious beer candy made from Henry Weinhard's beer. One of their best confections is called lemon pie candy. A rectangle of filling that tastes like a fresh lemon pie is dipped in white chocolate. All candies here are made in small batches using no preservatives, no starch, and no food colorings or artificial flavorings. These are real candies, made the real old-fashioned way.

PHILLIPS CANDIES, INC.

217 Broadway
Seaside, OR 97138

CREDIT CARDS: Yes

CALL FOR CATALOG

RETAIL STORE: Yes

PHONE: 503-738-5402

FAX: 503-738-8326

MINIMUM ORDER: No

SALTWATER TAFFY AND ROCKY ROAD

Steve Phillips' family has owned this seaside candy shop since 1939, when they bought out the original owners who'd made candy here since 1897. Although this is a full-line shop that makes good, fresh, candies and chocolates in hundreds of varieties, they have made their reputation with two products: saltwater taffy and Rocky Road.

The taffies, made from original recipes dating back to the nine-teenth century, are a far cry from the mass-produced, rocklike, over-sweet taffies one sees in most airport shops. These taffies are soft, sweet, and laced with butter and cream. My personal favorite is the butter one, a translucent amber, which blends the very best of butter's natural taste with that of caramelized sugar into a soft, chewy bite that is unforgettable. You can choose from a dozen flavors.

Of all the American candies that have been maligned, maltreated, and mass-produced to no good end, Rocky Road stands as the candy most in need of having its past glories revisited. Steve Phillips has done it. He makes his own mazetta—marshmallow cream without preservatives—and adds to it fresh walnuts and pure, first quality milk chocolate in the combination that first made Rocky Road famous. This is the real McCoy, folks. Don't ever order it unless you're prepared to order it again.

SUCKERS SIMPLY SUCKERS

B rookie Durkin made lollipops at home for her teenaged boy to sell at school for a little extra spending money. Her son, legally blind, soon sold them out so fast she quickly had to make more. Brookie made the rock hard little baseballs using great flavorings: cinnamon, sour cherry, some with butter. It wasn't long before she had a sucker business on her hands.

Now, Brookie Durkin's sent this kid all the way through the University of Arizona on her sucker money, and the business has flourished because the suckers are beautiful. They come in 62 flavors—a good many with liquor—and they remind people of their childhood.

Order these little hard balls on a stick in blackberry, peanut butter, butter rum, or any of the other ka-zillion flavors. And just remember that these suckers started out as one mom's love for her son, and her wish to give him a leg up. I think it's the love you're tasting in Brookie's suckers.

THE LICKER CANDY COMPANY
1600 East 2nd St.
Winslow, AZ 86047

CHECKS OR MONEY ORDERS ONLY

CALL FOR CATALOG

RETAIL STORE: Yes

PHONE: 800-637-8377
602-289-4815

MINIMUM ORDER: Yes

The Confectionery

R & R HOMESTEAD KITCHEN

803 Morning Glory
   Lane
De Pere, WI 54115

~~~~~~~~~~~~~~~~

CREDIT CARDS: Yes

CALL FOR CATALOG

RETAIL STORE: Call for
   directions

PHONE: 414-336-8244

MINIMUM ORDER: $8.00

HOMESTYLE HOT FUDGE

Getting to know Ruth Roffers is kind of like rekindling an old relationship with your favorite aunt, the one who used to send boxes of chocolate chip cookies to you at camp. If you're staying overnight in Ruth's B&B, you can just feel Ruth's warmth.

Her B&B is truly her home: "The kids had all grown up and we had these extra rooms." Indeed you can choose from a Colonial, Victorian or Country room. You'll be in a peaceful neighborhood with a swimming pool, plenty of shade, and lots of lovely green grass. On the way to Aunt Ruth's—go ahead and call her that—you'll want to claim her for a relative, you'll drive through quaint villages, orchards, and gorgeous Wisconsin scenery. This is a place to relax.

Ruth will send you a jar of her signature hot fudge sundae sauce if you just ask. This is not some fancy gourmet hotsy-totsy Belgian chocolate confection; no, this is good all-American comfort food that will make your heart swell. It's made from cocoa, sugar, evaporated milk, soybean oil, corn syrup, and vanilla, then put up in honey jars. The big temptation is to eat it out of the jar with a spoon. Resist. Heat it a moment in the microwave and pour it over good quality vanilla ice cream.

PARADIGM FOODWORKS INC.

5775 S.W. Jean Road
Suite 106A
Lake Oswego, OR
   97035

~~~~~~~~~~~~~~~~

CREDIT CARDS: Yes

CALL FOR CATALOG

PHONE: 800-234-0250
   503-636-4880

FAX: 503-636-4886

MINIMUM ORDER: No

CHOCOLATE SAUCES AND SCONES

Lynn Barra began her food-packing business with a master's degree in science and a love of chocolate. Some eleven chocolate sauces later, she turned her scientific mind and her not inconsiderable energies to other products.

Now you can buy some exquisite scone mixes from Paradigm. The sweet cream lingers in the memory like a soft kiss. The golden orange is equally good. She also sells locally cold-pressed hazelnut oil—what she calls Oregon crude—and walnut oil. Her dessert sauces are legendary and each one is better than the last.

Choose from Haute Fudge sauce in several flavors: grand marnier, deep dark fudge, Bailey's Irish cream, or raspberry. Amaretto, hazelnut, and cafe espresso round out the Haute Fudge series.

The caramel sauces are equally good: spiced caramel, Jamaican praline, and vanilla caramel are so good you may want to eat them with a spoon. Additionally, she makes a bright, clean-tasting apple cider jelly, lemon curd, and currant jelly.

Her standards are high. Her products are excellent.

CHOCOLATE ADDICTS BEWARE

CHOCOHOLICS
P.O. Box 890
Trinidad, CA 05570

I may not have been a chocoholic before I opened these jars, but now? This is mainlining chocolate. And no wonder. Rita Harris blends best quality chocolate with whipping cream, sweet butter, and pure vanilla. Don't start this. You'll never be able to stop. Trust me on this. I speak from experience.

This ecstasy in a jar comes in various forms: chocolate ambrosia with almonds and apricots, bittersweet spreadable chocolate (apply directly to hips and thighs), truffles in a jar, hazelnut paté, and macadamia nut chocolate caviar. You'll want to hide each one of these from every other person in the household. They are too good to share. Well, maybe with just one person.

For those who are already hooked—and show it, Rita's even made a very low-fat, sugar-free chocolate butter, sweetened with Nu-traSweet®, and with Simplesse® as the fat replacer. She's the first in the country to make chocolate sauce sweetened with NutraSweet®, making it appropriate for diabetics and dieters. Only 9 calories a spoonful and a rich chocolate flavor.

CREDIT CARDS: Yes

CALL FOR CATALOG

PHONE: 707-677-3405

FAX: 707-677-3985

MINIMUM ORDER: No

The Confectionery

Creative Calorie Counting

Personally, I prefer Rita's Creative Calorie Counting Chart—included with every order. Some of her best tips:

Other People's Food: A chocolate mousse you didn't order has no calories. Ask your companion to order and you can taste about half of it.

Anything produced, purchased, or intended for minors is calorie-free when eaten by adults. This category covers a wide range, beginning with a spoonful of baby food—consumed for demonstration purposes—up to and including fudge made to be sent to children in college.

Anything eaten in front of the TV has no calories. It may have something to do with radiation leakage which negates not only the calories in the food but the memory of having eaten anything.

Nothing smaller than 1-inch has calories. This includes chocolate kisses, maraschino cherries, cubes of cheese, or thin slices of salami. These are too small to be considered real food and therefore have no calories.

Food taken medicinally: feed a cold, starve a fever. Or is it the other way around? You can't be too sure. Feed both. It's time-tested medical advice and we all know medicine has no calories.

Charitable foods, such as girl scout cookies, pancake breakfasts, and bake sale goods all have a religious dispensation from calories. Don't take my word for it. It's in the Bible.

Hard-To-Get-Foods: Pre-packaged foods are notoriously high in calories when opened with scissors. Fight with them and open the package with your own two hands and the calories expended to open the package equals the calories about to be consumed. Honest.

Fancy Sundaes from C.C. Brown's

Buster Brown: banana, scoops of vanilla and chocolate ice cream, fresh-chopped roasted almonds, whipped cream, and a pitcher of bubbling hot fudge

French Nougat: vanilla ice cream, marshmallow, fresh raspberries, chopped roasted almonds, and whipped cream

Royal Mocha: mocha ice cream and syrup, crunchy peanut topping, and whipped cream

Cinderella: layered in a tall glass, a sliced fresh peach, vanilla ice cream, sliced strawberries, lemon sherbet, chopped fresh pineapple, roasted almonds, and whipped cream

Golden Mocha Sundae: three scoops ice cream, roasted almonds, whipped cream, and a pitcher of smoking-hot mocha sauce

HOLLYWOOD SUNDAES

Since 1929, the kids from Hollywood High have been coming to C.C. Brown's for his famous "last act" sundaes. Sitting in high-backed booths, inhaling the intoxicating perfume of cream and chocolate, they've ordered countless hot fudge, mocha, or hot caramel sauce sundaes. Some he serves in the store. Some he sends out in hot cups with liveried chauffeurs to stretch limos waiting out front. But now, in cans that look like Campbell's soup, he also sells his hot fudge and caramel sauces for the home larder.

The sauce is a thick, dark, rich caramel flavor, either chocolate or vanilla. Brown worked 20 years to perfect the right blend of cane and corn sugars. To this he adds chocolate, cocoa, whipping cream, dairy butter, egg whites, salt, and pure vanilla. Place the can in boiling water until it heats through, pour over ice cream, and just pretend—for a minute—that you went to Hollywood High. This is the sweet stuff dreams are made of.

C.C. BROWN CO.
7007 Hollywood Blvd.
Hollywood, CA 90028

CHECKS OR MONEY ORDERS ONLY

RETAIL STORE: Yes

PHONE: 213-464-9726

MINIMUM ORDER: Yes

The Confectionery

245

REAL PENNSYLVANIA PRETZELS, POPCORN BALLS. OTHER GOOD STUFF.

CHEESE STRAWS

Cheese straws are as endemic to the south as Southern accents. The perfect hostess gift, a standard for cocktail parties, and a favorite at Christmas time. They're simplicity itself: flour, salt, cheese, paprika, and individual secret ingredients according to whose recipe you're using. Which brings us to Aunt Lizzie, who just turned 85.

Ann Randalls, 41, and Ginna Kelley, 39, loved Aunt Lizzie's version and, about five years ago, began making them for Christmas gifts. Randalls worked at that time as an accountant for an insurance company and Kelley taught music in the schools.

Before long, people began to joke that they'd be willing to pay somebody to make the *de riguer* bites before the holidays started up. Randalls and Kelley were in business.

"Fun is just as important as making money," says Kelley. And fun they've had. They've pulled all-nighters. They've travelled to food shows on both coasts. They've both had to quit their other jobs to keep up. They've gone from a hand-cranked cookie dough press to more sophisticated equipment and additional help to get those cheese straws baked.

Buy the straws in various sized red tins, or red-checked or cello sacks. They're festive to look at and impossible to quit eating.

**AUNT LIZZIES
CHEESE STRAWS**

80 West Viking
Cordova, TN 38018

CHECKS OR MONEY
ORDERS ONLY

CALL FOR ORDER SHEET

PHONE: 901-756-5668

MINIMUM ORDER: No

The Confectionery

Josiah Bent's Common Cracker Pudding

Whiz up the crumbs in a food processor and you'll have improved on this hundred-year-old recipe.

Butter a 3-quart, deep dish earthenware casserole dish. Add crumbs, 2½ cups of the milk, sugar, cinnamon, salt, and butter. Bake in a 350°F. oven until the pudding is puffed and set. Add the raisins after 30 minutes, stirring completely. Pour the last part of the milk around the edges and continue to bake, uncovered, until a knife inserted into the middle of the pudding comes out clean, about 2½ to 3 hours.

1 cup raisins, plumped over steam for 5 minutes

2 cups common cracker crumbs

6 cups milk, divided

1 cup sugar

½ teaspoon cinnamon, or to taste

1 teaspoon salt

1 tablespoon butter

BENT'S BAKERY SPECIALTIES

7 Pleasant Street
Milton, MA 02186

CHECKS OR MONEY ORDERS ONLY

CALL FOR CATALOG

PHONE: 617-698-5945

MINIMUM ORDER: No

WATER CRACKERS

The Bent water cracker has been made continuously by this company since 1801. Originally, it was sold town-to-town by Josiah Bent from saddlebags. It is nothing more than stone-ground wheat flour and pure spring water, hand-formed and baked in a Dutch oven, somewhat similar to the hardtack that was a staple on sailing ships. Primarily, it is valuable as a backer to cheeses because of its neutral flavor, and for the fact that it will keep in the pantry until hell freezes over. It has traditionally been used, crumbled and mixed with sweet clams and salt pork, to make the original New England clam chowder.

Boiled in Oil Jumbo Virginia Peanuts

In 1953, after having three babies in eighteen months—a daughter, then twins—Mrs. Hubbard knew she couldn't go back to teaching school, so she began boiling peanuts using an old family recipe and selling them at the drugstore. Pretty soon, friends began asking her to ship them out for gifts, and her mail-order business was launched.

Today, the Hubbards prefer direct mail-order because the peanuts are perishable. What you get when you order is a two-pound tin of giant-sized peanuts that have been water-blanched, then boiled in coconut oil. This labor-intensive method produces a peanut like you've never tasted before. They come salted or unsalted, and are crisp, crunchy, and flavorful. Keep them in the icebox, Miz Hubbard says, or even in the freezer.

HUBBARD PEANUT CO.
P.O. Box 94
Sedley, VA 23878

CREDIT CARDS: Yes

CALL FOR CATALOG

RETAIL STORE: Call for directions

PHONE: 804-562-4081

FAX: 804-562-2741

MINIMUM ORDER: No

Latin Crunch

Garrapinadas may be a new term to you, but it's been known to Latin Americans since the 1700's. Basically, these are peanuts hand-coated with a sweet, sugary coverture. This is an ancient process, brought forward from the time confectioners used a special copper pot over an open fire, and tossed nuts and seeds in with boiling sugar until a roasted confection resulted that was rugged, wrinkled, and incredibly delicious.

Roberto Rosenfield still makes candies using this ancient hand-coating process. He coats both almonds and peanuts. Don't eat these the first time unless you're prepared to order them again. They make modern nut candies pale by comparison.

LA LUNA FOODS
P.O. Box 53
Oxford, MS 38655

CHECKS OR MONEY ORDERS ONLY

CALL FOR CATALOG

PHONE: 800-234-2084
601-234-2264

MINIMUM ORDER: 1 case

The Confectionery

CAROLYN'S PECANS

P.O. Box 1221
Concord, MA 01742

CHECKS OR MONEY
ORDERS ONLY

CALL FOR CATALOG

PHONE: 800-656-2940
508-369-2940

FAX: 508-369-8212

MINIMUM ORDER: $10

SUGARED PECAN CANDIES

Don't eat the first sweet, salty, cinnamony pecan that Carolyn sells. You'll find yourself eating the whole cello pack. Carolyn handcooks these pecans, way up in Massachusetts, then mixes them with a perfectly blended mixture of sugar, salt, and cinnamon. She also coats them with chocolate. And offers them salt-free. Perfect stocking stuffers provided Santa comes late enough so that the elves don't get them first.

The pecans Carolyn starts with are huge. Mammoth fancies they're called in the trade. These tasty bites are luxe, luxe. Try them.

JULIUS STURGIS PRETZEL HOUSE

219 East Main St.
Lititz, PA 17543-2011

CREDIT CARDS: Yes

CALL FOR CATALOG

RETAIL STORE: Yes

PHONE: 800-227-9342
717-626-4354

FAX: 717-627-2682

MINIMUM ORDER: No

GENUINE PRETZELS

There are pretzels and there are pretzels, and Julius Sturgis has been baking them in original, 200-year-old brick ovens. Well, not actually Julius. He was here in 1861. Now it's Michael Tshudy who oversees the production of these extra crunchy, extra tasty pretzels that are individually wrapped and packaged in good looking tins for shipment.

For the pretzel connoisseur, they come six ways: plain, penny hard, unsalted, cheese, oat bran, and no-salt oat bran. And pretzels have been coming on since 610 A.D., when a monk discovered a simple twist of dough could represent children's arms folded in prayer. He called his little bits of baked dough *Pretiola,* or little reward. And pretzels have been a little reward ever since.

*Linda
Eckhardt's
1995
Guide to
America's
Best Foods*

DOWN HOME JUNQUE FOOD

THE HUMPHREY
COMPANY

11 Magnolia Drive
Cleveland, OH 44110

So, your mother wouldn't let you buy popcorn balls or cotton candy when you were a kid and visiting the park. Wouldn't let you order salt water taffy either. Now you can fill up on all the old-fashioned park food you want. The Humphrey Company, which serviced Cleveland's old Euclid Park, sells popcorn balls. (I was so ashamed. I didn't want to like them, but I kept running out into the backyard to hide and eat another one.) They also sell candy kisses, and old-fashioned popcorn that pops up white, fluffy, and beautiful.

And it all comes in adorable tins—one that looks like a popcorn wagon, another that looks like a roller coaster, a big cannister decorated like a carrousel, and a huge assortment named after a ride called "The Flying Turns" that's like an all-day pass at the park. It includes 50 original-flavor popcorn balls, four bags of candy kisses, and two 2-lb. bags of premium white popping corn. Yum.

CHECKS OR MONEY
ORDERS ONLY

CALL FOR CATALOG

PHONE: 216-481-7575

FAX: 216-481-7575

MINIMUM ORDER: No

The Confectionery

ESPRESSO BAR

Besides mail-order sources for fine coffee beans, there are flavored cocoas and teas from the world over. Crackers and biscuits, shortbreads, cookies and fruitcakes, mousse cakes, bundt cakes, loaf cakes, jam cakes, and other sweet delights.

A jug of wine, a loaf of bread—and thou beside me singing in the wilderness—oh, wilderness were paradise now!

—EDWARD FITZGERALD (1809–1883)

BESIDES MAIL-ORDER SOURCES FOR FIVE COFFEE BEANS, THERE ARE FLAVORED COCOAS AND TEAS FROM THE WORLD OVER.

You can serve tea and screw, Arlington.

—JAMES CAGNEY to his servant in *Jimmy the Gent*, 1934

GREATEST COFFEE ROASTER

PEET'S COFFEE
P.O. Box 8247
Emeryville, CA 94662

CREDIT CARDS: Yes

CALL FOR CATALOG

RETAIL STORE: Call for
    directions

PHONE: 800-999-2132

MINIMUM ORDER: No

I became a born-again coffee lover after we'd moved to Menlo Park, California and I discovered Peet's in the strip center on the Camino Real. I'd never even thought much past inhaling the aroma when the Folger's can popped open, but once I began walking by Peet's on my way to another store—and even the sidewalk and the parking lot were perfumed with the aroma—I couldn't resist. Before long, I'd bought a grinder and two or three kinds of coffeepots, and had experimented with just about every kind of arcane coffee I'd never heard of before. But no matter what I and my family tried, we kept going back for more. The coffee was that good.

Their dark-roasted coffees start with the very best arabica beans and then showcase the flavor by careful deep roasting. These coffees are stunning. No coffee is sold more than a week after it's been roasted, so not only do you get a complex, interesting flavor, but you get coffee so fresh you'd have to own a coffee plantation yourself to get it any better.

Don't hesitate to ask a bunch of questions when you start to buy your coffee. These people are coffee nuts. They love to talk about it. You'll probably learn more than you ever wanted to know.

Highly recommended are the Major Dickason's blend, the French Roast, and the Italian Roast. No other coffee roaster in America, that I know of, can touch these three flavors.

Peet's offers coffees from South America, Africa, and the Pacific in light, medium, and full-bodied dark roasts. They offer seven regular and seven decafs. No funny stuff. No weird flavors. Just the best damn coffees you ever tasted.

And if that weren't enough, they're also superior tea merchants. They carry more than thirty varieties and of course have green teas, black teas, semifermented teas, and blends.

Ten Peet's stores are sprinkled throughout the San Francisco Bay area. If you're planning a trip, bring along an extra carry-on athletic bag. You can fill it up with Peet's. Of course, the people sitting around you on the plane may attack and try to relieve you of the prize.

Espresso Bar

GREEN MOUNTAIN COFFEE ROASTERS

33 Coffee Lane
Waterbury, VT 05676

CREDIT CARDS: Yes

CALL FOR CATALOG

RETAIL STORE: Yes

PHONE: 800-223-6768
     802-244-5621, Ext. 166

FAX: 802-244-5436

MINIMUM ORDER: 1 lb.

GREEN EARTH COFFEE ROASTERS

B ob Stiller and the Green Mountain folks follow beans from the tropical rain forests to their own roaster in New England and onward to the ultimate customer. They began a Coffee Kids Club to try and help out the children of coffee workers. They give nearly ten percent of their annual profits to non-profit and community-based organizations.

But back to the coffee. They buy only top quality arabica beans, from around the world, then roast them in a variety of ways to produce first quality coffees. Choose rare Jamaican Blue, Kona Mountain, Mocha Java, or Celebes Kalossi, among others.

They make a variety of blends including a good one they call

Nantucket, and another known as Harvard—guaranteed to make you smart or at least feel smart, and a dark, rich blend they call Jamie's. Join a coffee club and they'll send you coffee and supplies on a regular basis. Want it decaffeinated? They've got it. Like those flavored coffees? They've got those too. Need a Chambourd French press coffeepot? They've also got those. If it's about coffee, these folks have it. Even cool tee-shirts.

PEERLESS COFFEE COMPANY

820 Oak St.
Oakland, CA 94607

CREDIT CARDS: Yes

CALL FOR CATALOG

RETAIL STORE: Yes

PHONE: 800-227-3054

FAX: 510-763-5026

MINIMUM ORDER: 5 lbs.

PEERLESS COFFEE

R oasting beans since 1924, Peerless Coffee Company's Columbian was recently judged the best in a blind taste test by a panel of judges, including Culinary Institute of America luminaries. The judges said the coffee was sweet, balanced, with a subtle finish and a good balance of complex flavors.

Peerless has one small retail shop near Jack London Square in Oakland. Most of its business is wholesale to upscale grocers, restaurants, and delis. The mail order business makes it possible to get gift packs made to order.

John Vukasin, a Yugoslavian immigrant, established the business and now his youngest son George, along with wife Sonja, run it. It's still a small operation, with George picking out by hand the first quality arabica beans they'll be roasting.

The Vukasins also supply fine quality teas from the world over, including Chinese, Formosan, Japanese, and specially blended teas including Irish Breakfast, Earl Grey, and Russian Caravan. They also offer blended herbs including chamomile, rose hips, spearmint, and scented teas. Try the black currant. It's sweet and fruity.

NORTHERN CALIFORNIA COFFEE ROASTER

Coffee, cream, and social justice come to you with every cup of Thanksgiving coffee you drink from Paul Katzeff. Paul started out as a social worker helping JFK develop public housing. He worked in New York and came to love justice and a good cup of coffee.

He later moved to California's redwoods and with his wife Joan, started Thanksgiving Coffee. Putting his money where his mouth was, he bought coffee from small growers and co-ops, eliminating the middlemen who historically took the profits. He began with Mayan, Aztec, and Inca Harvest coffees. Thanks to Paul, growers in Guatemala, Mexico, and Peru have made more money than they ever dreamed of. He's also raised enough money to build a school in Guatemala, buy trucks for a Mexican co-op, and help develop a sustainable agriculture program in Peru.

Choose from dozens of varieties—from Ethiopian to Zimbabwe and everything in between. Call for a catalog. He also sells splendid teas under the Royal Gardens label and all sorts of tea and coffee paraphernalia. He even has a coffee club, where your choice of coffee is shipped on a regular basis. He roasts only the best. You'll see.

THANKSGIVING COFFEE CO.

P.O. Box 1918
Fort Bragg, CA 95437

CREDIT CARDS: **Yes**

CALL FOR CATALOG

RETAIL STORE: **Call for directions**

PHONE: 800-648-6491
707-964-0118

FAX: 707-964-0351

MINIMUM ORDER: **No**

Espresso Bar

257

THE FRENCH CONNECTION

3000 E. 32nd Ave., #32
Denver, CO 80206

~~~~~~~~~~~~~~~~~

CREDIT CARDS: Yes

CALL FOR CATALOG

RETAIL STORE: Yes

PHONE: 800-877-3811
303-399-1616

FAX: 303-399-2323

MINIMUM ORDER: No

GOURMET HOT COCOA MIX

Quick! What comes to mind when you think of ski lodges and snow. Hot chocolate, right? That's what came to mind for Michael Szyliowicz who, along with his mom Irene, owns a confectionery in Denver. Well known, and with a devoted following, the Szyliowicz family has been handmaking caramels, white chocolate, and cocoa truffles for several years, but only when they stumbled into the hot cocoa business did their operation go through the roof.

They're cocoa is one of those *Voila* moments. They used confectioner's quality cocoa, added fine grain sugar, pure milk and cream powder, and cinnamon. Suddenly, they had a chocolate that was deep, deep brown in color and in flavor, aromatic with the scent of chocolate and cinnamon, and within a year, they couldn't make it in the back of the store anymore. Now they're up to seven tons of cocoa and counting.

Once you try it, you'll be hooked. Another in the "just-add-water" sweepstakes, all you do is stir the powder together with hot water. The tin is quite handsome too. If you're looking for a hostess gift for your ski vacation, this is it. Of course, you will have drunk all of it by the time you're ready to go home, but so what. You'll soon be joining the others who agree this is the Best of Denver.

McSTEVEN'S

P.O. Box 3961
Vancouver, WA 98662

~~~~~~~~~~~~~~~~~

CREDIT CARDS: Yes

CALL FOR CATALOG

RETAIL STORE: Call for
directions

PHONE: 800-547-2803
206-944-5788

FAX: 206-944-1302

MINIMUM ORDER: No

FLAVORED COCOA

Not only are teas and coffees delicious for teatime, cocoa is a perennial favorite as well. Pat McCormick has taken cocoa one better. She has created spicy and flavored varieties: amaretto, mint, raspberry, hazelnut, vanilla, and many more. Also available are kid's cocoas, including peanut butter and banana nut, as well as lemonade mixes.

She also creates some other smashing mixes, including a white chocolate hot drink mix, plus brownies, muffins, and much more. When we stirred up the raspberry brownies, we thought we'd died and gone to heaven. Such a rich, deep, chocolate flavor and all perfumed with the aroma of raspberries.

Her packaging is exceptional. The white chocolate drink mix comes in a glorious white box with pen and ink penguins adorning it. The white chocolate vanilla drink mix comes with pandas. Either would make a great grandkid gift and they come under that fabulous "just-add-water" category.

Cocoa mixes come in more than 20 flavors. Cappuccino sprinkles are available in half a dozen varieties. She also sells Dutch baking cocoa, spicy baking cocoa, and a product she calls Milk Coolers/Steamers. For those who want to take their cappuccino to new heights, she offers raspberry, mint, amaretto, blueberry, and peach mixes for milk that can then be steamed.

TEA FOR TWO OR TWO THOUSAND— AND EVERY KIND YOU CAN THINK OF

STASH TEA COMPANY

P.O. Box 910
Portland, OR 97207

CREDIT CARDS: Yes

CALL FOR CATALOG

PHONE: 800-547-1514
503-684-4482

FAX: 503-684-4424

MINIMUM ORDER: No

Here in the Northwest, we're used to drinking Stash tea. It's all that's served in the best restaurants. The aroma of Earl Grey permeates our favorite breakfast joint and it's always and only Stash. The company started in the seventies supplying herbs and herbal cigarettes to health food stores. They kind of slid into the tea business and now are one of the nation's biggest suppliers of specialty and fine tea products.

The name Stash originated with the captains of sailing ships who were often given best quality teas as gifts in the various ports of call. The captains then hid their best tea, their "stash," for special occasions. We won't ponder the other reasons for this name by the company's owners. Leave it at the fact that they offer the best quality teas and tea products you can buy.

With more than 70 varieties—call for a list—you can buy tea loose, in foil-wrapped tea bags, or in paper-wrapped tea bags. We're particularly taken with the pitcher-sized paper pouches for iced tea. Our favorite blend—Currant—is a mix of black tea and currants that yields a bright red, refreshing iced drink that is punch, plain and simple.

Others we adore are Gunpowder, a green tea, Jasmine, Formosa Oolong, Sri Lanka, and Irish Breakfast. The list is too long to repeat here. But having both black and green teas, as well as herbal teas, on hand is a real luxury—and a healthy one at that.

Espresso Bar

CRACKERS AND BISCUITS, SHORTBREADS, COOKIES AND FRUITCAKES, MOUSSE CAKES, BUNDT CAKES, LOAF CAKES, JAM CAKES AND OTHER SWEET DELIGHTS.

Chocolate lovers enjoy unvarying health and are least attacked by a host of little illnesses which can destroy the true joy of living.

—BRILLAT-SAVARIN (1755–1826)

BED, BREAKFAST, AND BISCOTTI TO GO

CITY DUNKERS
159 North Main Street
Ashland, OR 97520

John Reinhardt's the kind of fine baker who wins competitions hands-down over others. He's a quiet sort of guy, who bakes breakfasts most mornings with his wife Carmen, in their Bed and Breakfast. The customers are usually so taken with John's breads and pastries they keep coming back for more.

Afternoons, John and Carmen serve tea to their guests and John's biscotti became so popular he began bagging them up for the guests to take along in the car. Now, you can buy them by mail. They are light, they are airy, they are heavy with scent and flavor. Order Cinnamon Pecan, Orange Almond, Chocolate Hazelnut or Lemon Walnut. Each one tastes better than the last.

If Shakespeare's on your agenda this year for a vacation, visit Ashland and stay in John and Carmen's home. They have four guest rooms and do such a good job they were named one of the 50 best Bed and Breakfasts in the U.S. A good part of that is due to John's baking. Believe me.

CREDIT CARDS: Yes

CALL FOR CATALOG

RETAIL STORE: Yes

PHONE: 800-888-6891
    503-488-2901

MINIMUM ORDER: No

Espresso Bar

SAN ANSELMO'S
COOKIES

P.O. Box 2822
San Anselmo, CA
94979-7590

CHECKS OR MONEY
ORDERS ONLY

CALL FOR CATALOG

PHONE: 800-229-1249

FAX: 415-492-1282

MINIMUM ORDER: No

CALIFORNIA BISCOTTI

You can't quit eating these things. These little dippers are crisp, subtle, complicated, and not too sweet. Jane Cloth-Richman makes traditional Italian biscotti in lots of mouthwatering flavors: ultra chocolate mint, chocolate raspberry walnut, chocolate macadamia, chocolate pecan toffee, chocolate-dipped almond (to die for), chocolate-dipped espresso, and chocolate-dipped orange. Roasted almonds are sprinkled on many flavors. And ground cinnamon sparks several others.

In addition, she's made traditional anise, almond, cinnamon raisin, lemon, and double chocolate walnut. And even though she makes 30,000 biscotti a day, and still has the brass to call them handmade, she's keeping the quality consistent by using only the best ingredients.

Jane and her husband Jeff, began with an ice cream shop in their home town of San Anselmo. This was in 1984. Soon they were both stuck in the back, rolling out the ever more popular twice-baked cookies. Meanwhile, their 4-year-old helped out by trying to give away all the candy in the front of the store. Within a year, they'd hooked up with a good graphic artist and decided to jettison the retail business and concentrate on making the best cookie around and packaging it attractively, to pair with the burgeoning espresso-cappucino craze. Talk about timing. Now they see that biscotti is growing past the trend stage, and will soon be as mainstream as the bagels they grew up on in Brooklyn. Their biscotti are certified kosher and classify as dairy for all seasons except Passover.

They've grown through several rented cooking sites and have now built a big plant. They've grown their family too, and have added a baby sister named Jenna, who thinks its pretty neat that mom and dad make teething biscuits for a living.

Linda Eckhardt's 1995 Guide to America's Best Foods

SAN FRANCISCO BISCOTTI

SWEET ENDINGS
1935 Lawton St.
San Francisco, CA
94122

Y ou want to talk about a company well-named—this is it. The biscotti is so good it will make a lump in your throat: lemon butter bars made with lemon curd, and almond lace cookies so delicate and rich, they melt in your mouth.

All these and a variety of American- and European-style cookies are made by Olga Harris-Deans in a bakery located on Lawton Street in San Francisco's foggy Sunset District. Step in the bakery and the aroma of baking butter and sugar will assail your senses. You may never want to leave.

Order cookies from Olga and it's better than a package from Mama. With eight flavors of biscotti, she even makes and sells an Oat Bran Biscotti (this tastes better than its healthful name might sound), and a polenta cookie that's become a real hit.

They'll send out the biscotti or other cookies baked to order, just for you or your party. They use only the best ingredients. They're sticklers for quality control. Try them. You'll like them.

CHECKS OR MONEY
ORDERS ONLY

CALL FOR CATALOG

RETAIL STORE: Yes

PHONE: 415-665-4748

MINIMUM ORDER: No

OLD-FASHIONED HOMESTYLE CAKES AND COOKIES

**SWEET THINGS
BAKERY**
1 Blackfield Drive
Tiburon, CA 94920

F or cookies that ship better than you can do it from home, and that taste as good as those your grandma made, this is it. These cookies and cakes are a real hazard to have around. You won't want to do anything but eat the whole box, all by yourself, once you take the first whiff of the fabulous baked butter and sugar smell that emanates from the box.

They offer chocolate chip cookies, ginger crisps, chocolate chews, turtle brownies, apricot bars, and raspberry buttons. Where's that glass of milk? And the packaging is terrific. Each bakery box is tied up with a red ribbon that says *Sweet Things* on it. For a little love present, this is it.

For a bigger gift—maybe a hostess or birthday party bash—try their Hungarian Coffee Cake or Apple Cream Cake. Also available are Lemon or Poppyseed cakes or Brandied fruitcake. They come packed in bright red tins and are as homey and good as watching old movies on A&E.

Alison Masters, the home baker with the vision behind all this

CREDIT CARDS: Yes

CALL FOR CATALOG

RETAIL STORE: Yes

PHONE: 415-388-8583

FAX: 415-388-8581

MINIMUM ORDER: No

Espresso Bar

goodness, has a straightforward view towards baking: she just wants to present homestyle American baked goods like she remembered eating as a kid. Trust me. It's better than most of the stuff that any of us had as a kid. It's what we wished for. Now you can have it. Promise not to cry when it's all gone.

VICTORIA'S KITCHEN

P.O. Box 995
Gualala, CA 95445

CHECKS OR MONEY ORDERS ONLY

CALL FOR ORDERING INFORMATION

PHONE: 707-884-4995

FAX: 707-884-4995

MINIMUM ORDER: Yes

VICTORIA'S SECRET

Victoria Fahey's Ginger Snaps don't quite snap, and I guess that's the secret. They more or less melt in your mouth, they're so aromatic and good. Gingered up with a spicy flavor that lingers and lingers, the secret to former chef Victoria's success is that she not only jazzes up the flavor with powdered ginger, but uses a generous dollop of crystallized Thai ginger as well.

The cookies are big, moist, and chewy. They contain no preservatives and store well in the freezer. Once you eat them, you'll experience a lovely ginger-clovey aftertaste. That taste comes from the freshly ground cloves she uses. These are some of the best store-bought cookies we've sampled. We recommend them. And now I'll tell you my secret. I nuke 'em a moment in the microwave and serve them warm. The air in the kitchen drips with ginger and clove. The cookies do melt in your mouth. Sometimes I can even get away with saying I slaved all afternoon over a hot stove to make them.

HUNT COUNTRY FOODS

P.O. Box 876
Middleburg, VA 22117

CREDIT CARDS: Yes

CALL FOR CATALOG

PHONE: 703-364-2622

FAX: 703-364-3112

MINIMUM ORDER: No

GOOD LUCK COOKIES

Want to wish somebody good luck? Send Best of Luck Scottish Shortbread cookies in the shape of horseshoes, complete with nails, packed in a good-looking, square, shiny red box, and your message will be received.

Maggie Castelloe and her husband, Barnard Collier, dreamed this up. They make the horseshoe-shaped cookies and farriers' nails in several flavors. Original buttery,

ginger, and chocolate. The cookies are made with rice flour, wheat flour, pure dairy butter, and a blend of sugars. They're slow-baked and hand-stamped so that you get a golden, chewy cookie.

Of course, the horsey set loves these. But so will you once you taste them. They taste as good as they look and sound.

AMERICAN SHORTBREADS

A blue box about the size of a brick with gold lettering and the handscripted name *Hedgehaven* hints at good things inside. And so there are. Linda Hedge's American shortbreads—with their pinked edges and their Oregon stamp—taste as good as they smell, and that's saying something.

Linda took an old family recipe for shortbread, then branched out to make several purely American flavors: hazelnut, chocolate, poppyseed, chocolate hazelnut, and Lumpy Bumpy, that contains whole hazelnuts, walnuts, almonds, raisins, and apples. Soon, people were begging her for more. But for the moment, Linda's said, Enough!

Now, Linda's shortbreads are privately-labelled to a good many "basket" companies, but you can buy them direct. She makes each batch by hand, kneading the dough so that you get a moist, buttery cookie with a fine crumb. I only hope she doesn't get too successful and buy machines to do all this stuff. The cookies just aren't the same when they're not handmade.

GET YOUR DESIGNER COOKIES

T he most beautiful cookies in the baking business. More than 150 designs in three flavors: gingerbread, butter, and shortbread cherry crisp. These cookies are cut, iced, and decorated with classic icing to make a durable gift cookie with a message.

Cookies are available for every occasion: holidays, weddings, birthdays, you name it. If you want to celebrate with cookies—custom-designed to suit your purpose—give a call. These cookies are gorgeous. They'll design one just for you.

HEDGEHAVEN SPECIALTY FOODS
P.O. Box 230803
Portland, OR 97281

CREDIT CARDS: **Yes**

CALL FOR CATALOG

PHONE: **503-643-9562**

FAX: **503-644-0986**

MINIMUM ORDER: **No**

SUGARBAKERS
1251 Gardner Way
Medford, OR 97504

CHECKS OR MONEY ORDERS ONLY

CALL FOR CATALOG

PHONE: 503-773-8763

FAX: 503-773-8763

MINIMUM ORDER: **3 Dozen**

Espresso Bar

MRS. TRAVIS HANES' MORAVIAN SUGAR CRISP, INC.

431 Friedberg Church Road
Clemmons, NC 27012

CREDIT CARDS: Yes

CALL FOR CATALOG

PHONE: 919-764-1402

FAX: 919-764-8637

MINIMUM ORDER: No

MORAVIAN SUGAR CRISP COOKIES

Evva Hanes began helping her mother, Mrs. Travis F., make Moravian sugar crisps back in the 1950's. People drove out to the Hanes farm to pick up these thin, flavorful, crisp cookies, the recipe for which originated in the part of Czechoslovakia known as Moravia. Evva's husband remembers mixing cookie dough in a baby bathtub.

Now, thirty-five years and no advertisements later, Evva, Travis, and their grown kids' Mike and Mona, have to employ a virtual army of grandmothers to keep up with the demand.

Travis mixes up 5,000 pounds of dough every week. Yet every cookie is still rolled by hand and cooked precisely. Then stacks of cookies are hand-wrapped in white napkins and placed in tins or cardboard tubes for mailing.

They don't hold to old-fashioned ways just for the heck of it. These cookies are simply too delicate to withstand machine-handling. But watch those well-muscled women working over the dough with rolling pins, and you'll believe it when Evva Hanes says they get their cookies to come out so thin and crisp by one means: elbow grease.

These crisp and delightful cookies come in five flavors: sugar, lemon, chocolate, butterscotch, and the most popular—ginger—made with the traditional Moravian blend of cinnamon, nutmeg, ginger, and cloves.

LYNN'S INCREDIBLE EDIBLES

3704 Silver Oaks
Danville, CA 94506

CREDIT CARDS: Yes

CALL FOR CATALOG

PHONE: 800-532-2805
510-736-0719

FAX: 510-736-5068

MINIMUM ORDER: No

COOKIE COTTAGE

Lynn Newman isn't exaggerating when she calls her cookies incredible: melt-in-your-mouth lemon butter balls, double chocolate indulgence cookies, cinnamon-scented rugelach, and delicate, heart-shaped linzers with delicious raspberry preserve hearts. All Lynn's cookies taste like ones you'd make yourself, if you had the time and a good recipe to begin with.

And to top it all off, Lynn packages these cookies in those decorated adorable cottage boxes that give you something to keep. Her friend, Ann Von Thaden, makes the boxes, and Lynn makes the cookies to fill them. She uses her grandmother's Russian recipes for the cookies and the results are dynamite.

BENNE WAFERS AND CITRUS COOKIE BITES

BYRD COOKIE COMPANY

P.O. Box 13086
Savannah, GA 31406

~~~~~~~~~~~~~~~~

CREDIT CARDS: **Yes**

CALL FOR CATALOG

RETAIL STORE: **Directions included in text below**

PHONE: **912-355-1716**

FAX: **912-355-4431**

MINIMUM ORDER: **Yes**

African slaves introduced sesame seeds to the United States. They hid bags of the seeds on their person for good luck in the journey. The Byrd Cookie Company has been making and selling "benne wafers" since the Twenties when Mr. Byrd took a recipe for these old slave cookies and began hand baking and delivering them in his Model-T Ford to local area grocers.

The Byrds were onto the notion of mini-cookies decades before the big boys at Nabisco figured it out. They've added several flavors to their popular benne seed wafer: Razzberry, a prize-winning Key Lime Cooler cookie, and Cinnamon Chips. From Mr. Byrd's original method for making nine dozen cookies every ten minutes by hand, to the modern plant where blinking, winking, silver and white machinery cranks out 60 million cookies a year, the third generation of Byrds still control every step of the process.

They use nothing but the best ingredients—Dixie Crystals granulated sugar, cake flour, fresh eggs and a light dusting of powdered sugar—and pack their cookies in distinctive square tins.

Although the plant and cookie shanty are not the easiest thing to find on your vacation to the low country, it's worth the drive. You're likely to see egrets flashing in the air, a mysterious fog rolling over the land, and shrimp boats bobbing in the tide. Just keep driving. You'll find it.

From I-95 North take exit 16. Turn right on Highway 204 (Abercorn Street). Go 8 miles, then turn right onto Montgomery Crossroads. Go 4 miles until Montgomery Crossroads dead-ends into Skidaway Road. Turn right and at the first light, turn left onto Norwood. Go about a half a mile and you'll see Byrd's on the right of Skidaway and Norwood. Once you're in the cookie shanty, you can mix and match southern food products and they'll make you a custom gift basket to send to the folks back home. Suckers for the grandkids. Jam for Aunt Lily. They've got a good selection to choose from. And don't forget some benne seed wafers—for your own streak of good luck.

Espresso Bar

267

DIVINE DELIGHTS

24 Digital Drive
Novato, CA 94949

CREDIT CARDS: **Yes**

CALL FOR CATALOG

RETAIL STORE: **Yes**

PHONE: **800-443-2836**

FAX: **415-382-7599**

MINIMUM ORDER: **No**
(May 1 to September
30, add $5 per order
for summer shipping.)

KING CAKES

2397 Hwy 43 North
Picayune, MS 39466

CREDIT CARDS: **Yes**

CALL FOR CATALOG

RETAIL STORE: **Yes**

PHONE: **800-669-5180**
601-798-7891

MINIMUM ORDER: **No**

PETIT FOURS AND FANCY CAKES

I thought petit fours existed only in *New Yorker* short stories from the fifties. But no, they're still made. And they're still as awe-inspiring as great fiction—just two bites of heaven—when made by Angelique and Bill Fry. In fact, these may be the only real ones left. They're certainly as divine as the dream ones. Each miniature butter cake is interlayered with marzipan, buttercream, smooth truffle cream, and fruit fillings. Then they're decorated elaborately and boxed elegantly. The remarkable thing about them is that they're not all that fragile. Order a box and you can have tea for days and days and the cakes will still be meltingly perfect.

If you're going to San Francisco for a vacation, pop over the bridge to Larkspur and visit their 1125 Magnolia Street Bakery in Larkspur, about a mile up the road from Bradley Ogden's Larkspur Inn. It's a full service bakery offering best quality muffins, breads, pies, cakes, those redoubtable petit fours, as well as other items that might strike the baker's fancy that day.

Call for a catalog and you can choose from petit fours, praline cheesecake, pumpkin teacake, or trufflecots—a splendid confection that begins with Australian glacéed apricots filled with a bittersweet truffle, then bathed in a bittersweet chocolate coverture. Also available are melt-in-your-mouth butter cookies, brownies, biscotti, poppy seed pound cake, lemon marzipan cake, a divine chocolate decadence cake, and a carrot walnut torte. Each one is better than the last.

MARDI GRAS CAKES

S herri Brown makes Kings' Cakes for New Orleans' Mardi Gras celebrations. Lots of Kings' Cakes. As many as 12,000 for the short happy holiday before lent. Sherri inherited this business from her mom, who improved on the traditional cake by adding a cream cheese filling so that you get the combination of a sweet, raised dough around a sweet, creamy filling. They had so much success with that, they then added other fillings, until now they offer more than 15 varieties. And they'll make one to fit your fantasy.

Even better are their other cakes: chocolate almond mocha cream, chocolate chip pecan cream, and poppy seed almond cream cakes are all light, full of flavor, and delicious. These cakes ship well and would be great for a birthday.

You can order a wedding cake here. It's still a small bakery and Sherry will do all she can to make your wedding cake unique to your wedding. Call and talk.

DARK VICTORY

D avid Glass is a good democrat. He made Bill Clinton's dessert, and got a thank you note for his trouble that he has—guess what—framed. Clinton's only now discovering what New York foodies have known for several years. David Glass's chocolate mousse cake—a flourless cake made only from bittersweet chocolate, butter, sugar, eggs, and cocoa—looks, feels, and tastes like the result of a love affair between a brownie and a truffle, with the intense chocolate mousse resting on a crusty, crunchy bottom. David apprenticed in France and claims he extracted the recipe from a French chef who was on her deathbed. She got well, but not before he got the recipe. Way to go, David.

David's also added a delectable New York cheesecake and a chocolate-covered cheesecake to his list of accomplishments.

If you're in New York, pick up one of David's cakes from the refrigerated sections at Zabar's or Balducci's (see Index for addresses). His cakes are stocked by upscale stores in cities across the U.S. but if you—like I—live in Backwater, USA, don't despair. Just call David up and order. He'll send it out Second Day Air. You're dark victory is at hand.

DESSERTS BY DAVID GLASS

140–150 Huyshope
Hartford, CT 06106

CREDIT CARDS: **Yes**

CALL FOR CATALOG

RETAIL STORE: **Call for directions**

PHONE: 800-328-4399
203-525-0345

FAX: 203-727-0717

MINIMUM ORDER: **No**

Espresso Bar

Authentic Junior's Cheesecake

Preheat the oven to 450°F. Coat sides and bottom of an 8-inch springform pan with butter, then dust generously with graham crackers. Refrigerate the pan.

In a mixer or food processor fitted with the steel blade, mix sugar and cornstarch, by pulsing. Add cream cheese and pulse to blend. Stir in the egg and pulse again to mix. Add heavy cream and vanilla and process just until mixed. Spoon the batter into the prepared pan. Bake in preheated oven until the top is golden brown and it's done, about 45 minutes. Cook on a rack at least 3 hours then refrigerate, covered.

2 tablespoons unsalted butter

graham crackers

⅞ cup sugar

3 tablespoons sifted cornstarch

30 oz. cream cheese, room temperature

1 extra-large egg

½ cup whipping cream

¾ teaspoon vanilla

JUNIOR'S CHEESECAKE

386 Flatbush Ave. Extension
Brooklyn, NY 11201

CREDIT CARDS: Yes

CALL FOR CATALOG

RETAIL STORE: Call for directions

PHONE: 800-826-CAKE (Nationwide)
718-852-5257 (In New York)

MINIMUM ORDER: No

BROOKLYN'S BEST CHEESECAKE AND DINER

Think about a diner in downtown Brooklyn. The sort of place you can sit on the stool, order up your bagel and lox, or a big, home-made pastrami sandwich on their very own club rye bread. Sit there, and before long, you've felt the heartbeat of Brooklyn. People down the counter strike up a conversation. The waiter pours you an extra cup of coffee. You've eaten so much of the free coleslaw, pickles, and beets you're feeling guilty. You've found your spiritual home.

Sherry and Kevin Rosen, grandchildren to Junior's founder, Harry Rosen, rebuilt the restaurant after a big fire in 1981 because, as they said, "We're a landmark." Everybody in the neighborhood was mighty relieved, let me tell you.

And for those who want a bite of old Brooklyn, order a cheesecake. You'll feel safe ordering from Junior's. It's one of the best places in New York to get the fabled New York dessert. They ship out 2,000 cakes every month. Order Original, Black Forest, Marbled or Flavor-of-the-Month. For Thanksgiving, they make an outrageous Pumpkin with cinnamon. We found the Original cake to be light, rich, and full-flavored. We topped it with some local blueberries. It was heaven. We'll order one again.

And if you're in Brooklyn's downtown, stop in for breakfast. They'll put a platter of Danish and various Kaiser rolls and bagels on your table before you even order. It's just the sort of place your Jewish mother believes in: eat, eat, you'll feel better.

THE OTHER GREAT NEW YORK CHEESECAKE: S&S

MOREY & DOREY'S EXTRAORDINARY CHEESECAKE COMPANY

3733 Riverdale Ave.
Riverdale, NY 10463

You'll have heard of the famous S&S Cheesecake if you've ever hung out for long in Manhattan. This is it. The traditional smooth, tart, creamy, silky pie that slides down your throat before you want to swallow. It's that good. You just want to hold it in your mouth.

One of the best things about this cake, besides the taste, is that it's freezable and refreezable. Take it out of the freezer, cut off a sliver or two, replace it in the freezer. Warm the slices to room temperature and top with blueberry preserves, or fresh strawberries, or our favorite—chopped bananas and walnuts.

Anyway you want it, this is an authentic New York-style cheesecake.

CHECKS OR MONEY ORDERS ONLY

CALL FOR CATALOG

PHONE: 800-822-5369

FAX: 718-548-1743

MINIMUM ORDER: No

HEAVENLY CHEESECAKES AND GERMAN SHEPHERDS

NEW SKETE FARMS

P.O. Box 128
Cambridge, MA 12816

If you're in the Saratoga area, stop by the New Skete Monastery. It's easy to get there. Just follow Route 29 east through Schuylerville and Greenwich, then continue down Route 372 into the little village of Cambridge. They're just a mile out of town and it's well-marked. You'll spot the three onion domes of gold before you even get there. This is the ultimate respite from the hustle-bustle of busy Boston or New York. It's peaceful and it's splendid in its isolation.

These nuns make a heavenly cheesecake in several flavors: chocolate, kahlua, and chocolate amaretto. They also make eggnog and pumpkin. Their brandied fruitcake is first rate. And their latest product is an apple walnut cake. Each cake is more divine than the last.

The monks at the monastery breed and train German Shepherd dogs. They also operate a smokehouse and smoke hams, bacon, Canadian bacon, sausage, and poultry. They also offer a 15-bean soup mix, a whole grain pancake and waffle mix, maple syrup, full-bodied cheddar cheeses, and cakes.

Stop in on a weekend and the gift shop will be full of people buying cakes, hams, and maybe even a puppy. It's that kind of place.

CREDIT CARDS: Yes

CALL FOR CATALOG

RETAIL STORE: Call for directions

PHONE: 518-677-3928

FAX: 518-677-2378

MINIMUM ORDER: No

Espresso Bar

271

MIDWAY PLANTATION

HC-62, Box 77
Waterproof, LA 71375

CREDIT CARDS: Yes

CALL FOR CATALOG

RETAIL STORE: Call for directions

PHONE: 800-336-5267

FAX: 318-749-3576

MINIMUM ORDER: No

OLD-FASHIONED SOUTHERN JAM CAKES

Nan, Jim and little Jimmie Jo Huff live in a great big old plantation house in the middle of a rice field way down in Louisiana. The house was built in 1834, and, typical for the period, was plunked right in the middle of a field. Jim still plants cotton, but now he also makes a good living off popcorn rice and a good many orchard fruits. If you've never seen a working plantation, and you're close by, call for directions and drive out. Nan's made a cute little shop in one room and there she sells some of the Plantation's prepared foods.

Their own organic popcorn rice is, of course, first on the list, put up in cloth bags. This rice is as aromatic as popcorn and makes any pilaf zing. You can almost smell the rich fertile Mississippi Delta in every single bite.

Nan also makes jams. Her Plantation Plum is our favorite. But perhaps her best-loved product is a line of cakes that she only bakes on order. You call for a cake, Nan makes it and ships it out. It comes really fresh. Made in either one- or three-pound rounds, these luscious cakes include Main Street Mayhaw Jelly Cake, Cloud Nine Muscadine Jelly Cake, Pompous Plum Jam Cake, and Garden Gate Dewberry Jelly Cake. These are old-fashioned plantation cakes. They'll freeze for up to a year, and are good in the refrigerator for months.

Jan's also invented a fun product she calls Oatmeal Crunch. A dry mix with wild cherries, it's great sprinkled on top of vanilla ice cream.

*Linda
Eckhardt's
1995
Guide to
America's
Best Foods*

272

COUNTRY CAKES

Deanne and Blaine Matthews wanted a country life for their children. They bought a big farm house in 1979, then figured out a way to make it pay. They began making cakes. Now, of course, they've become a cottage industry in the truest sense of the word, and their cakes are known worldwide.

Our personal favorite is the lemon rum cake. It's like a pound cake, moist, sweet, laden with rum, and a cake that's earned its name: Sunshine Cake. The 1¾-pound cake comes in a metal tin and is a good keeper.

Whenever we feel like being totally decadent, I call up Deanne and have her send out a fudge brownie torte. It's simply outrageous. Rich, chocolaty, and finished with a toasty oatmeal crust, all it needs is a dab of whipped cream. She also makes an apple crumb torte as old-fashioned as sleigh bells. Her heirloom fruit and nut cake, made with honey, cream, butter, eggs, and spices is what fruitcakes ought to be.

Deanne uses no artificial flavors or preservatives. And even though her cakes do keep well, that's become sort of a joke around here. Whenever a Matthews' cake comes through the mail slot, we just sort of fall on it. We can't help it.

OLD-FASHIONED YELLOW BUNDT CAKE

When Marge Murray sends you a bundt cake, you know it's homemade. It comes home-wrapped in foil and in a plain box. You open up the box and the aroma of home just bursts from the box. You want to make Marge Murray an honorary aunt.

Marge lives on an orchard farm and makes this 3-pound 12-serving bundt cake just like grandma did. It's sweetly scented, it's fluffy, it's no wonder it won a blue ribbon at the Stephans County Fair.

This isn't a classic pound cake, but more of a traditional Farmer's cake. Made with farm eggs, flour, sugar, shortening, salt, soda, buttermilk, and vanilla and almond extracts, it has the added advantage of being a good keeper. Marge makes these one at a time.

Marge recommends toasting a slice and serving it with orange marmalade. However, around here, we eat it the way my husband

MATTHEWS 1812 HOUSE

P.O. Box 15,
250 Kent Road
Cornwall Bridge, CT
06754-0015

CREDIT CARDS: Yes

CALL FOR CATALOG

RETAIL STORE: Call for directions

PHONE: 800-662-1812
203-672-0149

MINIMUM ORDER: No

MARGE'S COUNTRY KITCHEN

Rt 1, Box 164 A
Duncan, OK 73533

CHECKS OR MONEY ORDERS ONLY

CALL FOR CATALOG

PHONE: 405-255-0753

MINIMUM ORDER: No

Espresso Bar

Joe's mother would have wanted. No matter what I cooked when she'd come to dinner, at the end, she'd turn to me in her bland, non-threatening, totally demanding way and ask, "Honey, don't you have a little plain cake?" This is what mama had in mind. Exactly what mama had in mind. It's homemade cake, the way mama used to make it.

HOMEMADE LOAF CAKES

Ed Tutin bought an old bakery and began turning out the most delicious old-style loaf cakes. The kind that don't need any icing and keep a long time. Order Lemon Walnut—smells good before you even take the first bite. Or Cranberry Orange, flecked with whole cranberries. Coconut Apricot Macadamia Nut and Boston Brown Bread make up the rest of his luscious loaf cakes.

He also makes a traditional Danish cookie called Peber Nodder. Small as pebbles, these delectable bites are packed in tins to match the season and are decorated with traditional Danish designs. Delicious.

OLD-TIME CHICAGO BAKERY

Here comes a tongue twister. When Joseph Dinkel met George Dickel, guess what happened? Dinkel, who bakes in Chicago, was taken with the whiskey that Dickel makes in Tennessee and he determined to make a Dinkel-Dickel cake that could be doused in this fine Tennessee sour mash. This idea kicked around, just talk really, and became part of the family legend. Years and years later, Dinkel's grandson, Norm, Jr., perfected the bundt cake that is now shipped from the bakery and is known, ig-nominiously, as The Sip'n Whiskey Cake. Made from whole wheat flour, raisins, pecans, eggs, and milk, this cake is moist, mellow, not too sweet, and has enough

YOUR DARN TOOTIN IT'S SOO GOOD

416 Main Street
Glenwood, MS 38930

CREDIT CARDS: Yes

CALL FOR CATALOG

RETAIL STORE: Yes

PHONE: 800-999-2669
  601-453-8150

MINIMUM ORDER: No

DINKEL'S BAKERY

3329 N. Lincoln
Chicago, IL 60657

CREDIT CARDS: Yes

CALL FOR CATALOG

RETAIL STORE: Call for
  directions

PHONE: 312-281-7300

FAX: 312-281-6169

MINIMUM ORDER: No

sour mash in it to make you get up and try a Tennessee Two-Step. We kept trying to be circumspect about it—to only eat it in thin slivers. The cake sent to us lasted about three days. We liked it a lot.

If you're in Chicago, stop by Dinkel's old-fashioned bakery. It's a classic German-style bakery located in the Lakeview neighborhood. And worth a stop on anybody's tourist trip. The glass cases and bins tumble over with a wide variety of best quality German-style baked goods: everything from stollen to muffins to brownies. With coffee, it's fuel to keep you rolling all day.

SAN FRANCISCO'S FRUIT AND NUT PATÉ

In a grand gesture, Barbara Srulovitz has agreed to custom-bake her famous Fruit and Nut Paté. It's the quintessential product for the nineties. It's healthy, it's low-fat, it's sweet without having sugar. The paté has no honey, no citron, no candied fruits, and no chemicals. The classy 2-pound cake is lovely used for a Christmas gift and the larger Savarin serves as a wedding cake quite often.

The paté is made of Turkish and California apricots, prunes, dates, gold and black raisins, figs, almonds, walnuts, and pecans. She adds a mere 2 tablespoons of flour, less than one egg, and a dash of vanilla—then after baking she adds a quick misting of amaretto—unless you ask her to leave that off. The paté is full of fiber, low in calories, and compatible with most diets. Gourmands love it, fitness folks love it, diabetics, and weight watchers love it. I love it.

Order anything from a mini-loaf to a banquet block—40 ounces in a ring. For special occasions, Barbara decorates the tops with seasonal dressings: plum jam, cranberry relish, chocolate drizzle, fresh fruit of the season—kumquats and kiwis for Christmas, red flame grapes and lemoned bananas for summer.

Barbara will work with you to make your special event even more special. And the cake will not ruin your diet.

THE FLOUR ARTS PANTRY

5668 Oak Grove
Oakland, CA 94618

CHECKS OR MONEY ORDERS ONLY

CALL FOR CATALOG

PHONE: 510-652-7044

MINIMUM ORDER: No

Espresso Bar

EILENBERGER'S BAKERY

512 North John
Palestine, TX 75801

CREDIT CARDS: Yes

CALL FOR CATALOG

RETAIL STORE: Yes

PHONE: 800-831-2544
903-729-2253

FAX: 903-723-2915

MINIMUM ORDER: No

FANCY FRUITCAKE

The people of Palestine, Texas are so grateful to the Eilenberger's for making fruitcake, they put up a big plaque at the edge of town commemorating the business. And no wonder. German immigrant, F.H. Eilenberger, started the business here in 1898 after baking a few seasons in Galveston and Fort Worth. Through several generations and a good many permutations of the recipes, we arrive at the present where the Eilenberger's best product is a cake made with Australian glacéed apricots and Texas pecans. Along with their other cakes, they ship out thousands of fruitcakes all over the world.

Eilenberger's Pecan Cake is a dense, flavorful, not-too-sweet style of fruitcake. The cake is a full third of good pecans blended with chewy dates, golden pineapple bits, big red cherries, and a honey batter. As the Eilenbergers say, "Bring a little bit of Texas to your table."

Eilenberger's makes a full line of German Texas-style fruitcakes that they pack in tins decorated with dogwood blossoms. Apple Cake, Chocolate Amaretto, Chocolate Pecan, Walnut Cake and their Original Famous Fruitcake. All are rich, handmade cakes. Visit the bakery on North John Street in sleepy little Palestine. It's the original location and still baking.

MARY OF PUDDIN HILL

P.O. Box 241
Greenville, TX 75403

CREDIT CARDS: Yes

CALL FOR CATALOG

RETAIL STORE: Call for
directions

PHONE: 903-455-2651

MINIMUM ORDER: No

*Linda
Eckhardt's
1995
Guide to
America's
Best Foods*

BEST FRUITCAKE YOU COULD ASK FOR

Mary Horton Lauderdale's Pecan Fruitcake, baked by following her great-grandmother's recipe, was the hands-down winner with our focus group for the best fruitcake. The first ingredient is the famous Texas pecan, a small, oil-rich, taste-packed variety. Pineapple, cherries, and dates are held together with a little egg batter. This fruitcake comes in a 1¾-pound or 2¾-pound loaf, or a giant 4½-pound ring. It is so rich and moist, it's more confection than cake.

Mary first made this cake for sale one Christmas to raise some extra money. The first year she sold 500 pounds of it. She mixed the cakes in dishpans, cracked the nuts herself, and used fruits her parents donated to the cause. That was 1948. Lots of things have changed, but they still haul out the dishpans for the ladies to employ every September as they brace for the Christmas onslaught. Snapping on rubber gloves, these ladies hand-mix their dishpans full of sticky batter until it's well blended, then they hand-pack it into baking pans.

Simply to die for is their Pecan Praline Pie. Chock full of native pecans in a chewy praline made with butter and sugar and packed into an old-fashioned pie crust. It's a good keeper and smashing with a cup of Earl Grey.

Sybil's Outrageous Brownies with Raspberry Sauce

Thaw the raspberries and force through a sieve to get as much juice as possible. Discard pulp and seeds.

In a small saucepan, soften the cornstarch in cold water. Stir until completely dissolved. Stir in raspberry juice. Cook over low heat until sauce is slightly thickened and becomes opaque. Sauce can be made ahead and refrigerated for days.

Cut three brownies diagonally into four triangles. Spoon raspberry sauce into a circle in the center of a dessert plate. Place three brownie triangles on the sauce with the points of the triangle pointing towards the "top" of the plate. Garnish with a sprig of mint and fresh raspberries in season.

Three brownies will serve four people this way.

Eckhardt's suggestion for Raspberry Rustica—good for anyone who's free of the French influence and doesn't have diverticulitis. Skip the straining business with the raspberries. Whole berry sauce has more body and looks better.

20 ounces frozen or fresh raspberries

½ cup cold water

4 teaspoons cornstarch

WHOA . . . THESE ARE BROWNIES

It's a fact of life in the cottage kitchen business that overstatement is the rule. So many companies give themselves grandiose names that you just have to sigh. But what can I say? Sybil Wilkins is simply stating a fact. Her brownies are outrageous.

Packed in an airtight tin, they arrive dense, moist, flavorful, and packed with a chocolate wallop you won't soon forget. Keep them in the fridge and they're good for two weeks. Put them in the freezer and they're ready for your next impromptu tea party.

Sybil began catering 11 years ago and served these brownies to raves. Soon the requests came so fast and furious that she just made brownies. Last year, she sold twenty-five tons.

Visit her store at 1525 Moreno in San Diego and you'll find the confection offered in seven varieties. It's outrageously rich, sinfully fudgy, and really satisfying. Made with premium ingredients from scratch. No wonder they taste like mama's.

Available in chocolate with or without walnut, white chocolate with nuts, praline, chocolate peanut butter chip, chocolate macadamia, and white chocolate macadamia. Free recipes come with every order.

SYBIL'S OUTRAGEOUS BROWNIES & NATURAL FOOD PRODUCTS

9932 Mesa Rim Road
San Diego, CA 92121

CREDIT CARDS: Yes

CALL FOR CATALOG

RETAIL STORE: Yes

PHONE: 800-423-9303
619-450-6811

FAX: 619-450-0110

MINIMUM ORDER: 1 unit

ANNA, IDA & ME
1117 West Grand
Avenue
Chicago, IL 60622

CREDIT CARDS: Yes

CALL FOR CATALOG

RETAIL STORE: Yes

PHONE: 800-729-2662
312-243-2662

FAX: 312-243-5533

MINIMUM ORDER: Yes

MANDEL BRODT

Linda Kleiman, along with her mom, Sally, and the recipes of her grandmothers, Anna and Ida, has brought us old-fashioned mondel bread (also known as mandel brodt to the purists, Jewish biscotti to the rest of us). Linda, known in her business as "me," learned how to make these rich, tasty, twice-baked bites from a grandmother, who when asked where *she* learned to bake these cookies replied, "I went to Mondel Bread College."

Packed in tins and boxes, these traditional Jewish cookies keep well—provided you can keep out of them. Choose cinnamon, raspberry, apricot, poppyseed, lemon, anisette, orange walnut, chocolate chip or choco'lot.

Rugelach is their newest product. A small pastry pinwheel, it comes stuffed with raspberry, apricot, almond, date, pistachio, prune, or chocolate chips. Yum. Just like Anna and Ida used to make. For noshing, there's nothing nicer. Stop in the store when you're in Chicago, and you can get all of Linda's products hot out of the oven to take along on your vacation.

*Linda
Eckhardt's
1995
Guide to
America's
Best Foods*

278

A BAKER'S SECRET WEAPON

CHEF'S SHADOW

2433 Walnut Ridge
Dallas, TX 75229

CREDIT CARDS: Yes

CALL FOR CATALOG

PHONE: 800-833-6583
214-484-5533

FAX: 214-484-5493

MINIMUM ORDER: No

Bebe Ablon started her professional life as a social worker. But she was a fabulous baker and people at the office where she took in her home-baked goods were forever telling her, "I haven't had a rugelach like this since I ate at my grandmother's table."

In a small way, she began catering by selling her homemade products to high-end gourmet stores in Dallas. Before long, Neiman Marcus heard about her. She's been in their catalog ever since. Harry and David, Cavanaugh Lake View Farms—all have called on her to be their shadow in baking. Hence, she call's herself the Chef's Shadow.

Order from her directly and you can get homemade goodies like your grandmother baked, provided your grandmother was this good. Try her rugelach—rich and dripping in nuts and delicious with cream and cream cheese. She also makes what has been called the best carrot cake in America. Somebody even called *Gourmet* magazine to get them to ask her for the recipe. She makes heavenly brownies, muffins, and chocolate chip cookies. Lately, she's added mandel brot, a sort of Jewish biscotti, to the line.

Having a party? She still caters in the greater Dallas area and if you live far away, will send a dessert tray made to order with cookies, brownies, or the famous carrot cake. This chef will be your shadow. She doesn't even mind if you take credit. She's used to it.

BAKLAVA YOU'D KILL FOR

DESSERTS ON US

100 Ericson Court
Suite 105
Arcata, CA 95521

CHECKS OR MONEY
ORDERS ONLY

CALL FOR CATALOG

PHONE: 707-822-0160

MINIMUM ORDER: No

Another of the backwoods foodies, Emran Essa's makes a world-class baklava. And no wonder. Before living in the deep woods of California's north coast, Emran called the area around Syria home. And Lord, can Emran cook.

How can I begin to describe this exemplary pastry to you? Dripping with California honey and fine butter, the baklava is stuffed with both almonds and walnuts in a phyllo dough. The top is generously sprinkled with dazzling green pistachios. The aroma of honey and nuts assails your nose before you take the first bite. Your mouth will water, your eyes will close.

Emran Essa's baklava is quite simply the best baklava on the planet earth.

Besides the original version, Emran also makes a chocolate

Espresso Bar

279

baklava, adding gourmet chocolate chunks to the original recipe. Also available is a meltingly soft and sweet coconut baklava, and an apricot baklava that adds the tart sweet taste of genuine California apricots to the traditional Mediterranean desserts.

Emran Essa proves once again that not all good cooking is done in world-class cities. Some world-class cooking is done way out in the woods. But, thank gawd, the big UPS truck still stops. You can get it even if you don't have time for a trip to Arcata.

HONEST TO GOD DANISH PASTRIES

There was a time, not so long ago, when if you didn't have a Danish bakery in your neighborhood, you couldn't even begin to comprehend the true meaning of the term "Danish." Forget about those son-of-a-bakery versions sold in grocery chains. Lehmann's will air-ship genuine Danish Kringle—thin, crisp, and dripping with sweet butter—in fourteen flavors. These flaky, heady pastries come in pecan, almond, walnut, raspberry, apricot, prune, date, cherry, apple, strawberry, pineapple, blueberry cheese, and chocolate, among others. Made with all natural ingredients and no added preservatives, these Kringles melt in your mouth. You can also order other authentic Danish-style pastries, cookies, cheesecake, or apple cake. They'll even send you a Danish wood Kringle platter, decorated with Danish folk art designs. And, if you're really in to it, join the Kringle-of-the-Month Club. You may never eat a doughnut again.

LEHMANN'S BAKERY

2210 Sixteenth St.
Racine, WI 53405

CREDIT CARDS: Yes

CALL FOR CATALOG

RETAIL STORE: Yes

PHONE: 414-632-2359

FAX: 414-632-4473

MINIMUM ORDER: No

Linda Eckhardt's 1995 Guide to America's Best Foods

MOON PIE AND AN RC PLEASE

MOON PIES
(CHATTANOOGA
BAKERY)

P.O. Box 111
Chattanooga, TN 37401

CREDIT CARDS: Yes

CALL FOR CATALOG

PHONE: 800-251-3404

FAX: 615-266-2169

MINIMUM ORDER: 1 case

If you're from the South you can forget about Mom and Apple pie. Moon Pies are it. The quintessential American experience for children, the Moon Pie is a round gush of marshmallow between two graham cracker cookies, dipped in chocolate, vanilla, or banana frosting. And to wash it all down, order an "RC" or, if you can find it, a Delaware punch.

So beloved is the Moon Pie that it has its own Culture Club. International, if you please. The Moon Pie is beloved for many reasons. Perhaps one of its best functions is helping the thin and haggard to gain weight. Should you need this aid, here are suggestions for its use.

* The Island Delight: a Moon Pie floating in a bowl of Molasses.
* The Honey Bun: a Moon Pie drowned in a cup of pure honey.
* Eskimo Divinity: two Moon Pies covered by a quart of ice cream.
* Moon Pie Jubilee: a vanilla Moon Pie covered with vanilla ice cream and cherries. Pour on some brandy and ignite. Keep a bucket of water handy.

Breakfast Beauty: a vanilla Moon Pie covered with butter and blackberry jelly.

The good people at the Chattanooga Bakery do require that you order a case of 12 Moon Pies, but what the hey. If you like your Moon Pies, you'll want to lay in a supply.

Espresso Bar

281

Mother Sperry's Easy Hard Sauce

And I quote:

"Cream one stick soft butter with ½ cup powdered sugar. Whip until light. Add 2 tablespoons good brandy. Beat until fluffy. Chill. That's it. It's that simple."

MOTHER SPERRY'S PLUM PUDDING

1416 East Aloha St.
Seattle, WA 98112

CHECKS OR MONEY ORDERS ONLY

CALL FOR CATALOG

PHONE: 206-329-8631

MINIMUM ORDER: No

REAL PLUM PUDDING

Yes, there is a Mother Sperry. In fact, there are two mothers, who live across the street from each other, and have joined up to make a good old-fashioned plum pudding, balancing fruits and spices with brandy. When you cut into this dark brown blob, it simply drips with butter. As Mother says herself, this is the great leap backward. The pudding weighs only 26 ounces, comes in a slick red box, and will easily serve six, and maybe eight, anytime within the next couple of years. Between the booze and the butter, this cake may have a longer shelf life than the rest of us. And there aren't any artificial preservatives or chemicals to muck the thing up.

Linda Eckhardt's 1995 Guide to America's Best Foods

OLD-FASHIONED SUGAR PIES

MRS. WICK'S PIES

100 Cherry St.
State Rd. 32
Winchester, IN 47394

At the polar opposite from the fancy European entries in the sweets' sweepstakes stand Mrs. Wick's old-fashioned pies. The original Sugar Cream, plus Pecan, Peanut Butter, German Chocolate and Pumpkin Cream pies make up the varieties available by mail. But the Sugar Cream is the *raison d'etre* for Mrs. Wick's. They're so sure their recipe is the best, they've patented it. Sometimes called the Indiana Farm Pie, it's made with cream and sugar, no eggs, and has at least 40 percent butterfat. One of the reasons it tastes so good is that it's baked in a lard crust. Loathsome old lard still makes the most flavorful crust. Stop in the adorable bakery, located in an ancient red brick building, and you'll find an even broader selection.

Wick remember's his grandmother putting an unfilled pie shell in the oven, pouring sugar cream filling inside, then sitting on a stool in front of the oven and stirring the filling with her finger until the mixture became warm. Wick can't stir all the pies he makes today, but he decided people don't actually mind the fact that the filling is thicker on the bottom than on the top. The crust is just like homemade, the filling as sweet and bland and delicious as something your Great-Aunt Susie might have sent over for Sunday dinner. Wick sends these out frozen, six at a time, and you can keep them on hand for Thanksgiving dinner or other festive gatherings. After a heavy winter dinner, this pie is perfect. Wick's pies say one thing: Home at last.

CHECKS OR MONEY ORDERS ONLY

RETAIL STORE: Call for directions

PHONE: 317-584-8401

FAX: 317-584-3700

MINIMUM ORDER: 6 pies

Espresso Bar

GREAT GROCERIES

Forget Fauchon. Forget Harrod's. Every single thing you ever imagined available by mail order and to the local shopper in America's Grand Grocery Stores. Best local and regional sources for American and imported goods. All ethnic supplies, exotic hardware from Europe, Africa, and Asia—strange things you never thought you needed. Available here with one phone call or one mind-boggling visit.

"Supernatural"—perhaps. "Baloney"—perhaps not. There are many things under the sun.

—HALLIWELL HOBBS to Ned Sparks in *Lady for a Day*, 1933

**ANDRONICO'S
MARKET**

1200 Irving St.
San Francisco, CA
94122

CREDIT CARDS: Yes

CALL FOR CATALOG

RETAIL STORE: Yes

PHONE: 800-522-4438

MINIMUM ORDER: No

GOURMET GROCERIES

Frank Andronico first opened his grocery business in Berkeley 65 years ago. His grandson, Bill, who runs the store today, says, "He'd be blown away by the exotic stuff."

Now, Andronico's has five specialty grocery stores in the bay area of California as well as a thriving mail order business for custom and standard gift baskets. Their flagship San Francisco store is worth a stop for tourists. Besides dazzling produce, a deli, an espresso bar, a bakery, an innovative sandwich bar, and other perishable comestibles, see the exhibition Chinese kitchen, order a custom pizza, ask for short order pastas, or sit down for a hofbrau sandwich.

I went to a party catered by Andronico's in San Francisco and it was overwhelming: Spit Roast Pomegranate Chicken, Bow Ties with Pesto, and fine focaccias were among the more divine offerings.

Ask for the brochure showing their ten diverse gift baskets. Everything from Italy to the rain forest is represented. They'll also custom-pack a basket for you. Just call them.

BALDUCCI'S

424 Avenue of the
Americas at 9th st.
New York, NY 10011

CREDIT CARDS: Yes

CALL FOR CATALOG

RETAIL STORE: Yes

PHONE: 800-822-1444
(Nationwide)
800-247-2450 (in NY)

MINIMUM ORDER: No

*Linda
Eckhardt's
1995
Guide to
America's
Best Foods*

A VEGETABLE STAND MADE GOOD

This is New York's premier grocer when it comes to exotic fruits and vegetables. Every item is perfect. Whether you're looking for fresh Italian flat leaf parsley or porcini, Balducci's has it. Stroll their crowded aisles and try to take in the vast array of world-class groceries they offer—cheeses, breads they make on-site, and ready-made deli items among others. Don't leave without buying a focaccia. It's not New York without a visit to Balducci's.

They conduct a brisk mail order business, shipping out lots of bread and other exotica to people who used to live around there and moved on to other climes, and to the most discriminating cooks who know if they can't get it in Kansas City, they can sure as hell get it from Balducci's in a couple of days.

CHILE HEAD HEAVEN

THE CHILE SHOP
109 E. Water St.
Santa Fe, NM 87501

Y ou say you like chiles? Love the romance of the Southwest? So does Su-Anne Armstrong. So much so that she's opened a shop right off Santa Fe's main square that offers chiles in every conceivable form. Chile powder, pure New Mexico red chile, Hatch mild chile, and dried New Mexico Green chile, whole and in powder. A long list of more arcane dried chiles are also available: chipotle, habanero, ancho, pasilla, negro, guajillo, cascabel, and pequin to name but a few.

Su-Anne has also hand-picked some terrific salsas, vinegars, pastas, pestos, mustards, and salad dressings—anything, so long as it's highly seasoned with chile. She's even gone so far as to track down chile Christmas lights, chile candles, chile candies, Montezuma Mexican recipe sauces, Posole, anasazi beans, and even a terrific looking chile dinner bell. Naturally, there are chile dishes, chile mugs, chile earrings, and paper mache chiles.

She'll send out gift boxes—everything from a Chile Sampler and Santa Fe Favorites, to her own Select Box-of-the-Year. My personal favorite from the comestibles department is the Native Chile Wreath that's full of red chiles, tiny corns, seed pods of all kinds, gourds, garlic, and pricklies. It's the flavors and textures of New Mexico, dried and put into a wreath.

This is a must for walking tours of downtown Santa Fe, and a great catalog for those who left their hearts in New Mexico's high desert country.

CREDIT CARDS: **Yes**

CALL FOR CATALOG

RETAIL STORE: **Call for directions**

PHONE: **505-983-6080**

FAX: **505-984-0737**

MINIMUM ORDER: **No**

CAJUN COOKING AND COFFEE WITH CHICORY

COMMUNITY KITCHENS
P.O. Box 2311
Baton Rouge, LA 70821

I 've never quite figured out whether *Beignets*, Louisiana's square, deep-fried doughnuts are supposed to be eaten for breakfast when you get up, or after you've stayed up all night, just to kind of steady you until you get back to the hotel after a night of revelry in the Crescent city.

Served dusted with powdered sugar, alongside a steamy cup of chicory coffee, this is the breakfast that's made for New Orleans' natives and served all over the city at stand-up bakeries.

Buy Community's own coffee and their beignet mix and you can almost hear the Mississippi lapping at the banks. Call and ask for their

CREDIT CARDS: **Yes**

CALL FOR CATALOG

RETAIL STORE: **Call for directions**

PHONE: **800-535-9901**

FAX: **800-321-7539**

MINIMUM ORDER: **No**

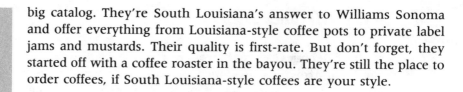

big catalog. They're South Louisiana's answer to Williams Sonoma and offer everything from Louisiana-style coffee pots to private label jams and mustards. Their quality is first-rate. But don't forget, they started off with a coffee roaster in the bayou. They're still the place to order coffees, if South Louisiana-style coffees are your style.

COOKWORKS

318 S. Guadalupe
   Street
Santa Fe, NM 87501

~~~~~~~~~~~~~~~~~~

CREDIT CARDS: Yes

CALL FOR CATALOG

RETAIL STORE: Yes

**PHONE: 800-927-3357
   505-988-7676**

FAX: 505-988-1886

MINIMUM ORDER: No

YOUR SOUTHWESTERN PERSONAL SHOPPER

A necessary part of Santa Fe's Guadalupe District Walking Tour, Cookworks is a store that sells fine foods of New Mexico and beyond. Way beyond. You could think of Cookworks as your personal shopper for Southwestern and imported fine foods.

They send gift baskets all over the world. We were particularly taken with their Santa Fe Seasons, a "Six Seasonings" mix of dry herbs, and a "Flavors of New Mexico" blend of garlic, saffron, cumin, oregano, and chilies. With recipes and serving suggestions, these make for fine Southwestern dinners.

Also staggering in taste and presentation were *Le Beune Tradizioni, Tipiche Della Calabria,* Italian mushrooms and wild herbs packed in extra virgin olive oil and sent out in a gorgeous hex green jar. Also delicious and beautiful is another Italian import, *Cipolle alla Brace,* a grilled onion in olive oil condiment packed in a good-looking hex jar.

Exotic teas including Fortnum & Mason and Kushmicoff teas from Paris are also available. They sell lots of exotic hors d'oeuvre, including Scottish salmon, Russian caviar, frozen canapes, chips, dips, and salsas. Having a party? Need help? Call them up.

*Linda
Eckhardt's
1995
Guide to
America's
Best Foods*

SACRAMENTO'S GOURMET GROCER

CORTI BROTHERS
5810 Folsom Blvd.
Sacramento, CA 95819

CREDIT CARDS: Yes

CALL FOR CATALOG

RETAIL STORE: Yes

PHONE: 916-736-3800

FAX: 916-736-3807

MINIMUM ORDER: No

Darrell Corti not only sells fine food and wines, he also offers a virtual gold mine of information about the food scene in central California and the world. Darrell can tell you how much it rained in Italy this year and what that means to the olive oil crop. He'll seek out the finest handmade comestibles in the neighborhood—like Eduardo's handmade pasta from San Francisco. Not only will he sell it to you, he'll tell you where the eggs came from that went into it— Petaluma. He'll even track down an arcane cookie from a Tuscan spa and offer it for sale—*Cialde della Nencia,* a wafer filled with almond paste and sugar. It's not available outside the spa except through Darrell Corti's.

Darrell is also an innovator in his own backyard. He kept seeing the bitter oranges fall from the trees around California's capital and knew they'd make great marmalade. He made a deal with the state and now harvests a limited number to make his rare and wonderful Capital Vintage Marmalade. He also makes a traditional mincemeat that's made to be aged. This man can cook. Trust me.

Order oils, vinegars, sherries, wines, chestnut pancake mix—his stores change with every season. Get on his mailing list. Your horizons will broaden deliciously.

CREOLE COOKING LESSONS AND FOODS

CREOLE DELICACIES
533 Ann Street
New Orleans, LA 70116

CREDIT CARDS: Yes

CALL FOR CATALOG

RETAIL STORE: Yes

PHONE: 504-523-6425

FAX: 504-523-4787

MINIMUM ORDER: No

Next time you're in New Orleans, drop by Jackson Square and pick up a tote bag full of genuine Creole food products to take home. Or, better yet, call and book yourself into the cooking school they offer at #1 Poydras Street, Store 116 on the Riverwalk. This way, you can learn to make a real roux, or jambalaya. And you can learn what makes for authentic creole and cajun dishes so that you can make them at home.

And if you don't quite know the difference between Cajun and Creole, here's your chance to get it straight. Creole is basically the uptown cousin to country food developed by the French-speaking Acadians who settled in Louisiana's bayous after they'd been banished from Nova Scotia. This is a cooking style that's distinct. Chicken

Great Groceries

Maque Choux, Andouille Sausage Jambalaya, and Dirty Rice are a few of the fine dishes you can learn about here.

They'll send you a brochure listing everything from pralines to Cajun cooking mixes. We especially like and recommend the popcorn rice from Le Riz. For a real taste of the bayou, order a Cajun 6-Pack. That's six different Louisiana hot sauces packed in a wooden crate. It's a perfect gift for those who left their heart in old New Orleans. And if you don't have the chance to take cooking classes, ask them which one of the many Cajun cookbooks they sell you should start out with. My personal favorite is *Talk about Good!* I've cooked from it for years. It's great.

MUSEUM-QUALITY GROCERIES

After you've been uptown to the Met, a visit to Dean & Deluca should be next on your list for a look at the possibilities that are New York. Here's a food emporium where the lettuce has been groomed as if it were going out on a date. The breads are arranged in the case so artfully you can't bring yourself to disturb the display by buying one. The olive oil choices are stupendous. The Nova salmon is outrageous. The aroma is heady. It's just part of your education to stroll through this store whenever you visit the Big Apple.

Meanwhile, if you're sitting back in Little Snap, and need some rare comestible—say chestnuts to roast by your open fire—call them up. They'll send whatever your little heart desires right out. Never mind that you have to hock the Buick to pay for it. You won't even mind. And that's the truth.

DEAN & DELUCA

560 Broadway at Prince
New York, NY 10003

CREDIT CARDS: Yes

CALL FOR CATALOG

RETAIL STORE: Yes

PHONE: 800-221-7714
    212-431-8230

MINIMUM ORDER: No

CREOLE COOKING SUPPLIES

GAZIN'S CAJUN CREOLE CUISINE

P.O. Box 19221
2910 Toulouse Street
New Orleans, LA 70179

Here's the wish book for all things Cajun. Order Sauce Pirogue, a sauce mayo for South Louisiana, genuine New Orleans French Bread, or some fig preserves like Mama used to make. If it's from Louisiana, Gazin's probably carries it in their Cajun Creole Grocery Store and catalog.

Order a dozen frozen bobwhite quail or some wild game sausage. Sample Elmer's Gold Brick Ice Cream Sundae Sauce or Turbinado Vanilla Sugar made from Louisiana sugar cane. Choose from andouille Cajun sausage, Pig Stand Barbecue Sauce, choice lump crabmeat, Trappey's Gumbos and Sauces, or New Orleans Red Beans and Bacon. Try the Konriko rices—wild pecan, artichoke, or cajun pilafs. Order Cajun Upside Down pickles, French Market coffee with chicory, Beignet Mix from the Cafe du Monde, even Camellia red kidney beans, just like they sell at the Winn Dixie in the Quarter. It's all just a phone call away. And do stop in the store next time you're in the Crescent City.

CREDIT CARDS: Yes

CALL FOR CATALOG

(There is a $1 charge for the catalog, which includes a coupon for $1 off any item.)

RETAIL STORE: Yes

PHONE: 800-262-6410
   504-482-0302

FAX: 504-827-5391

MINIMUM ORDER: No

Great Groceries

HOT STUFF

227 Sullivan St.
New York, NY 10012

CREDIT CARDS: **Yes**

CALL FOR CATALOG

RETAIL STORE: **Call for directions**

PHONE: **800-466-8206**
212-254-6120

FAX: **212-254-6120**

MINIMUM ORDER: **No**

CONDIMENTS FROM HELL

Top Tamale David Jenkins has become addicted to all things peppery and hot. Now this was a problem in Old New York which—although it certainly has a plethora of foodstuffs from around the world—was a little shy of the hot stuff.

But David fixed that by opening a store on the West Side (near West 3rd Street) that sells every good hot thing you might have dreamed of, and some you haven't. This shop, which he aptly calls Hot Stuff, (subtitled "The Spicy Food Store"), was a hit from the moment it opened in 1991. He's built a loyal clientele. No wonder. He's got everybody who's willing to give it a go addicted to the capsicum as well.

David stocks hot stuff from Mexico, India, Louisiana, the Southwest, Thailand, Indonesia, Texas, Florida, the Caribbean in all its permutations, Vermont, Turkey, and even Yugoslavia. Order Melinda's XXXtra Hot Sauce from Belize. This is mainline "Hot Dope" and it's truly addicting.

Get your bulk spices here, your Bloody Mary mixes, your Ristras, your strings of dried chiles and your New Mexico wreaths. David expands his stocks daily. At this moment, he is chock full of Cajun products, habanero sauces, hot mustards, dried and canned exotic peppers from Mexico, New Mexico, and Peru. Get your Thai curries, your hot oils, your Chinese hot zinger stuff, your barbecue hot stuff, salsas out the kazoo, and best of all, sweet hot stuff, including Jamaican Busha Browne, a medium hot banana chutney. Our favorite. This place is fun to shop in, one of the Best-of-Manhattan, and it's a gold mine for mail order. Call up David and order.

*Linda
Eckhardt's
1995
Guide to
America's
Best Foods*

292

KANSAS COOKS

Sunflowers, Dorothy, and the Wizard of Oz. That's what they grow in Kansas and that's what Sue Goldman sells. Sunflower seed cookies, all manner of sunflower souvenirs, and Prairie Dog Chow, which is a crunchy corn crisp.

For a look at all things Kansas, call Sue and ask her for a catalog. If you're in the mall at Clifton Square in Wichita, stop in and see the complete Kansas trip: Sandhill Plum Jelly (delicious and made with authentic wild Kansas sandhill plums), wheat treats, Buffalo sticks and jerky, single cob popcorn, sunnywheat bread mixes, a Wyatt Earp Super Snack, and the Kansas Cookbook. If it's Kansas, Sue Goldman probably has it.

BEST OF KANSAS

5426 East Canal
Wichita, KS 67208

CREDIT CARDS: **Yes**

CALL FOR CATALOG

RETAIL STORE: **Call for directions**

PHONE: **800-593-5566**

FAX: **316-682-5566**

MINIMUM ORDER: **No**

JAPANESE GROCERIES

Here's your source for nori, sushi supplies, and all things Japanese. They have chopsticks, rices, buckwheat noodles known as *soba*, miso, dried fishes, sake, soy, and every last living thing you could ever need if you want to cook Japanese. They'll ship it out. You can just bow to the UPS man when he delivers. It will be the courteous thing to do.

KATAGIRI

224 E. 59th St.
New York, NY 77024

CREDIT CARDS: **Yes**

CALL FOR CATALOG

RETAIL STORE: **Yes**

PHONE: **212-752-4197**

MINIMUM ORDER: **No**

Great Groceries

LITTLE INDIA STORE

128 East 28th St.
New York, NY 10016

CREDIT CARDS: Yes

RETAIL STORE: Yes

PHONE: 212-683-1691

MINIMUM ORDER: No

INDIAN GROCERY SUPPLIES

One of the most staggering sensory experiences you can have is a trip through this Indian Emporium. The aromas go so far past the word *Curry* that it simply doesn't apply. You'll think ginger, you'll think curry, you'll think asafetida before it's all over. Because it's all here. Every single item you'll ever see in any Indian cookbook: garam masala, mustard seeds (black and yellow), saffron, tamarind, dals, fennel, fenugreek, and ghee. Nighella, Panchphoran, it's all here. They'll put the herbs, spices, and rices you desire in little brown bags and send them right out. They have everything for New York's burgeoning Indian population: pots, pans, utensils, Indian soap operas on video and in paperbacks, packaged goods, spices by the gunny sackful, and fresh fruits and vegetables. This is a must see for New York visitors, and mandatory for the rest of us who want to cook the good foods that Julie Sahni tells us about in her fine Indian cookbooks, including *Classic Indian Cooking*.

MAISON GLASS

11 East 58th St.
New York, NY 10022

CREDIT CARDS: Yes

CALL FOR CATALOG

RETAIL STORE: Yes

PHONE: 212-755-3316

MINIMUM ORDER: $15

GRAND GROCERIES

Carrying more than 3500 items, both domestic and imported, they have everything from Caspian Caviar to rattlesnake, from lebkuchen to their famous fig pudding. Ask for the catalog. It's a great wishbook.

*Linda
Eckhardt's
1995
Guide to
America's
Best Foods*

294

ITALIAN GROCERIES AND SUPER SUBSANDWICHES

MANGANARO'S
488 9th Ave.
New York, NY 10018

CREDIT CARDS: Yes

CALL FOR CATALOG

RETAIL STORE: Yes

PHONE: 800-472-5264
212-563-5331

FAX: 212-239-8355

MINIMUM ORDER: No

S elling Italian groceries on the Upper West side of Manhattan for nearly a hundred years, the Manganaro family has a formidable reputation for quality, for purity, and for authenticity. They were making and selling genuine Italian foods long before the Italian craze hit the country, and will no doubt continue selling Italian—long after it's been replaced by the next craze.

Meanwhile, should you need advice about authentic Italian goods to buy, this is the source. They sent me biscotti that redefined the product. Light and airy as a meringue, perfumed with almond, these crisp biscotti begged for a good dipping wine. You can also purchase real polenta, fine imported DeCecco and Divella pastas, Panettone, Torrone Nougats, La Tempesta Cioccolotti, and DiCamillo Italian cookies.

Best quality olive oils and balsamic vinegars are sold here. Stop in the store and order hot foods ranging from cannelloni to tripe and pasta. Make a sandwich, get a salad. Help yourself to the antipasto bar. This is old New York. Still the same. They've even kept the counters. And if you can't get there, just ask them to ship you a gift basket. Get a copy of their family cookbook and you'll be guaranteed—Buon Gusto!

Great Groceries

Homemade Chili Powder

Over medium heat, warm a dry skillet then shred chiles by hand, discarding seeds and membranes, and toss them into the skillet. Stir with cumin, cloves, and allspice until all the spices are toasty and aromatic. Stir constantly. Pour this mixture into a blender or food processor fitted with the steel blade. Add oregano leaves and paprika. Process until pulverized. Store in a clean jar with a tight-fitting lid.

3 large Chiles Pasilla, dried

1 large Chile Negro, dried

1 large Chile Ancho, dried

1 dried cayenne (optional)

½ tablespoon cumin seeds

¼ teaspoon whole cloves

3 allspice berries

2 tablespoons dried oregano leaves

1 tablespoon paprika

MO HOTTA-MO BETTA

P.O. Box 4136
San Luis Obispo, CA
93403

CREDIT CARDS: Yes

CALL FOR CATALOG

PHONE: 800-462-3220

FAX: 805-545-8389

MINIMUM ORDER: No

Linda Eckhardt's 1995 Guide to America's Best Foods

CHILI HEAD CATALOG

Here's the catalog for chili heads. They've collected products from around the world and listed them in a catalog that can only be described as Capsicum Voluptuary. If you want a quick, one-stop-shop for the hot stuff, call up and get this catalog.

They stock habanero hot sauces from Island Delight to Apocalyptic. They also carry hot sauces from Doc's Jamaican Hellfire to Voodoo Jerk Slather, as well as Indonesian sauces, Mexican sauces, and Hawaiian sauces and rubs. If it's hot, it's here.

Looking for salsas? Their catalog lists pages of them. You can order Pedro's fresh tamales here, and enough dried chiles to keep you in the hot stuff for life. Also order curry pastes and provisions, salsa ties and salsa bowls, freshly minced ginger and Wasabi chips, coconut milk and Tandoori paste. The catalog's 45 hot pages. It's fun to read. What is it about hot stuff that brings out the sexy metaphors? Don't wonder, just enjoy.

HUNGARIAN SPECIALTIES

PAPRIKAS WEISS
1546 Second Avenue
New York, NY 10028

CREDIT CARDS: Yes

CALL FOR CATALOG

RETAIL STORE: Yes

PHONE: 212-288-6117

MINIMUM ORDER: No

For years and years, this Hungarian grocery store has supplied New Yorkers with Eastern European groceries and spices. Here's where you can order many imported European products you hardly see in this country. They carry thousands of items from Hungarian Salami to Australian glacéed Fruits. They offer peppers, cheeses, and spice grinders. This New York fixture has been importing European foods for most of this century. They have an enchanting catalog that lists all the hundreds of herbs and spices they sell, plus all the arcane European hardware. It's a real wishbook for those of us who are kitchen gadget junkies.

MEDITERRANEAN GROCERIES

G.B. RATTO, INT. GROCERS
821 Washington St.
Oakland, CA 94607

CREDIT CARDS: Yes

CALL FOR CATALOG

RETAIL STORE: Yes

PHONE: 415-832-6503

MINIMUM ORDER:

Ratto's carries a good selection of imported olive oils and all Mediterranean-type foods, as well as grains and meals in a list as long as your arm. They also sell lots of beans, seeds, and glacéed fruits. They have an enormous catalog that lists everything from soup to nuts, along with specialties from Indonesia, the British Isles, Israel, Argentina, Brazil, India, West Africa, and Italy.

Order pomegranate juice, red palm oil, vindaloo paste, cassava meal, and treacle drops. I agree with John Thorne, curmudgeonly author of *Outlaw Cook,* in his assessment of their housebrand olive oil as one of the best and least expensive. It's a robust, round-flavored oil, good for both cooking and using in salad dressings. Heck, I'd even rub it in my hair and on my body. It's that great.

They also offer good red and white vinegars made from California wines aged in oak. Their own handmade spice blends are fascinating. Order a *berbere*, a taco, or a Greek seasoning—they blend it themselves. The flavors will be fresh and new.

Do go in the store if you're in this area of California, just across the bay from San Francisco. The grocery store is fun and you can order a sandwich at the cafe from 11–2—a nice break from looking at all those ingredients. Come Friday nights and have a light supper and a little live opera. Yes, opera. Get your reservations. You'll need them.

SANTA FE SELECT

369 Montezuma #345
Santa Fe, NM 87501

CREDIT CARDS: **Yes**

CALL FOR CATALOG

RETAIL STORE: **In the Plaza Market**

PHONE: **800-243-0353**
   505-986-0454

FAX: **505-986-0640**

MINIMUM ORDER: **No**

THE GREAT SOUTHERN SAUCE COMPANY

5705 Kavanaugh
Little Rock, AR 72207

CREDIT CARDS: **Yes**

CALL FOR CATALOG

RETAIL STORE: **Yes**

PHONE: **800-437-2823**

FAX: **501-663-0956**

MINIMUM ORDER: **No**

Linda Eckhardt's 1995 Guide to America's Best Foods

SANTA FE TASTES

Darby Long's got the Santa Fe tastes down pat and will put them together for you in a gift basket or box. From her hand-chosen products you can get Chavos Cookies, Jackrabbit Java, Hogwash Marinade, Smokin' Cactus Salsa, Spaghetti Western Pasta Sauce, Three Banditos Salsa Verde, Jalapeno Peanut Brittle and Cowboy Caviar. Although all these names sound kind of silly when you read them in a list, the products do taste good. Because Darby Long's careful to choose products that taste good first, and sound good second.

HOT STUFF FROM LITTLE ROCK

Handy Ensminger has assembled a dazzling array of sauces in his Little Rock store. He's got barbecue sauce every which way from Sunday. He's got relishes, he's got condiments, he's got hot sauces out the kazoo, and salad dressings, pasta sauces, marinades, dessert sauces, and a bunch of good cookbooks.

If it comes from the south or southwest, Randy Ensminger has tasted it and may have put it in his store or catalog. Call and find out.

IMPORTED SALAMI AND SUCH

TODARO BROTHERS
555 Second Ave.
New York, NY 10016

CREDIT CARDS: **Yes**

CALL FOR CATALOG

RETAIL STORE: **Yes**

PHONE: **212-679-7766**

MINIMUM ORDER: **No**

Another of those delicious little New York stores, Todaro carries all things Italian. The ceiling is hung so heavily with salami and cheese you think you're going to bump your head. The aisles are so narrow you have to turn sideways past the polenta to get anywhere. You won't mind. This place is like a mini-trip to Italy.

They offer a vast assortment of Italian cheeses, oils, and breads. Their catalog lists 50 varieties of pasta, from conchiglie to tortellini to ziti. They also offer balsamic vinegar, unfiltered oils, panettone, pandoro, prosciutto, salsiccia abruzesa, and lots of mushrooms. This is Little Italy.

ITALY IN CALIFORNIA

VIVANDE, INC.
2125 Fillmore St.
San Francisco, CA
94115

CREDIT CARDS: **Yes**

CALL FOR CATALOG

RETAIL STORE: **Call for directions**

PHONE: **415-346-4430**

FAX: **415-346-2877**

MINIMUM ORDER: **No**

Carlo Middione presides over a food emporium in California that rivals *Fauchon* in Paris. A cafe, a grocery store, a deli, the store is the heartbeat of its Pacific Heights neighborhood. Middione is author of the acclaimed *The Food of Southern Italy*, and his store and worldview are one of America's treasures.

Along with his wife, Lisa, Carlo personally selects essential Italian products to import: the cheeses, the arborio, the polenta, the olive oils, the flours. He also sells imported pastas, sausages, antipasti, biscotti, and selected Italian sweets. They not only ship nonperishable items, but made-in-the-shop seasonal house foods, and fresh foods in refrigerator packs. Call and ask what they're cooking this week. You will not be disappointed. This is unpretentious, authentic Italian cooking. The kind that would make Fellini weep. You'll want to eat all day. Although it's quite impossible to say what's best, his memorable almond poppyseed bars are something we order again and again.

The store is a must-see for San Francisco visitors. You may have to beat off the tourists from the tour buses with a stick, but elbow your way into the deep narrow shop. It's wonderful. Buy two or three kinds of olive oil. Have a lunch break with Carlo, and try his southern Italian specialties.

Great Groceries

WILLIAMS SONOMA

P.O. Box 7456
San Francisco, CA
94120

CREDIT CARDS: Yes

CALL FOR CATALOG

RETAIL STORE: Call for
the name of a store
near you.

PHONE: 800-541-2233

FAX: 415-421-5153

MINIMUM ORDER: No

EPICURE'S GROCERIES AND SUPPLIES

Chuck Williams calls this simply "A Catalog for Cooks" and unless you have been cooking for the past twenty years on a cruise ship that never came to port, you know that this catalog—above all others—and these stores—scattered around the country in good neighborhoods—are the places to order from and shop. They offer foodstuffs, gear, recipes, and tableware that I would rob banks to lay hands on. Chuck Williams makes you want to cook. And to that end, I am getting up from this chair this very moment to go make the tomato asparagus pasta sauce recipe I saw in the catalog today. You see what I mean?

The original stores are in the bay area: San Francisco, Sonoma, and Palo Alto. Call and ask for the name of a store near you. They've gone through a major expansion and you might not have to drive far to find one. Once you get in the store, hang onto your pocketbook. You will want to spend money. I guarantee it.

ZABAR'S

2245 Broadway
New York, NY 10024

CREDIT CARDS: Yes

CALL FOR CATALOG

RETAIL STORE: Yes

PHONE: 212-496-1234

MINIMUM ORDER: No

KITCHEN TCHATKAS

For the kitchen-challenged, this is the store of choice. Chock full of every gadget and doodad ever dreamed of, as well as comestibles exotica and not so exotica, this is the Upper West Side's answer to Nirvana. Turn sideways to pass through the aisles and aisles, and floors and floors of pots, pans, coffeemakers, cookie cutters, bread machines, bagels, European chocolates, and hard-to-find ethnic ingredients. If you look long enough and hard enough, you'll probably find that needle in the haystack you're looking for. Zabar's has everything. If you can just find it. Perhaps it's easier just to call and ask them to send the catalog. It's a more orderly, sane way to shop Zabar's, but not nearly as much fun.

*Linda
Eckhardt's
1995
Guide to
America's
Best Foods*

300

ITALY COMES TO MICHIGAN

ZINGERMAN'S DELICATESSEN

422 Detroit Street
Ann Arbor, MI 48104

Let Paris have Fauchon. Let London keep its Harrod's. Let New York have Dean & Deluca. In Ann Arbor, they've got Zingerman's, and it's a world-class deli, cafe, and grocery store.

They import the best that the Mediterranean has to offer. They bake fine European-style breads every day that they'll ship by mail order. They have a cafe with a dazzling array of sandwiches to keep the college crowd happy. Zingerman's may, in fact, be the center of the world. At least of Michigan's world.

Here you'll find a world-class selection of cheeses, teas, corned beef and pastrami, oils, vinegars, fruits preserves, and pastas. You name it. If it's the best, they probably have it. When I was searching for a fabulous product called Manicaretti that I saw at the Fancy Food Show in San Francisco, where did they send me? Zingerman's. Manicaretti is, by the way, the finest line of Italian pastas, polentas, rices, olive oils, and pantry items that I know of.

The pasta begins with stone-ground hard winter wheat, is mixed with pure well water, then extruded over dies more than a hundred years old. The pasta is then air-dried for 56 hours. All these details combine to give you exquisite pasta, with a texture and taste you've never experienced before.

Pair a Zingerman's sauce with imported Manicaretti pasta and imported Parmigiano Reggiano cheese. It's an opera. Don't forget a loaf of Farm Bread. That's mandatory.

CREDIT CARDS: Yes

CALL FOR CATALOG

RETAIL STORE: Yes

PHONE: 313-663-3400

FAX: 313-663-3400

MINIMUM ORDER: No

Great Groceries

INDEXES

A wonderful bird is the pelican, his bill will hold more than his belican. He can take in his beak, enough for a week, but I'm darned if I know how the helican.

—DIXON MERRITT (1879–1954)

There really is a grapevine in the food business. You know somebody who knows somebody who knows somebody that makes a great cookie, or a fabulous bread, or smokes a salmon better than anybody in the world. Would you please write to me and tell me about that person and their product?

This is an ongoing project and the book will be updated every year. Let me hear from you in the summer and I'll be glad to present new products to the focus group for inclusion in later editions of the book.

Send information to: Linda Eckhardt's Guide to America's Best Foods
108 Bush Street
Ashland, OR 97520
FAX: 503-482-2760

P.S. If you found a memorable food stop on your vacation this year, write and tell me about it. And don't forget to ask them if they ship their products to out-of-town customers. If they do, I want to hear from them—provided you think their food products taste great.

And we meet, with chicken and champagne, at last . . .

—LADY MARY WORTLEY MONTAGU (1689–1762)

COMPANIES

RECIPES

STATE-BY-STATE

Indexes